BY MARC STEPHEN GARRISON

FINANCIALLY FREE:
ADD $20,000 (OR MORE) A YEAR TO YOUR INCOME
THROUGH PART-TIME REAL ESTATE INVESTING

HOW TO BUY YOUR OWN HOME IN 90 DAYS

HOW TO BUY
YOUR OWN
HOME
IN 90 DAYS

HOW TO BUY YOUR OWN HOME

IN

90

DAYS

□ □ □

MARC STEPHEN GARRISON

MAIN STREET BOOKS

Doubleday
New York   London   Toronto   Sydney   Auckland

A MAIN STREET BOOK
PUBLISHED BY DOUBLEDAY
a division of Bantam Doubleday Dell Publishing Group, Inc.
1540 Broadway, New York, New York 10036

MAIN STREET BOOKS, DOUBLEDAY, and the portrayal of a
building with a tree are trademarks of Doubleday, a division
of Bantam Doubleday Dell Publishing Group, Inc.

The material in Appendix B is reprinted by
permission of the copyright owner,
Professional Publishing Corporation,
122 Paul Drive, San Rafael, CA 94903,
(415) 472-1964.
Library of Congress Cataloging in Publication Data

Garrison, Marc.
    How to buy your own home in 90 days.

    1. House buying.   2. Mortgage loans.   3. Real
property.   I. Title
HD1379.G37   1989   643'.12   88-30017
ISBN 0-385-24531-9

DEDICATION

□   □   □

The most powerful combination of emotions in the world is not in-spired by any grand cosmic event, nor is it found at the movies, in novels, or in history books. It is found by a parent who, after locking the doors at night, heads up the stairs. Picking up a few toys on the way up, the parent places the toys quietly in the child's room, then in the dim light stops and sees eternity while gazing down on the sleeping child.

I am grateful that my wife DeAnn and my children Ryan, Kelly, and Hunter have helped make our house a home and our home a glimpse of heaven.

Without that feeling, I never would have seen the utter importance of homeownership and the need for the strategies I've written about in this book.

ACKNOWLEDGMENTS

□   □   □

Special thanks to Russ Galen for his enthusiasm and support, to Rachel Klayman for her superb and insightful editing, to my son Ryan for his love, and to my wife and parents for their support.

CONTENTS

□ □ □

HOW TO BUY
YOUR OWN
HOME
IN 90 DAYS

INTRODUCTION

□   □   □

"Nothing better symbolizes the end of post-war prosperity in the United States than the fading American Dream of home ownership. In recent years, the dream has become a nightmare for a growing number of Americans."
—Peter Dreier *in* The Nation

We Americans love our freedom—especially our freedom to dream. Why? Because we believe that it doesn't end there. That's what America is all about, isn't it? We believe that we can take a dream and make it real. Anything is within reach; if we can dream it, we can achieve it.

Unfortunately, there is a growing feeling that the time has come to wake up and put the dream aside. The inflation of the seventies was a splash of cold water bringing us out of our peaceful sleep; suddenly prosperity, so long taken for granted, is no longer assured. And, for the first time in fifty years, we can no longer afford to be a nation of homeowners. We're becoming a nation of renters, living month to month, with no bright future to look forward to. The American Dream—a home we can call our own, with lace curtains and a white picket fence—is becoming less and less real, little more than a daydream.

If you're reading this from the comfort of your own home, I don't have to tell you about the pride of ownership: that chest-swelling feeling that rises up when you pull into the driveway at night, or when you stand on the porch—*your* porch—and know you're the master of all you survey (at least to the sidewalk). I don't have to convince you that the joy of owner-ship is worth the added responsibility, or that the financial security that owning your own home brings is worth the early years of struggle. But if you don't own your own home—if you're contributing to some landlord's bank account—you might need convincing.

Let's face it: Chances aren't great that you'll end up owning more than a tiny piece of planet earth. Seriously, what will you end up with? A few clothes, a dozen pieces of furniture, a color television and a videocassette recorder (of course), a couple of cars, maybe a boat, and a home. And which one will be the greatest source of personal satisfaction? Which will make you feel that you've done more in this life than take up space? Which will make you feel like you belong? What do you mean, the television? It's that fuzzy kind of thinking that put you behind the eight ball in the first place.

The answer, of course, is a home. A home of your own. A piece of the rock. A place to have and to hold. That's what the American Dream is all about. And all I hear, everywhere I go, is that fewer and fewer Americans can afford to own their own homes. Well, if you're a member of the rent-ing majority, it's time to learn a trick or two. You *can* own your own home. If you're in a home right now and would love to step up to a nicer one, but don't know how, don't feel alone. Thousands are in the same boat. But don't despair, there are techniques whereby you can have your next home locked down within the next ninety days. That's what this book is all about. I'm going to take you by the hand and teach you how to buy your first or next home, step by step.

Before we start on this quest, let's take a minute or two to talk about homeownership. Just what went wrong? Why are foreclosures at an all-time high—higher even than during the Great Depression? And, just in case you're not convinced you need to own a home, why should you even bother?

If we look back to just after World War II, it's easy to see why postwar prosperity meant not only a chicken in every pot but a home for just about every family. In 1945 a VA (Veterans Administration) loan, with an interest rate of 4 percent and monthly payments of $25, could be secured by just about any veteran. Twenty-five dollars was a lot of money to a man bringing home $200 per month; house payments were a good 15 percent of a family's net income! But the chance to own a home made the sacrifice worthwhile. Thirty years later, in 1975, that old loan was paid off. And today Mom and Dad—or Grandma and Grandpa—own their own home free and clear. What a feeling!

We're not so lucky today. The average price of a home is approaching $100,000 across the nation; monthly payments equal one quarter to one third of a family's income—for the few families making enough to cover the payments. Husbands and wives are both working, and not always by choice. I don't wish to bore you with statistics, but the average price of a new home in 1970 was $23,400. Monthly mortgage payments were down around $250. Today, not twenty years later, the average home costs $90,000, with payments of $900 per month or more. And they keep going up. Twenty years ago one third of all homes sold went to first-time buyers; today that has dropped to less than 13 percent. In other words, the only people who can afford to buy homes are those who already own homes. Of course *they* can buy a home; they have equity from their old home—the one that appreciated in value over the last ten years. But what if you don't have a home, or the equity to help you? How are you going to buy your home?

What happened?

The culprit is inflation, a nasty beast that may seem to have been tamed. It's not. It may be sleeping, or it may be hibernating for a season, but inflation is a way of life. Monetary inflation is here to stay, because it's the grease in the machine of politics. To paraphrase a famous economist, inflation is the hidden tax. This book isn't the place for a lecture on economics, so I'll spare you the details. For the purposes of this book, I'll state as a premise that inflation is here to stay. Monetary inflation is *always* a result of an increase in the supply of money, which is controllable and controlled. Housing prices *will* go up. Rents *will* increase. We will see the average price of homes climb above $100,000, then above $200,000, then . . .

A while back I visited Northern Europe. It was amazing to me, an American, to talk to people living in countries where socialism strangles the very will to succeed. When I told them I made a living as a real estate investor, they were dumbfounded. Real estate investor? What kind of factory job was that? It took several minutes of explaining and reexplaining before they could even grasp the concept—and then it was usually with obvious doubt. The majority of Europeans live in tiny, cramped apartments, forty or more apartments per building. There is no place in their economic system for financial freedom. Homeownership is only a distant hope to most of them, and owning more than one home an impossible dream.

I'm here to tell you that we haven't reached that point yet; in fact, we won't reach that point for many more years. We just have to rethink our strategies for getting out of our apartments and into our homes. And we need to do it *now*.

Let's take a second to consider the benefits of homeownership. If you're sitting pretty in your rented home or apartment, thinking you really don't need all the costs and hassles that go with owning a home, consider the benefits of ownership:

1. *Steady Payments.* You may be paying $300 less each month than the Millers down the street, who just bought their first home. In fact, you may be gloating over the fact that they are eating their dinners squatting on the floor, while you enjoy your new oak dining table. But who's going to be laughing ten years from now, when you're still renting the same apartment and paying $300 *more* for your rent than they are for a mortgage payment? If they locked in a fixed interest rate, their payments are going to *stay right where they are.* Are yours? Have rents *ever* stayed level for more than a year or two?

For a real-life scenario, let's use facts and figures. Say you're paying $450 per month now for rent on your nice three-bedroom apartment, while the

Millers are struggling with $750 house payments on the $75,000 home they just bought—one of those so-so suburban homes, nothing to look at. Now let's throw in an average inflation rate of 5 percent over the next twenty years. At the end of that time, your rent will have at least doubled, to $900 per month. The Millers will still be paying $750. Sure, your income may have doubled, but so has theirs.

To make matters worse, rental rates are increasing faster than inflation. In the late 1970s, 40 percent of all renters were paying out more than one quarter of their disposable income in rents; today, 53 percent of all renters are in that same boat. In other words, renting is getting more expensive all the time. A full third of all renters today have to give 35 percent of their income to a landlord.

>   **2.** *Retirement.* Let's take the example above and jump ahead an-
>   other twenty years. Prices (and rents) have doubled again;
>   you're now paying $1,800 per month for the same apartment.
>   The Millers made their last mortgage payment ten years ago
>   on that old house that's now appraised at $300,000 (inflation is
>   working for the Millers now). Your working days are over, and
>   the combination of your pension (*if* you have one) and social
>   security (*if* the program still exists) isn't enough to support
>   you in such high style. Time to move into the one-bedroom
>   hovel at the end of the road. Don't take this one lightly; there
>   are too many retirees living in those dumps today who will be
>   moving out to permanent underground housing in the years to
>   come to make room for you.

By the way, if the numbers in the example above seem unrealistic, take the time to talk to a retiree. Find out from him or her how unrealistic $300-a-month rentals and $90,000 houses sounded in the forties. That kind of money could have bought a castle back then.

>   **3.** *Tax Savings.* Ah, Uncle Sam. What a pal—to the homeowner.
>   You see, he allows owners of real estate to deduct mortgage
>   interest payments from their income. In the first years of an
>   amortized loan, most of the payment goes to paying the inter-

est. Greater deductions means less tax paid. It makes dollars and sense to own a home.

As an added bonus, you can either take the money in April—as a refund—or you can take home more every week. For every $1,000 in allowable tax write-offs you have, you can claim one extra exemption on your new W-4 form. More exemptions means a higher take-home pay every week.

But that's not all. There is also a tax-free savings account built into owning your own home. Called the "over 55 rule," this onetime exemption allows a principal resident seller age fifty-five or over to claim a once-per-lifetime $125,000 exemption on his home sale profits. What this means is that, as a homeowner, you will able to sell your home after you turn fifty-five, move into a smaller, less expensive one, and legally avoid paying any tax on up to $125,000 of your profit. You then could use that tax-free $125,000 any way you chose. Not bad at all.

Uncle Sam is even nicer to landlords; in addition to the interest deduction, he allows the landlord to *depreciate* his rental property. Depreciation is Uncle Sam's way of compensating the poor landlord for the fact that his buildings are losing value every year—even though they are actually *gaining* value as real estate continues to appreciate.

4. *Forced Savings.* We Americans are notorious spenders. If we have a dollar we spend it; if we have a nickel . . . well, what can you buy for a nickel anymore? We save less than 5 percent of our disposable income, making us just about the worst savers in the world.

In the comedy movie *Brewster's Millions,* a young man has the chance to inherit $300 million—if he can spend $30 million in thirty days without having anything to show for it. If, at the end of the month, he owns any assets at all except for the clothes he is wearing, he doesn't get diddly (in the words of the movie). It was interesting to see how he spent his money. Did he buy a house? Of course not; he rented two floors of a hotel for a cool million. Why? *Because renting is one of the best ways to spend your money and have nothing to show for it.*

Having house payments is a lot like having a forced savings account.

Every month, when the check goes to the lender, another bit of principal is paid off. Only a tiny sliver at first, but toward the end of the loan's life almost the entire payment is applied to the principal. So every month we're putting money in the bank. If you're renting, that's exactly what you're doing: helping the landlord meet his or her monthly payments. Keep it up long enough and you'll end up paying off his entire loan. Now, who do you want to help more: yourself or your landlord?

5. *Appreciation.* This factor has already been mentioned in passing, but let's look at its full potential. Let's take our average home of today, valued at $90,000. What will it be worth ten, twenty, thirty, forty, and fifty years from now? It depends on how much appreciation real estate experiences in the meantime. Professional economists can't agree on the price of tomatoes next week, so your guess is probably as good as mine. In the following chart you can choose the appreciation rate you think will be most likely: 3, 5, 7, 9, or 11 percent. I think anything below 3 percent is unrealistically pessimistic, and anything over 11 percent unnecessarily optimistic. Go ahead: Take your best guess and see what the home of the future will be worth—but remember, you're betting your financial future on that guess.

HOUSING APPRECIATION CHART

□

Assumption: A $90,000 average single-family home experiences appreciation rates from 3 to 11 percent during the next fifty years.

Appreciation Rates	0 Years	10 Years	20 Years	30 Years	40 Years	50 Years
3%	90,000	120,952	162,550	218,454	293,583	394,552
5%	90,000	146,601	238,797	388,975	633,599	1,032,066

Appreciation Rates	0 Years	10 Years	20 Years	30 Years	40 Years	50 Years
7%	90,000	177,044	348,272	685,103	1,347,701	2,651,132
9%	90,000	213,063	504,397	1,194,091	2,826,848	6,692,177
11%	90,000	255,548	725,608	2,060,307	5,850,078	16,610,834

Example: A basic $90,000 house today would appreciate to $685,103 in 30 years if we had a mild 7% inflation rate on housing.

Now do you see what I'm talking about when I say appreciation? The price of *everything* may increase at the same time, but without real estate as a hedge, you have nothing to protect you from the ravages of inflation.

A quick note to those who might feel that even 3-percent inflation in housing is too high. In 1986 Coldwell Banker did an intensive study showing housing appreciation rates in all fifty states. The highest appreciation during that year was 47 percent in Providence, Rhode Island. The median housing appreciation rates were between 15 and 26 percent. I personally don't think 11 percent is too high.

6. *Stability.* For yourself, for your family. If you grew up in a house, with Mom and Dad, this may need no explanation. A home is your own personal castle. It's your fortress. An apartment—or a rental house—can't offer the same sense of permanence. We Americans are a mobile people, and yet at the same time we like to sink our roots into whatever soil we inhabit. We love to stake out our own territory and enjoy the feeling of stability that comes only with ownership.

7. *Freedom.* We take our freedoms seriously. Nobody, but nobody, tells us what to do—except the landlord. Ownership allows freedoms that renters barely dream of. You can have your MTV or Lawrence Welk, and you can have it anytime, day or night. (It's much easier to wake the neighbors in the next room

than the neighbors down the street.) You can paint the fence black or white or green or red (or not at all). You don't have to get written permission to have pets or waterbeds or *children.* Yes, there are more responsibilities when you own your own home, but ask any owner whether or not those extra chores are justified.

8. *Pride.* Owning your own home does something that renting can never do: It gives you a sense of proud accomplishment. You feel—rightly—that you've done something worthwhile. The money that goes out every month doesn't just line some landlord's wallet; it's money you're paying yourself for having had enough on the ball to buy your own home. Put a home-owner and a renter in the same room and listen for a while. When they discuss where they live, which one holds his or her head high and which one's head is bowed? I'm not suggesting that homeowners are superior people, but it's undeniable: There is something about owning your own home that makes you sit a little straighter, stand a little taller, and feel as though you have a place in the world.

9. *Community Involvement.* Until you buy that first home, you'll always feel like you don't quite belong fully in the community. You may even feel homesick for a place that exists only in your mind. It's hard to care about the community when you're just another transient in an apartment building full of renters. Even if you rent the same house for five years, you'll always find yourself on the outside looking in. That feeling might not be true in a society of renters, such as those communities I visited in Europe. It might not be true in the America of the twenty-first century. But *this* America is a different story. You're not a full-fledged member of the community until you're a homeowner. Do you know any stable business people or mayors who rent? Not long ago I was driving through a small town. On the radio, broadcasters asked for public assis-tance. Flooding was imminent and the community needed vol-

unteers to help fill sandbags. Curious, I stopped at the designated site and watched with wonder as hundreds of citizens scurried like stirred-up ants, filling and stacking sandbags. That cohesive quality of community involvement just doesn't exist in rental areas.

Buying a home isn't a prerequisite for community involvement; nor will buying a home obligate you to run for mayor. But buying a home *will* make you feel more like you're a part of the neighborhood—and of society at large.

10. *Responsibility.* Every member of your family will learn lessons in responsibility when you own your own home. For adults, there is added responsibility in the form of more yard work and housework. If the faucet leaks or the dishwasher breaks down, there won't be a landlord to call. Again, the benefits and pride of accomplishment outweigh the sacrifices ten to one, and the lessons learned will be passed down from generation to generation.

Speaking of generations, children can learn more responsibility in a house than they can in an apartment. There are wonderful opportunities to teach your children how to take care of the yard, or to raise animals, or to grow a garden. Working together on their home, parents can show their children how to take pride in ownership. Single adults can use their home not only as a tax haven, but as a lucrative investment. And mature Americans can view their own home as a haven from the ravages of inflation as they enjoy the benefits of the sacrifices they made thirty years or more ago, when they tightened their belts and took the homebuying plunge.

□   □   □

THE PERIL OF PROCRASTINATION

□   □   □

There was a time, maybe back when Mom and Dad were just getting started, when it was possible to save up enough for a down payment. It took a couple of years, but the sacrifice was worth it. If you tried the same strategy in the seventies and eighties, you know by now the folly of such a tactic. By the time you've saved the necessary $10,000, prices have risen again and you need another $10,000 for the same house. You struggle to save again, only to find that by the time you've put aside another $10,000 they want $10,000 more. And it just goes on.

There is an alternative. Actually there are several alternatives, and I'll cover each in turn. For now, let's start with the knowledge that you need to buy a home and you need to do it *now*.

In this book I'm going to show you, one step at a time, how to locate, negotiate, and finance your first or next home right now. I'm not going to teach you the tools that worked in the forties and fifties—or even the tools for the sixties or seventies. You need tools that will work for the nineties. I'll give you the tools you need, but it won't work without commitment from you. This is a do-it-yourself course, and even though I'm your teacher, I can't do it for you. If you want to own your own home within ninety days, you'll have to spend time each of those ninety days working hard. Sorry, that's the bottom line. If you're willing to work—and work hard—you'll find a place you can call your own.

The rest of the book is composed of steps. You can't graduate from this class unless you follow every step to the letter. If I say jump, I'll expect you to jump just as high as you're able. If I say prepare a net worth sheet and show you how (and I will), you had better do it. If I tell you to draw a picture of a pink elephant and mail it to your best friend, then do it.

As a further incentive, if you do *everything* in your power to follow my instructions and you still cannot locate your first home, write to me and we'll discuss it. In my investing career I have seen people literally taken from an unemployment line and taught how to buy property with none of their own money, without a job, and without credit. If each of them could do it, why not you? Nevertheless, if you get stuck, please drop me a line. Write to:

Marc Garrison
M. S. Garrison and Company
P.O. Box 1096
Orem, Utah 84057

What more can I offer? If you really want a home of your own, and if you're ready and willing to work, turn the page and let's get started.

DETERMINE HOW MUCH YOU CAN AFFORD

☐   ☐   ☐

Ninety days. Not much time if you're living in an apartment now—especially if you're never quite sure where next month's rent will come from. And yet here I am promising to put you in your first or next home within that short period. The truth is, there are a few desperate cases that may be close to hopeless. It would be foolish on my part to suggest that someone who has been unemployed for nine years, who owes $90,000 on various credit accounts, and who is being pursued by the IRS is a likely candidate for the home-buyer-of-the-month award. However, even that person *can* buy a home—if he or she is willing to work hard enough.

Even for the majority of renters—who enjoy a decent income, who pay their bills, and who a few years back would have certainly bought a home —the dream seems distant today. Housing prices have skyrocketed in the seventies and eighties, leaving the nonowner hopelessly grounded. In Southern California, for example, the average price of a house was under $30,000 in 1970. Today the same house sells for $150,000 or more. A 10-percent down payment on such a house has gone from $3,000 to $15,000, and monthly payments on the balance (assuming an 11-percent interest rate) have shot up from $257 to $1,285! Average incomes have tripled since 1970, but housing prices have gone up 500 percent or more.

Is there any hope?

Of course there is. And while at this point it may seem nearly impossible, you'll find that, like most seemingly impossible tasks, it's just a matter of steps. How did anyone ever climb Mount Everest? One step at a time.

WHERE ARE YOU NOW?

□   □   □

Your first step is finding out where you are now—financially—and what you can realistically afford. Before you can even begin thinking about buying your first or next home, you need a very clear picture of your current financial situation. To help you, I've prepared a series of fill-in-the-blank forms that you can complete.* When you're finished, I'll have some specific recommendations that will fit your own personal situation.

There are three crucial elements in deciding how much you can afford

---

* In this book you will find a number of forms. You can fill in the blanks in the book, or, if you prefer, you can receive a complete set of 8 1/2" × 11" forms when you order the *Homebuyer's Tool Kit*, which is published by the National Committee for Real Estate Investment. *The Homebuyer's Tool Kit* not only includes all the forms you need, but also a four-cassette audio training course and workbook I've put together. Priced nationwide at $162, this guide is available through M. S. Garrison and Company to readers of this book for only $99. To order by credit card, call (801) 225-8777, or send your check to M. S. Garrison and Company, P.O. Box 1096, Orem, Utah 84057.

Average housing prices have risen 500 percent since 1970, while average incomes have risen only 300 percent.

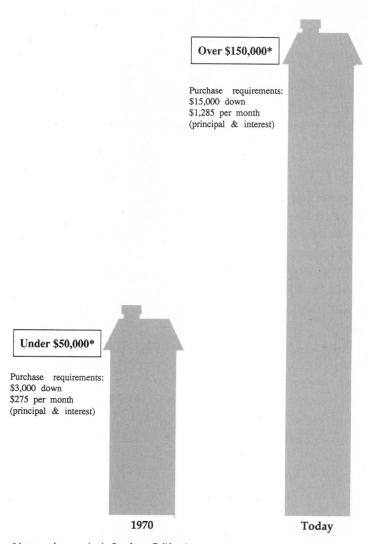

Over $150,000*

Purchase requirements:
$15,000 down
$1,285 per month
(principal & interest)

Under $50,000*

Purchase requirements:
$3,000 down
$275 per month
(principal & interest)

1970

Today

*Average home price in Southern California

to spend on your home buying: cash, credit, and income. Let's take a closer look at each and figure out where you stand.

CASH

□ □ □

By cash I mean all the cash you can come up with in the next ninety days. The Personal Asset Information Sheet on page 17 will help you decide where your piggy banks are and how to crack them open. In each of the categories on the form, try to estimate market value—that is, how much you could sell each asset for if you had to. For example, you may think your collection of pocket lint is priceless, but how much could you get for it at next Saturday's garage sale?

As I warned earlier, following this program won't be easy; many assignments will require more than a few minutes to complete. I want you to take the time to walk through your apartment or wherever you live and carefully estimate the selling value of every item of salable property. Enter your estimates in the first column. Find out from a car dealer the blue-book value of your car. Check your sources before writing down a random number.

In the second column, write any amount owing on the item. For example, if your car's blue-book value is $4,500 and you still owe $2,000, enter $2,000 in the second column.

To get the figures for the third column, subtract any financing you still owe from the market value and enter the cash value. In the car example above, you subtract the $2,000 you still owe from the blue-book value of your car and then enter the $2,500 difference in the third column.

Carry the amount in the third column to the fourth column *if* you would be willing to convert the asset to cash for the purchase of a home. How about that lint collection? Assuming someone would be willing to pay $1,000 for it, are you willing to part with it? Or what about the gold piece you inherited from Uncle Zeb? It's worth $850 now . . . would you

Personal Asset Information Sheet

Name _Pt~ R~h~_   As of _1/4/98_

Description	Market Value	Financing	Cash Value
Cash on Hand	3,000		3,000
Checking Account	3,000		3,000
Checking Account			
Savings Account ~~MF~~	20,000		20,000
Savings Account MF Mgt	7,000		7,000
Savings Account 401K	6,000		6,000
Certificate of Deposit			
Certificate of Deposit			
Certificate of Deposit			
U.S. Government ~~Bonds~~	5,000		5,000
Corporate/Other Bonds			
Investment in Business			
Partnership			
Cash Value Life Insurance			
Cash Value Retirement			
Cash Value Profit Sharing			
IRA	33,000		33,000
Trust Fund	150,000		150,000
Personal Loans Owed You	0		
Automobile Value	20,000	5,000	15,000
Automobile Value			
Recreational Vehicle			
Jewelry			
Furs			
Collections			
Art			
Furniture			
Appliances			
Other (itemize):			
			242,000

Total Cash Value   _____
Total Available Cash (without borrowing)   _____
Borrowed Money (conventional sources)   _____
Borrowed Money (relatives)   _____

Total Cash Available (including borrowing)   # 242.000

237,000 possible
mortgage

17

Personal Asset Information Sheet

Name *Barbara Kline* _____ As of *March 13, 19--*

Description	Market Value	Financing	Cash Value
Cash on Hand	$ 200.00	$	$ 200.00
Checking Account	585.35		585.35
Checking Account			
Savings Account	244.00		244.00
Savings Account	1,245.45		1,245.45
Savings Account			
Certificate of Deposit	3,000.00		3,000.00
Certificate of Deposit			
Certificate of Deposit			
U.S. Government Bonds			
Corporate/Other Bonds			
Investment in Business			
Partnership			
Cash Value Life Insurance			
Cash Value Retirement			
Cash Value Profit Sharing			
IRA	2,000.00		2,000.00
Trust Fund			
Personal Loans Owed You	150.00		150.00
Automobile Value	4,500.00	2,000.00	2,500.00
Automobile Value			
Recreational Vehicle			
Jewelry	200.00		200.00
Furs			
Collections	550.00		550.00
Art			
Furniture	6,000.00	2,000.00	4,000.00
Appliances	750.00		750.00
Other (itemize):			
computer	1,500.00		1,500.00
mutual funds	2,000.00		2,000.00

Total Cash Value	19,124.80
Total Available Cash (without borrowing)	7,324.80
Borrowed Money (conventional sources)	6,000.00
Borrowed Money (relatives)	2,000.00
Total Cash Available (including borrowing)	$ 15,324.80

sell it? It's up to you; what are you willing to sacrifice to have a home of your own?

The last two items on the list are borrowed funds. The first is from conventional sources: savings and loans, credit unions, banks, your work, credit card advances. Do you have an overdraft protection on your checking account? How much is that worth? If you could get $500 out of it by writing a check, then there's $500.

The second source of borrowed money is relatives. If you don't know how much you could borrow from them, grab the phone and give them a call. Tell them you want to buy a home of your own and need their help. (Don't forget the in-laws—although you may want your spouse to do the calling.)

Borrowing from relatives (and close friends) may or may not increase your monthly debt burden, depending on the terms of the loan. Will your generous lenders be willing to wait a year before you begin repaying the debt? Will Mom and Dad wait indefinitely?

When you have entered all the information, add up all the amounts in the fourth column. That's how much cash you can get from your current assets within the next ninety days.

Use a pencil on these worksheets! You will undoubtedly want to make changes.

You should compare the totals carefully. In the example above, Barbara Kline has over $19,000 worth of assets but is willing to sacrifice only $7,324 for a home purchase. If she borrows the full $8,000 available, she will have $15,324 available for investing, but is that the best way to round up the money? As you'll see in the next section, she may be better off pulling the money out of her CD or selling some of her other personal assets.

INCOME

□ □ □

Any lender who is considering lending you enough money to buy a house is going to look at your income first. In most cases, the more you make the

Sources of Income

Name_____ Date_____

	Annual	Monthly
Salary	_____	
Salary	_____	
Salary, Spouse	_____	
Tips	_____	
Bonuses	_____	
Commissions	_____	
Royalties	_____	
Income Tax Refund	_____	
Investment Income	_____	
Child Support	_____	
Alimony	_____	
Other Income (specify):		
_____	_____	
_____	_____	

Total Monthly Income _____

Sources of Income

Name **Kevin Anderson**   Date **November 23, 19--**

	Annual	Monthly
Salary	$~~23,200~~ 30,000	# 1,933 1,800
Salary		
Salary, Spouse	~~12,000~~ 35,000	~~4,000~~ 2,100
Tips		
Bonuses	~~5,000~~	417
Commissions	30,000	1,800
Royalties		
Income Tax Refund	2,500	208
Investment Income		
Child Support		
Alimony		
Other Income (specify):		
Interest Income,	1,200	100

Total Monthly Income $ 3,658 5,700

more you can borrow. It's the old borrower's dilemma: A banker will lend you as much as you want—if you can prove you don't need it.

Income includes all *current* sources of income. When you fill out the form on page 21, don't count on the million-dollar inheritance you're expecting whenever Aunt Tilda has the good sense to pass on. Future income is irrelevant in this determination. Include such sources of income as alimony, child support, wages, tips, royalties, and so forth—any dependable, *verifiable* source. If your income tends to be sporadic, add up your estimated earnings for the previous year and divide by twelve. It's to your advantage to include every source of income you can think of, so think hard.

In all cases, use net income, not gross. How much are you actually taking home?

Your income level will have an enormous impact on how much a lender will be willing to lend. But income is only half the picture. Debt—that all-American pastime—will also be taken into consideration. How much do you owe, and whom do you owe it to? After all, you may be making $10,000 a month, but if your expenses are $11,000, you're not a great candidate for a mortgage loan.

On the Personal Liabilities form on the next page, list all liabilities (debts) in the first column. If you plan on borrowing that $500 from your overdraft, this is the place to take that payment into account. You don't have to record the loan from dad *if* he said you don't have to pay it back for ten years and *if* he is willing to sign a "gift letter" stating that you don't have to pay it back at all (such a letter will be required by any mortgage lender, to prove that the money wasn't really a loan). You must include housing expenses and any installment debt with eleven or more payments remaining (examples would be revolving charge accounts, credit union loans, car loans, and court-ordered alimony or child support). Do not include ordinary living expenses, such as rent and groceries.

In the second column write the monthly payment due on each debt. If you aren't required to make payments every month, calculate the monthly amount. (For example, if you make annual payments, divide the payment by twelve.)

Carry amounts in the second column over to the third for all long-term debts. A debt is long term if it consists of structured payments over a

Personal Liabilities

Name_____ Date_____

Description	Total Debt	Monthly Payment	Long-Term Debt Pmt.
MasterCard			
Visa			
Charge Cards:			
_____			
_____			
_____			
_____			
Accounts Due:			
_____			
_____			
Mortgage			
Loans from Insurance			
Child Support/Alimony			
Other Debts (specify):			
_____			
_____			
Totals			

Total Monthly Income _____

Less Long-Term Monthly Debt Service = _____

Net Monthly Income Before Personal Living Expenses _____

Personal Liabilities

Name _Sharon Whitaker_   Date _February 28, 19--_

Description	Total Debt	Monthly Payment	Long-Term Debt Pmt.
MasterCard	$ 1,400.00	$ 45.00	$
Visa	1,250.00	40.00	
Charge Cards:			
J.C. Penney	850.00	35.00	
Mervyn's	350.00	20.00	
Sears	585.00	40.00	
Accounts Due:			
Credit Union	7,686.00	214.40	214.40
Mom & Dad	6,000.00	100.00	100.00
Mortgage			
Loans from Insurance			
Child Support/Alimony		400.00	400.00
Other Debts (specify):			
Car Loan	2,500.00	187.60	187.60
Totals	$ 20,621.00	$ 682.00	902.00

Total Monthly Income $ 3,658.00

Less Long-Term Monthly Debt Service   − 902.00

Net Monthly Income Before Personal Living Expenses $ 2,756.00

period of a year or more. Your three-year car loan, for example, is a long-term debt. Revolving charge card debts, such as your VISA account, are not considered to be long term if you will pay off your present balances totally within the next eleven months; normal monthly charges which you pay off each month are considered part of your monthly living expenses. If the balance due fluctuates and the monthly payment varies accordingly, it probably isn't a long-term debt.

At the bottom of the form, total all columns. You can figure your *net worth* by subtracting your total liabilities from your total assets (which you found out on the Personal Asset Information Sheet).* The figure we need most for this exercise is your monthly net income less your long-term debt payments. That figure—net income available for living expenses—will determine how much mortgage money you can afford to borrow.

CREDIT

☐   ☐   ☐

A good credit rating is a must for the home buyer. You are bound to fall into one of three categories: good credit, bad credit, or no credit. Let's take a look at your credit rating and see where you are now.

Your Credit Report

When you apply for a credit card or a loan, the bank decides whether or not you are an acceptable risk by consulting your credit history. Contrary to common misconception, it is a credit-reporting company, and not the government, that is keeping your credit history on file. In the United

---

* Net worth is an important concept. Your net worth is what you would have left if you sold everything you owned and used the money to pay off everything you owe. Many Americans who don't own a home of their own have little or no net worth, and the Americans who do own a home almost always have their home to thank for whatever net worth they do have.

States there are five such companies. Each of them is a private agency with many retail clients. They gather information from public records and retail sources, and they put together a surprisingly complete history of your credit purchases and payments. If you've ever bought anything on credit or if you have even applied for credit; if you've ever filed for bankruptcy; or if you've ever had a lien against you, then you can be sure you have a credit file hidden away in those computers.

Most credit files contain basic information about you such as name, current address, employer, the position you hold, your spouse's name, and your social security number. Following this information, there are reports from the retailers and merchants from whom you have obtained credit. These listings show dates of your last transactions, your credit line, how much you owed as of the date of the report, and any past-due amounts. They also show who has requested to see your records. All records kept by credit-reporting agencies are kept as current as possible, and they show every credit transaction for the past seven years, with the exception of bankruptcies, which are retained on a consumer's record for ten years.

If you are young and just starting out in the credit world, or if you are a more mature person trying to recover from some past financial difficulties, there are steps you can take to improve your creditworthiness.

The best way to establish, or reestablish, your credit is through a secured Visa and/or MasterCard (secured means that you must establish a savings account to protect your credit line). In most financial institutions, your credit line will be someplace between 40 percent and 100 percent of your total savings account.

While it is sometimes difficult to find a financial institution that will accept an individual with no credit or poor credit, if you persist you will be able to find one. Your first step should be to ask the institution that you have your checking or savings account with. If they don't offer this type of account, ask them to refer you to another institution in your area that extends this type of account to consumers. Most bankers will know what their competition is offering to the public. If there are no institutions in your area that offer this program, contact one of the institutions outside your area that offers this type of account nationwide.

If you already have a Visa or MasterCard, you will not need to go through the above procedures.

Once you have obtained a Visa and/or MasterCard, secured or unsecured, your next step in building a strong, positive credit report is to apply for instant credit (sometimes called a courtesy card) at a major department or furniture store in your area. There are many stores across the nation that offer instant credit: Macy's, Broadway, Southwest, Diamond's, Foley's, Emporium-Capwell's, Goldwater's, Robinson's, Levitz Furniture, Pacific Stereo, and so forth.

The reason that most companies offer this service to the customers in their area is that marketing studies have found that most people do not make a special trip to the store to apply for credit—they go to a store to shop (in other words to spend money) and, if the instant credit is available, while they are shopping they apply for the card. The stores mentioned above plus many other stores across the nation will give you instant credit if you have a positive (good) Visa or MasterCard (secured or unsecured).

Be aware that a courtesy card is a *temporary* card that you can use until your permanent credit card is approved (same procedure as those stores that refer to it as instant credit). The very same day you get this courtesy card you should immediately use it. It is important to use your courtesy card immediately because when a company turns you down for a permanent card they also reject your right to use your courtesy card.

The first time you use your temporary card, be sure you buy something you really need, but if you are like most people you can always use socks, bed linen, or other items for yourself, your family, or your home. Remember that your purpose in charging at this point is to build your credit record. It is absolutely essential that you pay the charges in a timely way, which is another good reason to be modest in what you charge.

Just because you are approved for a courtesy card (instant credit) does not mean you will receive a permanent credit card. Even though you get turned down for a permanent card, you must pay off the amount you charged on your courtesy card in the agreed manner. Once you have paid off your account in full, it will be entered as a positive on your credit report. Keep applying for new courtesy cards while still maintaining your budget, and pay off each one within terms. Each time you pay an account as agreed it becomes a positive on your credit report.

If you are just getting started in the credit world, this is the best way to get off on the right foot.

Whatever your situation is at present, you should know your credit rating. In fact, I want you to find out your rating before we go any further.

There are two ways to see a copy of your credit report. The first is to apply for every credit card you can think of until you're turned down (Sears is a toughie for anyone who has never had credit). When you're turned down by one company or another, you can request, within thirty days, to see a copy of your credit report for free. If you don't want to bother applying for credit cards you can always request to see your report, but you'll have to pay a fee (usually $10 or less).

To find your local agency, look in the Yellow Pages under "Credit Reporting Agencies." They will be happy to show you your report and go over it with you in detail, explaining any problems that might cause trouble when you apply for a loan.

Good Credit

If the reporting agency tells you your credit is in good shape, congratulations. Go to the head of the class; you are probably ready to apply for your first mortgage loan. You can make your rating even stronger by borrowing money from your bank on a signature loan (an unsecured loan, based on your good credit and net worth statement). Borrow the least you can—probably $1,000—and pay it back on time. A record of prompt payments will go a long way in securing any type of future loan.

Bad Credit

If there is a problem with your credit history, and if it is your fault, contact the creditor immediately. Find out what you need to do to correct the problem and then do it. Make sure that when clearing up credit problems that you *never* pay off a delinquent balance until the company agrees to remove the problem from your credit record. If you wait to ask them to clear up the problem after you have paid, you will not have any leverage to get them to do it.

While you still owe money on the account, you have the creditor's attention; you also have something he wants—the money. So before you pay a dime on an unpaid/late account that is causing a negative item on your credit report, negotiate a *complete* removal. How? Very simple. Tell the creditor that you are willing to pay off the account *if* the creditor will agree to remove the account from your credit report. Furthermore, if the account is old enough, a creditor will often settle for less than the original amount. Don't hesitate to ask. The worst that can happen is that he will tell you no.

It is extremely important that you get the creditor to agree to sign a "fulfillment agreement," which guarantees removal of the negative account from your credit report in fifteen days instead of the usual seven years. That's a savings of 2,540 days!

Consider this: An unpaid account and a paid account remain on your credit report for the same amount of time—seven years from the date of last activity. So, if you pay the account without negotiating the fulfillment agreement, you are shooting yourself in the foot. You will have paid the bill and gained absolutely nothing. The creditor, once he is paid, has no further interest in you and certainly cares nothing for your creditworthiness.

When you begin to negotiate the removal of a bad credit rating on your account, start with the local branch of the company and work your way up to the national headquarters if necessary. Tell them that if they do not agree to sign the fulfillment agreement, you may not pay them. Be gentle and diplomatic, but very, very firm.

If the creditor refuses to negotiate and you refuse to pay, their only recourse is to sue you. Respond to the suit in court (always appear) and tell the judge you are willing to pay the account, but the creditor is unwilling to remove the account from your credit report. The worst that can happen is that you will end up with a judgment on your credit report which you should get removed later with a vacate order.

While you are going through the process of removing the negative from your credit report, have a "consumer's statement" placed in your credit file telling your side of the story. Doing so will help you get credit during this time period.

Always remember that your credit rating is essentially a borrowing license, and when your license is suspended, so is your ability to buy a home with traditional bank financing.

If the problem is not your fault—if, for example, you're sure you never ordered a set of underwater ski poles from Banzai International—you should tell the agency. They must, by law, contact the reporting creditor and attempt to verify the information they were given. If that doesn't clear up the problem, and if the creditor insists that you are the culprit, you have the right to have a letter from you included in your report, explaining your side of the story. Furthermore, you can insist that a revised report be sent to all credit-reporting agencies in your area.

Anyone with a bad credit history should follow these additional steps:

1. Many times a person with a bad credit history at one credit bureau should simply quit doing business with that credit bureau. In other words, before you apply for credit find out what credit bureau the credit grantor is a member of and, if this bureau has negative information on your report, don't apply!

2. Start the procedure to improve your credit with the credit bureau that is reporting the negative.

3. Apply to a credit grantor who is a member of a different credit bureau.

No Credit

The hardest situation in America to be in if you want to obtain credit is to be a person over the age of twenty-five who has never had credit before in his or her name. When you apply for a loan, stating that you have no credit history, banks simply do not believe you are telling the truth.

If you don't have a credit history, it's only because you don't have a credit card or a credit account anywhere. If you are new to the credit game, or if you're proud of yourself for having resisted the temptation to play with plastic money, you are in almost as much trouble as someone with poor credit. You're not a bad risk, perhaps, but you're definitely an unknown. What lender will give you $60,000 when you've never proven your ability to repay a debt? And getting that first credit card can be a real catch-22. You can't get a card because you don't have credit, and you don't have credit because you can't get a card!

The best way to get your credit off to a good start is to buy an appliance at any major department store, such as J. C. Penney, and to apply for credit at the same time. Offer to pay half the price of the item (such as a microwave or toaster oven) if they will allow you to charge the other half. They will have you fill out a credit application, but this time you'll be surprised at the difference in their response. Nine times out of ten they'll be happy to extend a small credit line—perhaps $200. Pay it off on time and you can apply to have it increased to $500 or more.

You'll find that one credit card will start an avalanche of plastic. Your second card will be even easier, and with two or three department store cards under your belt (or at least in your wallet) Visa and MasterCard are only an application away. But watch your step; the credit card carousel tends to spin faster and faster, and if you're not careful you can get hurt.

Another way to establish credit doesn't involve the use of credit cards. If you have a savings account, ask your banker for a small loan, using the savings as collateral. Deposit the borrowed money in a savings account at another bank and borrow money there to pay off the first loan. You'll lose a little money in interest payments, but you will quickly establish a good repayment track record with the bank itself *and* you will get to know the loan officers personally.

What can you do if you have a bankruptcy on your record?

Bankruptcy is the worst item on a credit report and is the only item that can remain for more than seven years. A Chapter 7 bankruptcy remains for a maximum of ten years, a Chapter 11 or 13 for seven years. (All three of these bankruptcy chapters involve reorganization of your debts. You must pay off your debt through a plan that you originate and is approved by the court. The bankruptcy remains on your credit report not only during the time you are paying off the debts but for seven years following the final payment.)

Even so, you are not eliminated from the credit world just because at one point in your life you may have had to file for bankruptcy. Millions of Americans have experienced bankruptcy. If you are one of them, you may find it hard to get your credit reestablished, but it is not impossible. Remember that bankruptcy is supposed to be a relief, not a penalty.

To show your bankruptcy in the most positive possible manner, you must do the following (or remove the bankruptcy):

1. Get a copy of your credit report. Make sure the bankruptcy is being reported correctly. If the date, amount, court, and other facts are wrong, you have the right to ask for a verification from the credit bureau. And if the credit bureau is unable to verify the bankruptcy, they must remove the bankruptcy from your credit report.

If you go physically to obtain your credit report from the credit bureau, do not agree to a consumer interview to discuss your credit report. Get your credit report, take it home, and study it until you understand it. In most cases, the credit bureau will not require that you sit through an interview. If the credit bureau does require an interview, be polite and sit through the interview. Do not agree or disagree with anything. You may say something that could affect you adversely in the future. If you have any questions regarding the credit report, ask a neutral person.

Look at your bankruptcy papers (if you don't have a copy, you can get a copy from the bankruptcy court). Review the credit report and compare the way the bankruptcy is listed on your credit report to the information on the bankruptcy papers. Check the amount, date, court, attorney. Look for something to disagree with.

Assuming that you find at least one discrepancy, write a letter to the credit bureau asking them to recheck the bankruptcy. Mail a copy of the credit report with the letter, *but* do not mail a copy of the bankruptcy papers.

After the credit bureau completes the process of checking the information on the bankruptcy, they must provide you with a new credit report at no charge. Check your new credit report to see if the credit bureau has made a change on the disputed item(s). If the credit bureau did not make the corrections regarding your dispute, it means that they did not perform the verification required by law.

If this situation occurs, the next step is the most important one and it takes the most courage. Take your original credit report and the new credit report down to the credit bureau and ask to speak to a manager. Tell them that you have caught them in a violation of the law, but that you are a reasonable person and do not want to sue them. (Even then the law says you can, and you may win big money.) You may also report the credit bureau to the Federal Trade Commission. *Try to make a deal that they remove the bankruptcy in return for your not suing them and for not reporting them.*

2. If the verification procedure does not remove the bankruptcy, you have the right to include a consumer statement on your credit report explaining the reason for the bankruptcy.

3. Make sure those accounts on your credit report that were part of your bankruptcy show on the report as being part of the bankruptcy and are not reported by the creditor as a charge-off or charged to profit and loss. Accounts that were part of the bankruptcy that are being reported otherwise give two strikes against you instead of one.

4. Check all five credit bureaus. In most cases you won't find your bankruptcy reported by all the bureaus. This gives you the opportunity to obtain credit from banks and businesses that use a credit bureau that does not show your bankruptcy.

5. Keep your mouth shut. Tell a banker about your bankruptcy only if he asks. You are not required to volunteer the information, but if asked tell the truth.

There are many banks and businesses that do not automatically eliminate you because of a bankruptcy—especially with the rate of individual bankruptcy at an all-time high.

If you would like some specialized help in clearing up your credit problems I would recommend that you contact the American Consumer Credit Alliance at 209-582-0800. From their offices in California, ACCA specializes in credit improvement and counseling services. I have personally met ACCA's president, Tim Taylor, and have seen the excellent work his organization does.

HOW MUCH HOME CAN YOU AFFORD?

□   □   □

Let's shift away from you and concentrate for a while on how much house you can afford. If houses were selling for $5 apiece, or if you had $100,000 under the mattress, you could pay cash. Unfortunately, they aren't and you don't. That means part or all of your purchase will have to be financed. You might want to finance the entire purchase, but most traditional lenders will insist that you come up with 10 percent (or more) of the price yourself. The part you come up with is the *down payment;* the portion that is financed is the *mortgage.**

How much down payment you can afford will depend on how much cash you have available and how much you have to pay in *closing costs.*† How much financing you can afford will depend on your income (from the second form) and your credit rating. If you've been doing your homework you should be ready to determine both.

According to the rule of thumb that has applied in the past, your gross income should be five times your mortgage payment. That was a fine rule —way back when it was applicable. In the 1950s, 70 percent of all Americans could afford mortgage payments using that rule; by 1975 only 40 percent could do so; and today the number of qualified buyers has shrunk

---

* The actual instrument may be a *trust deed,* instead of a mortgage and note, but for the purposes of this book we'll call it a mortgage in every case.

† Closing costs, also called *settlement costs,* are fees paid the day you actually take title to the property. We will discuss them in detail in Step #10.

to less than 20 percent. Even if we have enough gross income, we pay higher taxes today than our parents did at our age, reducing net income even further. It's time to find a new thumb to make rules by. (Later in this book you will learn about several different ways to finance a home without having to step onto the carpet at a bank.)

What you are going to have to do, no matter which way you choose to finance, is to determine how much payment and house you can afford. Traditional sources would assert that today you should plan on spending no more than 25–28 percent of your *gross* income on your monthly housing expense (including property taxes and hazard insurance). They also will say that your total monthly debt (housing expenses, long-term installment debt, personal loans, automobile loans, alimony, and child support) should not exceed 33–36 percent of your gross income. To me that is like saying that anyone who can't run a four-minute mile can't even consider buying their first or next home. Not everyone has that kind of extraordinary income. If I used those rules, I would have never purchased my first home at age twenty-two. My wife and I would still be trudging along trying to "be patient and save up."

Instead I took a chance, had a house payment that was almost 50 percent of my gross income, fixed up the home, and sold it for a $15,200 profit. That initial profit let me move into a nicer home with a down payment that was big enough to cut my house payment by 40 percent. I would suggest that you concentrate right now on your monthly net income as we have already defined it. You should anticipate spending no more that 40 percent of that income toward your principal and interest payment.

To put these ideas all together, the table on page 36 is the heart and soul of this first step. It takes everything we've done so far into consideration to help you figure out exactly how much you can afford to spend on your home. It automatically includes a factor for taxes and insurance charges that will be added to your monthly mortgage payment; it deducts hidden costs of home ownership, such as higher heating bills; and it will help you calculate all of the cash expenses involved.

You must know your net monthly income to use this affordability index. If your net monthly income before living expenses is $2,800, you would locate that figure in the monthly net income column. Looking across the

Housing Affordability Index ‡

Monthly Net Income	Max. Suggested Payment (Includes Principal & Interest Pmt. Only)	Maximum Suggested Mortgage Amounts at a Specific Interest Rate							
		9%	10%	11%	12%	13%	14%	15%	16%
$ 800	$ 240	$ 29,827	$ 27,348	$ 25,202	$ 23,332	$ 21,696	$ 20,255	$ 18,981	$ 17,847
1,200	360	44,741	41,022	37,802	34,999	32,544	30,383	28,471	26,771
1,600	480	59,655	54,696	50,403	46,665	43,392	40,511	37,961	35,694
2,000	600	74,569	68,370	63,004	58,331	54,240	50,638	47,452	44,618
2,400	720	89,483	82,045	75,605	69,997	65,088	60,766	56,942	53,541
2,800	840	104,397	95,719	88,205	81,663	75,936	70,894	66,432	62,465
3,200	960	119,311	109,393	100,806	93,330	86,784	81,021	75,923	71,388
3,600	1,080	134,224	123,067	113,407	104,996	97,632	91,149	85,413	80,312
4,000	1,200	149,138	136,741	126,008	116,662	108,480	101,277	94,903	89,235
4,500	1,350	167,781	153,834	141,759	131,245	122,039	113,936	106,766	100,390
5,000	1,500	186,423	170,926	157,510	145,827	135,599	126,596	118,629	111,544
5,500	1,650	205,065	188,019	173,260	160,410	149,159	139,256	130,492	122,699
6,000	1,800	223,707	205,111	189,011	174,993	162,719	151,915	142,355	133,853
6,500	1,950	242,350	222,204	204,762	189,576	176,279	164,575	154,218	145,008
7,000	2,100	260,992	239,297	220,513	204,158	189,839	177,234	166,081	156,162
7,500	2,250	279,634	256,389	236,264	218,741	203,399	189,894	177,944	167,316

‡ In using the Housing Affordability Index, use the monthly income figure from the liability worksheet, gross income minus long-term debt. Also note that your monthly payment will include not just a payment toward the principal (the money you are borrowing) and the interest, but also one twelfth of your annual property insurance premium and one twelfth of your property-tax assessment. Because of the wide range of prices on insurance and property-tax costs in the United States, we will base the monthly payment calculation on 30 percent of your net monthly income before living expenses. The monthly payment figure will represent a payment which includes principal and interest.

index to the right, you would see that your maximum suggested monthly principal and interest payment is $840. Keep in mind that $840 is only a suggested figure. Looking further to the right, you see several loan amounts under the different interest headings. If you feel that a 9-percent owner-financed loan on a home is feasible, then you're looking to buy a home where you'd be financing $104,397. If 12 percent seems more realistic, then you would look under that figure and find that the loan amount drops to $81,663 because of the increased interest charge. (That $23,000 drop in how much you can borrow because of the increase in interest rates is your first lesson in real estate finance. Terms make a big difference!)

Now let's figure out how much you can afford to pay. The chart shows the maximum amount, including principal and interest, that you can afford. Let's put this payment figure on the purchase price worksheet on page 38.

Do you like what you see? If not—if the results spell disaster for your homebuying plans, or if your case is borderline and you'd like to afford more than a one-bedroom shack in the country—don't get discouraged. Later we'll take a look at options available if you really don't have the money and/or the income to buy a house.

If you find that you can afford to buy, you'll likely have to lower your earlier expectations. With the surge of prosperity experienced after World War II, most baby boomers learned to expect the best of everything. We live with luxuries our parents only dreamed of. As a result, when it comes time to buy our first homes we start with the best—after all, we deserve nothing less. Unfortunately, reality—as revealed by the worksheets in this step—may be a sharp slap, waking you up. You may have to lower your housing sights even lower than your parents' original expectations, if only for a couple of years. But the sacrifice will be worth it. You'll own your own piece of America, and while you may be starting on the bottom rung, you'll have a foothold on the ladder of success.

None of the results of these worksheets is written in cement (in fact, they shouldn't even be written in ink). You can find ways to increase your income, can't you? Or you can sell that lint collection after all, increasing the cash available. Swallow your pride, promise your mother-in-law she can live with you when she gets old if she'll lend you $5,000 now. One way

Purchase Price Worksheet

Name _____ Date_____

Total Cash Available (within 90 days)   _____

Less Closing Costs (4 percent of mortgage amount
from Housing Affordability Index)   _____

Total Cash Available for Down Payment   _____

Total Mortgage Amount at _____% Interest   _____

Total Proposed Purchase Price   _____

Purchase Price Worksheet

Name __Douglas Piper__   Date __December 22, 19--__

Total Cash Available (within 90 days) $8,433.00

Less Closing Costs (4 percent of mortgage amount
from Housing Affordability Index)   2,220.00

Total Cash Available for Down Payment $6,213.00

Total Mortgage Amount at __11__ % Interest $52,300.00

Total Proposed Purchase Price $58,513.00

or another, you should be able to increase income or cash available and decrease your debts at the same time.

Whatever the results of this step, it's time to move on to the next: determining your housing needs.

DETERMINE YOUR HOUSING NEEDS

☐   ☐   ☐

In this step we'll throw out—or at least temporarily set aside—everything you did in Step #1. Let's forget the numbers, forget about what you can and can't afford, and think about what you really *want* in a home—and what you don't want. How about an indoor pool with a rollaway glass ceiling for those swim parties under the stars? A three-story mansion with an elevator from the underground garage? Five acres of wooded land, with your own private fish-laden stream? A modest eight-bedroom beach house on Maui?

Take a minute out of your busy reading schedule and dream. There are people living in homes just like the one you're imagining right now. Somewhere someone is bathing in that sunken heart-shaped bathtub you were just thinking about. And why are they in your dream home while you're where you are now? Because they dared to dream and then worked like crazy to fulfill their dreams. You can do the same.

Those dreams you have are important, but for now they may be unrealistic. One of the logjams people run into when they look for their first or next home is that they've got it in mind to buy the perfect home—or a place at least as good as the home they were raised in. They forget that Mom and Dad probably bought during the postwar expansion of the forties and fifties, when houses were selling for about what a small disposable import car sells for today. Housing was plentiful and cheap compared with today, and Mom and Dad bought without even realizing they were buying future equity. *Today we have to readjust our sights.* Reality insists that we set aside a few of our dreams for a year or two.

WHAT DO YOU NEED?

□   □   □

There is a scale that starts with absolute needs, such as enough food to keep starvation at bay and enough shelter to keep out the winter winds. At the other end of the scale are the impossible dreams, such as becoming ruler of the universe or the richest person in the world. Somewhere on that scale is the house you dream about; another house that you really think you could be happy with (the one that's only slightly larger than Mom and Dad's); and the one you will end up buying soon.

In your search for that first or next home of your own, you'll have to go through a narrowing-down process, wherein you will weed out the essential from the nonessential and your *wants* from your *needs, as you reconcile your dream home with reality.* It works something like this:

□   □   □

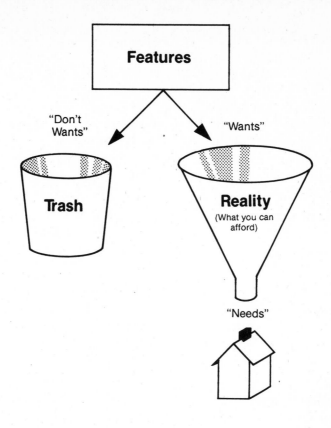

WANTS VS. NEEDS

☐ ☐ ☐

Following is a checklist that will help you decide which features you want, don't want, need, don't need, can't live without, and can't live with. Only you can determine whether or not you could live in a rundown section of town; only you can decide whether or not you really *need* six bedrooms and four bathrooms.

Rate each feature on a scale from one to five, as follows:

1. I love it; it would definitely be included in my dream home, and it's an important consideration in my house shopping.
2. I like it a lot, even if it isn't on my list of the best things in life. It would be a fairly important consideration.
3. I don't really care; I can take it or leave it.
4. I don't like it much, but I could live with it.
5. I can't stand that feature, and if my home had it I'd be embarrassed to invite guests over for a barbecue.

The last two columns are for the absolutes; that is, if you absolutely, positively must—or must not—have a particular feature in your home. For example, a person confined to a wheelchair may be dead set against having a two-story home, and rightly so; or a family of eight cannot live in a house with less than two bathrooms. If a particular feature is that important, place a check mark in either the Yes or the No column.

If you need help figuring out how to use the checklist, a filled-out sample follows.

As you looked at each feature in your mind, I hope you were wearing your reality glasses. If you put something down as an absolute must, is it really carved in stone? For example, I have three children and hopefully a few more on the way. I want at least a four-bedroom home, but how many bedrooms do I really need? Can we get by with two bedrooms for a couple of years, or would we drive each other right out the window? Likewise with the things we don't want. Perhaps you don't want to live in a "fixer" —one of those ramshackle, sixty-year-old homes—that will need a few months of hard work fixing up. Is it an absolute no, or could you live with it? Remember, our joint goal is to get you into a home of your own, and if you don't have money flowing into your bank account faster than you can empty it, you shouldn't narrow down your options so tightly that you close out a possible good deal.

Homebuyer's Checklist
Part 1

Name *Briarwood*   Date _____

Features	1	2	3	4	5	NO	YES
THE HOME							
Particular architectural style		X					
Number of stories	X						
BiLevel						X	
Split entry				X			
New home			X				
Existing home		X					
Number of bedrooms *4-5*		X					
Number of baths *2-3*		X					
Master bedroom	X						
Frame construction				X			
Hardwood flooring				X			
Carpet throughout				X			
Southern exposure					X		
Carport						X	
Garage							X
Basement							X
Kitchen windows		X					
Separate dining room		X					
Bedrooms on main level						X	
Expandability				X			
Air Conditioning	X						
Energy Efficient	X						
Gas heat		X					
Electric heat			X				
Oil heat			X				
Coal heat			X				
Fireplace		X					
Possible rental income				X			
Fixer-upper			X				
Investment value							
A home that doesn't look like the neighbors' homes			X				
THE NEIGHBORHOOD							
A particular neighborhood		X					
A neighborhood with a lot of families		X					

Features	1	2	3	4	5	NO	YES
NEIGHBORHOOD (continued)							
An all-adult neighborhood				X			
A neighborhood that's friendly		X					
A neighborhood that's private		X					
A cul-de-sac			X				
A street with a lot of traffic		X					
A quiet neighborhood		X					
Close proximity to a commercial or industrial zone						X	
THE YARD AND LOT							
A lot of sunshine		X					
A dark home during the daytime			X	X			
Private backyard			X				
Mature landscaping		X					
Fenced yard			X				
Swimming pool				X			
Patio		X					
Backyard deck	X						
CONVENIENCES							
Security system			X				
Appliances:							
Trash compactor				X			
Dishwasher	X						
Gas stove		X					
Electric stove			X				
Commuting time							
Near transportation			X				
Near schools			X				
Particular school district		X					
Near shopping		X					
Close to major roads or freeways		X					
Near your particular church		X					
Near community services:							
Library		X					
Parks		X					
Recreation centers		X					
Swimming pool		X					

1hr 10m

F Park

Homebuyer's Checklist
Part 1

Name *Denise Atwood*   Date *October 10, 19--*

Features	1	2	3	4	5	NO	YES
THE HOME							
Particular architectural style	X						
Number of stories		X					
BiLevel		X					
Split entry			X				
New home			X				
Existing home			X				
Number of bedrooms	4	3					
Number of baths	3	2					
Master bedroom			X				
Frame construction			X				
Hardwood flooring			X				
Carpet throughout		X					
Southern exposure				X			
Carport			X				✓
Garage		X					
Basement		X					
Kitchen windows		X					
Separate dining room		X					
Bedrooms on main level		X					
Expandability			X				
Air Conditioning		X					
Energy Efficient		X					
Gas heat	X						
Electric heat					X	X	
Oil heat					X		
Coal heat				X			
Fireplace		X					
Possible rental income			X				
Fixer-upper				X			
Investment value			X				
A home that doesn't look like the neighbors' homes		X					
THE NEIGHBORHOOD							
A particular neighborhood		X					
A neighborhood with a lot of families		X					

Features	1	2	3	4	5	NO	YES
NEIGHBORHOOD (continued)							
An all-adult neighborhood					X		
A neighborhood that's friendly		X					
A neighborhood that's private		X					
A cul-de-sac		X					
A street with a lot of traffic				X			
A quiet neighborhood		X					
Close proximity to a commercial or industrial zone				X			
THE YARD AND LOT							
A lot of sunshine		X					
A dark home during the daytime				X			
Private backyard		X					
Mature landscaping			X				
Fenced yard			X				
Swimming pool				X			
Patio				X			
Backyard deck				X			
CONVENIENCES							
Security system				X			
Appliances:							
Trash compactor			X				
Dishwasher			X				
Gas stove			X				
Electric stove	X						
Commuting time	1 hr.						
Near transportation			X				
Near schools		X					
Particular school district			X				
Near shopping			X				
Close to major roads or freeways	X						
Near your particular church	X						
Near community services:							
Library	X						
Parks			X				
Recreation centers			X				
Swimming pool			X				

FINDING THE HOUSE YOU NEED

□   □   □

Now that you've sorted the wants from the needs, you're almost ready to begin analyzing your specific real estate market. But to do so, let's take what you've already done and put it into a more usable format. The following form can be used by you or by any real estate agent to help you in your search. The second part of the home buyer's checklist defines your absolute needs (and absolute don't wants) and prioritizes your desire for other wanted features.

The form is mostly self-explanatory. In the first section, fill in what you're sure you can't live without; in the second, what you're sure you cannot live with; and in the third everything else that got a score of one or two in the first checklist—in order of priority.

To the right of each item is a space to verify that the property actually does (or does not) have the features you want. When you hand out these forms to real estate agents in your area, you can instruct them that these are the items that you are looking for in a home. Have them screen any available homes using these criteria. Make it clear that before you go out and visit anything they should either check off those items or have the seller check them off for you, so you don't waste time visiting a home that doesn't at least meet your lowest level of expectations. This one form can save you countless hours of looking.

Again, there is a filled-out example after the blank form in case you need help.

□   □   □

Homebuyer's Checklist
Part 2

Name(s) _____ Date _____

Address _____

City _____ State _____ Zip _____

Telephone _____

Real Estate Agent:

    Name _____

    Telephone _____

Property Owner:

    Name _____

    Address _____

    City _____ State _____ Zip _____

    Telephone _____

I (We) **must have** the following:	Target Property Evaluation (Excellent–Acceptable–Poor)
_____	_____
_____	_____
_____	_____
_____	_____
_____	_____
_____	_____
_____	_____
_____	_____
_____	_____
_____	_____
_____	_____

I (We) **do not want** the following features:

Target Property Evaluation
(Excellent–Acceptable–Poor)

_____

_____

_____

_____

_____

_____

_____

I (We) would like to have the following features
(in order of priority):

Target Property Evaluation
(Excellent–Acceptable–Poor)

Homebuyer's Checklist
Part 2

Name(s) *Mary Williams*   Date *September 29, 19--*

Address *1011 Cherry Creek*

City *Anytown*   State *CA*   Zip *92670*

Telephone *555-8120*

Real Estate Agent:

     Name *John Johnston*

     Telephone *555-9020*

Property Owner:

     Name _____

     Address _____

     City _____ State _____ Zip _____

     Telephone _____

I (We) **must have** the following:	Target Property Evaluation (Excellent–Acceptable–Poor)
at least 3 bedrooms	
at least 2 bathrooms	
carport or garage	
basement	
gas heat	
air-conditioning	
no more than one hour commute	

52

I (We) do not want the following features:

all-adult neighborhood
busy street
commercial industrial area

**I (We) would like to have the following features
(in order of priority):**

new home
4-5 bedrooms
3-4 bathrooms
master bathroom
carpet throughout
separate dinning room
private backyard
dishwasher
gas stove
near high school
Cape Cod style
split entry
frame construction

It's *almost* time to get out there and find your home. In fact, you've finished all the paperwork for a while, and with what you've learned I'll bet you're ready to run out the door and . . . hey, wait! Come back here. Sit back down and listen. Yes, the next step is to analyze your own area, but we're going to do it in a very organized, careful fashion.

If you've done everything I've asked you to do so far, congratulations; you're right on schedule and ready to move on to Step #3. In fact, you might not know it, but you are already miles ahead of the competition.

ANALYZE YOUR AREA

☐   ☐   ☐

We're all familiar with our own neighborhoods, and maybe even with most of the city or countryside around us. We know where the best stores are; what's available in the way of entertainment; if we're parents, we usually know where the best schools are—and the worst. We know where the city parks are, the library, the police station, and perhaps a church or two. We know where the "good" and "bad" neighborhoods are, and we know what areas to avoid late at night.

But what we don't realize is just how much housing prices are affected by location. That should be obvious; but just how much are they affected? And can you gauge that effect?

Most potential buyers fail to realize that location is one of the key determinants in the value of any home. The price of the same basic type of home can vary thousands of dollars if the home were located in various sections around town. Just think what that means: If you could pack a house onto the back of a pickup and move it across town, you could make a small fortune (disregarding moving, land, and hookup costs). Imagine moving that nice little three-bedroom (the off-white on the corner with the blue trim) from its location near the ball-bearing factory to the top of Snob Hill; it would double in value.

As we look at neighborhoods, we need to consider location as an important determinant of price. You also need to look at other factors concerning your neighborhood besides price. We need to look at the loan programs available in your area. You probably don't even know it, but under the rug of government red tape you just might have some special government financing available in your local area for buying your next home. Many states now are offering low-interest-rate insured loans for first-time homebuyers and owner-occupants.

After we get to know what loan programs are available and once we understand the area better, we need to look in depth at special services. Special services that might affect your buying decision and life-style include transportation, schools, churches, parks, libraries, shopping, and community fire and police protection. An understanding that you are not just buying a house but a whole neighborhood and all its features will lead you to a better knowledge of just where you'd like to live.

The first thing to do is to go out and get a map. I would suggest going down to the planning and zoning commission at your county office building and getting a county "plat" map. Such a map comes on blueprint paper and is quite easy to read. If you live in an area where more than one county is represented, you might want to go to a bookstore and buy the best local neighborhood street map you can buy. Make sure the map covers an area of at least several hours' transportation time from your place of employment. You should also get yourself a set of highlighter pens to make notes on the map with. These highlighters usually come in sets of five different-colored pens.

With this map in hand, you're ready to do a little work. I would suggest that you start by marking on the map where you work. Then lay the map out on a table and, as accurately as possible, draw a circle which represents the maximum commute you could live with from where you and your spouse work. Consider all transportation options which are available to you even though you may not like them, such as car, train, ferry, bus, van pool, and so forth. Having marked this map with your target area, you are now ready for the next step—*getting to know your housing search area.*

Pay a visit to a real estate agent in your area with your map. But before you show up at just any real estate office, do a little preparation.

1. Ask your friends, co-workers, and relatives if they have used a real estate agent recently in the purchase of a home. If anyone has, ask him or her if the agent did a good job. If they were pleased with the agent, ask for the agent's name and phone number. Start filling in the form headed "My Homebuying Team on page 59." This list should include at least three real estate agents. You might want make a copy of the form to organize your search for professionals to help in your homebuying efforts.

As you get a recommendation for a real estate agent, pencil in his or her name on this homebuying team directory sheet. If possible, include each agent's home phone number. As we go along, I'll show you how to complete your homebuying team list.

2. If you haven't been able to get at least three personal recommendations of agents from friends, open up your phone book and make some calls to some local real estate agencies. Use the following filtering process to find yourself a good agent to work with.

   • Ask to speak to the office secretary.

   • Identify yourself as someone who is interested in buying your first or next home.

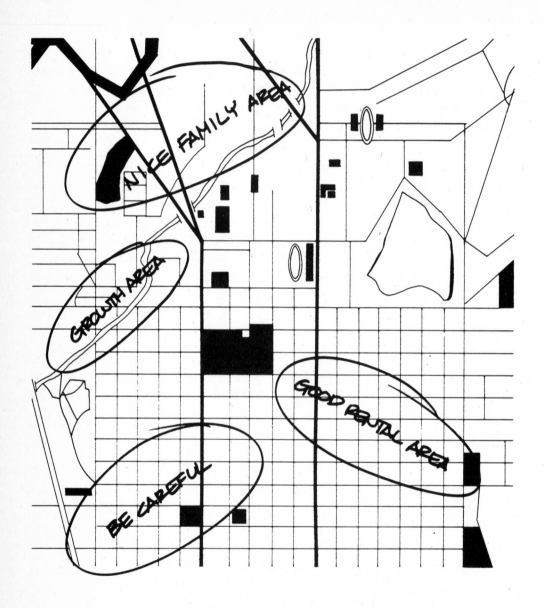

My Home-Buying Team

Resource	Address	Telephone
Real Estate Consultant	*P.O. Box 1096*	*(801) 225-8777*
Marc Garrison	*Orem, Utah 84057*	
Real Estate Agent		
Real Estate Agent		
Real Estate Agent	Gail Magnant	
Loan Officer		
Mortgage Broker	Chris Blanchard	
Title Officer		
Property Inspector		
Property Appraiser		
Real Estate Attorney		
Maintenance		

- Ask if there is an agent in the office who is particularly good and/or willing to work with first-time or step-up homebuyers. Try to narrow this down to one particular real estate agent in the office.

- When the secretary gives you a name, write it down on your list. Ask when the agent can be reached by phone. Write this information down on your list along with the phone number. You should also leave your name and number with the secretary, and request that the agent call you.

Continue this process until you have a list of at least three agents. Remember that these are quality agents, each of whom has been recommended as being good or whom you have prescreened by calling around. The next step is to set up an appointment with one of these agents. If you are married, make each appointment at a time where both you and your spouse can be present. When you arrive for the appointment, make sure to be on time and bring the map on which you've marked where you work and the area you'd consider buying in. Also, make sure to bring copies of your completed homebuyer's forms with you (this is essential).

Once you are seated with the agent, be friendly. Introduce yourself and your spouse; spend a minute getting to know each other. It would be wise to ask whether that agent is a member of the National Association of Realtors. The NAR is a member trade organization which subscribes to a high level of professionalism and enforces a rigid code of honest dealings in helping people with their real estate concerns.

You might also want to ask the agent how many homes he has sold in the last year and how many listings of homes for sale he has now. You should also ask whether he works full time as an agent or part time. If you are going to work with this agent, it is wise to find out about his track record and how much time he is going to have to help you. Once you have gotten to know the agent, then take control. Don't wait for the agent to ask you questions; you need to prove yourself to the agent and to get down to the most important matter at hand: buying your first or next home. With your spouse, go over with the agent each of the following points:

1. You are seeking to buy your first or next home. Show him your completed homebuyer's forms. Review with him your present financial situation and your housing needs.

2. Explain how serious you are about your housing search. Tell him you think your next step is to find out which areas are best to concentrate your search efforts in.

3. Explain that you are interested in working with a good agent in buying your first or next home. Right now he could help you by answering a few specific questions about the neighborhoods, housing prices, and financing options available in town.

If you are worried about forgetting a question, take this book with you. The act of using this book will show the agent how serious you are. Next:

1. Show him your map, point out where you work, explain that the circle represents your maximum allowable commuting distance from your job, and that you want to limit your house search to within that commute. Ask him to point out for you which areas he would recommend for a couple in your situation.

2. Ask him to explain his choices.

3. Ask him to look in his MLS (real estate agent's Multiple Listing Service) computer or book and review with you what the average homes have been selling for in those areas and what the high and low sales prices have been there in the past year.

4. Ask him what financing programs are available. In some states, there are state-guaranteed loans which offer special interest rate programs for first-time homebuyers. There are also other loan programs which offer special financing and fix-up money.

5. Let the agent know how serious you are about getting a home. Show him your homebuying team directory. Ask him to recommend a good loan officer to work with, a mortgage broker, a title company and officer, a property inspector, and a real estate attorney. Pencil in each of these recommendations. As you go see other real estate agents, ask them what they know about "Joe Johnson" as a mortgage officer, or one of the other professionals recommended to you. Listen to their opinions and make some notes about their recommendations on your homebuying team directory. When it comes time to use these professionals, you are going to be equipped with some excellent recommendations.

6. Tell the agent that you appreciate his/her help. Explain that you want to go look through those areas he has recommended and get a better idea of what they look like. If he offers to drive you around, by all means go, if you have the time. When you are through, thank him/her for his time. It's amazing how far just a simple thank-you goes in the real estate business (as elsewhere). Leave the copies of your completed homebuyer's forms with the agent. Make sure these forms include your address and phone number.

7. If you would like to continue working with the agent, commit yourselves to a specific course of action. Examples would be, "I will call you tomorrow to see what kinds of state loans you found out that we could qualify for," or "Let's meet again at your office at 6:30 P.M. and look through the homes that you think we might be able to buy."

Don't forget to say thank-you.

In performing this six-step process, you haven't wasted anyone's time. You have actually gotten to know the agent; he has also gotten to know you. He realizes that you are serious. Just the fact of bringing in the map and forms indicates you are miles ahead of the other people who come in. You asked for his help and thanked him for his time. If you felt impressed

Area Worksheet

Agent's Name _____

Phone _____

Recommended Neighborhood _____

Average Current Home Sale Price _____

Lowest Sale Price in Past 12 Months _____

Highest Sales Price in Past 12 Months _____

Commuting Time to Work _____

School District _____

School Bus Service (Yes/No) _____

Distance/Walking Time (minutes)

- Elementary School _____

- Junior High (Middle School) _____

- High School _____

- Church School _____

Types of Mass Transportation _____

Nearest Mass Transit Stop (minutes) _____

Distance/Travel Time

- Public Park _____

- Library _____

- Public Swimming Pool _____

- Recreation/Youth Center _____

- Ballpark _____

- Tennis Courts _____

- Fitness Center _____

- Jogging Track _____

- Golf Course _____

- Shopping Center _____

- Grocery Store _____

- Fire Department _____

- Police Station _____

- 24-Hour Pharmacy _____

- Post Office _____

- Hospital _____

- 24-Hour Emergency Room _____

Area Worksheet (continued)

Type and Condition of Neighborhood

- Single-Family Residences _____
- Well Maintained _____
- Rental Area _____
- Commercial Area _____
- Industrial Area _____

Is the Area so Near the Following Areas That Traffic, Noise, Pollution, or Safety Might Be a Problem?

- Airport _____
- Military Base _____
- Sewage Plant _____
- Trash Dump _____
- Railroad _____
- Industrial Area _____
- Energy Plant _____
- Highway _____
- Rock Quarry/Open Mine _____
- River _____
- Swamp _____

General Impressions

- Neighborhood's Assets _____
  _____
- Neighborhood's Liabilities _____
  _____

Notes _____
_____
_____
_____
_____
_____
_____
_____
_____
_____
_____

Area Worksheet

Agent's Name	Bill Johnson
Phone	226-2340
Recommended Neighborhood	Middlesex
Average Current Home Sale Price	$95,000
Lowest Sale Price in Past 12 Months	$67,000
Highest Sales Price in Past 12 Months	$106,000
Commuting Time to Work	45 minutes
School District	Middlesex
School Bus Service (Yes/No)	yes

Distance/Walking Time (minutes)

• Elementary School	5
• Junior High (Middle School)	15
• High School	15
• Church School	—

Types of Mass Transportation	bus
Nearest Mass Transit Stop (minutes)	10

Distance/Travel Time

• Public Park	5
• Library	5
• Public Swimming Pool	5
• Recreation/Youth Center	5
• Ballpark	5
• Tennis Courts	5
• Fitness Center	10
• Jogging Track	5
• Golf Course	25
• Shopping Center	5
• Grocery Store	5
• Fire Department	10
• Police Station	10
• 24-Hour Pharmacy	none
• Post Office	5
• Hospital	10
• 24-Hour Emergency Room	10

Area Worksheet (continued)

Type and Condition of Neighborhood

- Single-Family Residences   *mostly, some apartments*
- Well Maintained   *yes*
- Rental Area   *no*
- Commercial Area   *no*
- Industrial Area   *no*

Is the Area so Near the Following Areas That Traffic, Noise, Pollution, or Safety Might Be a Problem?

- Airport   *no*
- Military Base   *no*
- Sewage Plant   *no*
- Trash Dump   *no*
- Railroad   *no*
- Industrial Area   *no*
- Energy Plant   *no*
- Highway   *no*
- Rock Quarry/Open Mine   *no*
- River   *no*
- Swamp   *no*

General Impressions

- Neighborhood's Assets   *very nice – clean*

- Neighborhood's Liabilities   *a little far from work – but worth the drive*

Notes

with the agent, you will be back. If the agent wouldn't help you, or you didn't feel your questions were given good answers, call up the next agent. In any case, you should repeat this with at least three different real estate agents at different companies. You will not only be learning about your housing market, but you will be enlisting several professionals' help in finding your first home.

Make sure to save these agents' names, because we will be using the three good ones you find during the next steps. Make some notations about the agent and how he helped you so you won't forget who's who. Now go visit their recommended neighborhoods. As you drive round, highlight on the map where the schools, parks, and shopping centers are. Mark with a special color the things that appeal to you, such as parks, bus lines, and commuter parking lots. Fill in the information you received from the agent on the top of the worksheet on pages 63-64 and then score the neighborhood after driving through it according to the worksheet items.

When you're finished with the area worksheet from each area the agents have recommended, spread them out on a table and read them over one more time. If you are married, discuss with your spouse what you like about each area and what you feel the drawbacks are. This will help you start narrowing down your housing choices. Again, don't just work through one real estate agent and review one area. Follow this process with at least three different agents and review at least three different areas and neighborhoods. Ask for several different opinions. The efforts you put in here at this stage will reap benefits for years to come as you enjoy and grow in your new home.

TAP YOUR HIDDEN RESOURCES:
HOW TO BUY A HOME
WHEN THEY SAY YOU CAN'T AFFORD ONE

☐   ☐   ☐

The decision to buy a home has been made, and the options have been narrowed; it's time to take the information gathered in the earlier steps and put it to work. Fix that lousy credit rating; clean up those credit card bills; organize your time, money, and other resources; and get ready to take the plunge.

Organizing your resources means facing reality. Some of you, in looking at your net worth, may have come out squeaky clean, with immaculate credit and excellent cash resources. Others may have discovered a major problem. That imported stereo with the eight-foot boom-box speakers that you "just had to have," which exploded on its third use, may have now come back to haunt you. When you protested by not paying the bill, a bright scarlet letter might have been quietly put on your credit record. Even though the problem was eventually cleared up, your credit report says, in black and white, "6 months late in payments to XYZ Stereo International." Others of you may have discovered worse credit problems, or have found out that you have a lack of available funds for a down payment.

Those of you who don't have these problems are to be commended. If you have perfect credit and no problems with raising a down payment, simply review the forms you filled out in Steps #1–#3. Make sure each is filled out clearly and neatly. Make several copies of each form at a local copy center to have on hand when you start your housing search. Once that is done, you might as well skip the rest of this section and move on to Step #5.

For those who feel like there is a brick wall between you and your dream of a first or next home because of a credit problem or lack of down payment, don't lose heart. I want you to pay particular attention to the rest of this step. In this section I plan to give you some concrete steps you can use to lock in your first or next home now. I don't want you to give up. I want to share with you several almost secret techniques that investors use to acquire properties and lock down purchase prices without any cash of their own or embarrassing credit checks.

If you are willing to work hard and you have a steady income, I promise you these techniques will help you lock down a purchase price today without your having to have a lot of cash or a pristine credit rating. Over time, you can fix those things; by the time you do, though, housing prices will have increased and so will the down payments required. Waiting to buy later is like trying to chase an accelerating car down a long road. Each frantic step finds you farther and farther from your goal.

These alternative techniques will also work for those of you who have good credit but can't meet the standard qualifications of a large down payment and long job history. Alternative ownership techniques such as equity sharing, lease options, and joint ownership can allow you to lock in the price of your home now. These methods provide a solution to the homebuyer with a steady income who simply can't find a way to buy a home.

□   □   □

EQUITY SHARING

□ □ □

Equity sharing is a partnership between a homebuyer and an investor. It is a sharing of ownership in which the buyer lives in the home, is responsible for all maintenance and repairs, and makes the total monthly payments in return for 50-percent ownership in the property. With equity sharing, the buyer can get into a home with "nothing down," and, with the fulfillment of the responsibilities of maintenance and debt service, the buyer will receive one half of all the appreciation on the home and one half of all the tax benefits, interest deductions, and real estate tax credits associated with ownership. With equity sharing, the financial strength of an investor is teamed up with the hard work of the buyer to create a win-win financial situation. The investor, who puts up the down payment for the property and qualifies for any outside financing, receives a property with no management hassles, no negative cash flow, one half the appreciation, and, in many instances, tax deductions of up to one half the property taxes, improvement expenses, fire insurance, and depreciation write-off.

Who should be considering equity sharing?

- Anyone who is renting right now. Fifty-percent ownership for yourself is a lot better than collecting a bunch of rent receipts.

- Someone who has had past credit problems (foreclosure, bankruptcy, personal business failure, and so forth).

- Someone who doesn't have enough for a down payment or sufficient credit to qualify to purchase under normal conditions right now.

- Anyone who has transferred into an area but can't qualify until the home he left behind is sold.

- Someone who now owns a home but has troubles—financial, job, family health, or something similar.

In equity sharing, the financial strength of an investor is combined with your energy to get a house. The investor gets a piece of the action; you get a home. Your equity-sharing partner could be someone you know right now. Your parents and relatives might be the first people to turn to. It is a great way for a parent to help a child get into a home of his own. Your equity-sharing partner could also be your doctor, dentist, lawyer, someone you work with, or maybe someone you don't even know right now.

To review, in equity sharing the investor puts up the down payment and qualifies for any necessary loan. You, the homebuyer, then occupy the property, maintain it, and make the monthly payments.

In addition to the tax write-offs, no monthly debt service or negative cash flow, no maintenance, no management hassles, and all the other benefits we have described, the investor receives a negotiated percentage of the property's appreciation and a defined buy-out date by you, the homebuyer. With equity sharing, the homebuyer and investor set a time limit on the equity-sharing agreement. Usually, this period is set for at least five years from the purchase date. (I wouldn't suggest more than seven years for such an arrangement.)

During that time, the homebuyer receives the benefits of locking in the house price today, locking in the payments today, and getting into a home without qualifying, credit checks, down payments, or the other typical hassles. The homebuyer's only requirement is to maintain the property and keep current on the monthly mortgage payments. During that period of time the homebuyer can clean up his or her credit, gain tenure on the job, and put his finances in better order.

At the end of your equity-sharing agreement, you can renegotiate a new equity-sharing agreement, sell the home and split the profits, or buy out your partner's position. Whichever you chose, you both gain a lot in this win-win situation.

□   □   □

EQUITY-SHARING EXAMPLE

□ □ □

Let's use some actual figures and see how an equity-sharing situation over the next five years might work for you. To purchase a $90,000 home today, your investor would probably have to put up about $18,000 for a down payment. After calculating principal, interest, taxes, and insurance, you as the buyer would be paying about $750 dollars each month in total payments. After five years, with just an 8-percent inflation rate on housing, the home could easily increase in value to $132,240. That's $42,000 in appreciation that you and your investor/partner will share fifty-fifty. In addition, you will share fifty-fifty in the equity buildup from five years of loan payments. In this case, you'd also get half of the $2,466.37 principal reduction on the loan. Talk about having your cake and eating it too!

If after five years the home were to be sold, the investor/partner would get his original down payment back ($18,000) plus one half of the equity, which would be $42,000 equity buildup + $2,466.37 loan reduction = $44,466.37 total equity divided by two, which would equal $22,233.19. Each equity share partner would make $22,233.19, give or take a few dollars for closing costs. Beat's renting, doesn't it?

That means each partner would receive over $4,400 a year plus tax write-offs. The profit for the investor would be over 17 percent on his money (and that doesn't even include tax benefits). The homebuyer could then take his profit and buy his own home without an equity share partner and possibly have a few thousand dollars left over for cleaning up some credit or to finance that long-overdue trip to see Aunt Harriet, who lives in the Bahamas.

If you, the homebuyer, decide you don't want to sell the home and would like to stay, you also have the option of buying out your equity-sharing partner. This buy-out could take the form of several alternatives:

1. Go to the bank and refinance the home using your equity from the partnership as your down payment.

Equity Sharing

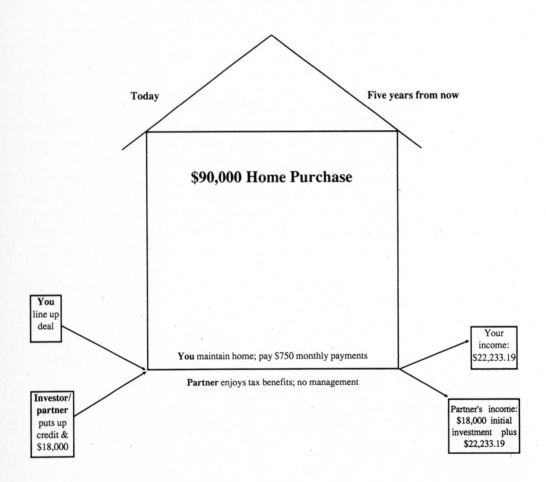

Today

Five years from now

$90,000 Home Purchase

You
line up
deal

You maintain home; pay $750 monthly payments

Partner enjoys tax benefits; no management

Your
income:
$22,233.19

**Investor/
partner**
puts up
credit &
$18,000

Partner's income:
$18,000 initial
investment plus
$22,233.19

2. Assume the first mortgage and create a second mortgage with your investor's equity. This second mortgage, strictly between you and your investor, would be secured against the home. You would negotiate, with the investor, the detail of interest rate, duration, and monthly payments.
3. Get a personal loan with your newly improved credit history and buy out the investor's equity.

Whichever alternative you chose, equity sharing has many benefits for you if you can't qualify for a home right now under "normal criteria." A key benefit in equity sharing is that, rather than a handshake and promise that in five years something will be worked out, an actual partnership agreement is drawn up pursuant to Internal Revenue Code Section 280 A, which outlines several rules of equity-sharing investments. While a hassle to fill out, these equity-sharing agreements help remove the risk and liability of being in partnership with another person. With the permission of Keith L. Moore, a California real estate broker who specializes in equity sharing, I'd like to share with you his equity-sharing forms.* These forms consist of three separate parts: a limited partnership agreement, a lease agreement, and a subscription and agreement to invest. While written for California, these agreements can easily be adapted by a local real estate attorney for your own particular state. (Refer to Appendix A for these forms.)

□   □   □

---

* A special note to brokers and professionals: Keith L. Moore is a California broker who has taken the equity share concept and started a revolutionary company in the area of homebuying. As a broker, he specializes in matching equity-sharing homebuyers and investors. For more information, contact him at EquiShare of California, P.O. Box 3855, Visalia, California 93278.

PUTTING EQUITY SHARING TO WORK FOR YOU

☐   ☐   ☐

If you are interested in equity sharing as a solution to your homebuying needs, you might want to call each of the three agents you talked with in Step #3 and tell them that you are interested in buying a home with an equity-sharing partner. Don't be surprised if they already have a partner in mind for you and perhaps some local equity-sharing forms available through their board office to close the deal.

Whatever forms you use, make sure, before you enter into any equity-sharing agreement, that you fully understand (and agree with) when the arrangement will end; what rights you have to buy out, assume, or sell your position; how you will be protected from the liability of a lawsuit or judgment against your partner; and who is responsible for major repairs during the equity share period. Also, make sure the forms you use are approved in your state.

If the agents don't have a client or other agent in mind who might be interested in being your equity-sharing investor, you should ask them to find you one. Make that a prerequisite to your working with them to find your home. Make sure they understand what equity sharing is by asking them to explain what it is. You should also talk, as we mentioned earlier, with relatives, friends at work, and professionals you deal with such as a doctor, dentist, or CPA. You might even want to advertise in your local paper under the "Personal Section" in the classified ads. Your ad might say something like this:

Invest with me in a local single-family
home. High yield, no management, no
negative cash flow, low risk. Call Marc at
(801) 225-8777.

When someone calls you on the phone, simply explain the profits that are available to them, explain equity sharing, and tell them how much you want to work with them to get into your first home. Honesty and sincerity will get you a lot further than a slick sales job.

LEASE OPTIONS

□ □ □

An alternative way to lock in the price of your first or next home is through a lease option. A lease option is similar to equity sharing, but it is a somewhat watered-down form of ownership. However, it can be every bit as effective as equity sharing. With a lease option, you negotiate the purchase price of a home, but the actual closing is set at a predefined date, usually several years in the future. In the meantime, your occupancy of the home is treated as a rental. The lease option then designates that a certain percentage of the rent that is paid prior to the exercising of the option (the closing) goes toward the down payment and purchase price of the home. You are renting a home for a specified period of time, at the end of which you have the option to buy at a purchase price established at the beginning of the agreement, using a designated percentage of the rent you've paid as part or all of the down-payment. (See Appendix B for a sample lease option form.)

The benefit to the seller is a tenant who is motivated to maintain the property and pay his rent on time and a set purchase price, terms, and date of closing for the home. The benefit to the buyer is a predetermined purchase price, a negotiated portion of what would normally be rent money going toward a down payment, and a "trial marriage" with the home and neighborhood. If, at the end of the option period, the homebuyer decides to back out of the situation, then the seller keeps any money that has accumulated toward the down payment as a percentage of the rent. The seller then simply finds someone else to rent or buy the home. The would-be buyer finds another home, neighborhood, or purchase price that better fits his situation.

Again, the advantages of lease options are immediate occupancy, established price and terms, a forced savings plan to help you save toward a down payment, and a trial period in the home to see if you really do like the home and the neighborhood. If you decide that you don't like anything about the home, you are not legally bound by contract or purchase to stay there. You would simply forfeit any option consideration and monies that have accrued toward the down payment from your rents.

WHO SHOULD CONSIDER USING A LEASE OPTION?

□ □ □

A dear friend of mine recently moved to the Big Apple, New York City. He wasn't sure, when he moved there, if he would end up staying on a permanent basis. So, he looked around town until he found a builder who needed to fill some empty condominium units. He made an offer to the builder, based on a lease with an option to buy, for a period of twenty-four months. He negotiated that a portion of his monthly payments would go toward the purchase price. He moved into a beautiful new condominium in New York City for nothing down. If he decides to stay, he already has the start of a down payment to buy the unit; if inflation drives the price of the condominium up, he still buys in two years at today's price. Between now and then, he gets the chance to test the waters and see if he likes his job there and if he likes his new home and neighborhood.

Lease options should be considered not only by people who are being transferred, like my friend, but also by young couples who don't have the capital or credit to buy a home today and by people who are moving up into a bigger and better home and want to see if the grass really is greener on the other side of the fence on a trial basis. Even retirees moving to a new retirement area can benefit. Recently, I appeared on a national radio show with Sonny Bloch whom I consider the best real estate expert on radio today. We fielded a call on Sonny's national real estate talk show from a retiree who had moved from back East to a retirement community in California. The essence of the call was that she hated her new home and wanted to move back to Queens in New York City. She had been in California only a few months but was ready to pack. Her problem was that she had sold her place in Queens and bought a new home in California.

Hindsight is twenty-twenty, but we could alleviate a lot of problems if we would understand that there is more than one way to skin a cat. She should have rented out her old place and either rented her new home or, if she wanted to lock in the price, used a lease with an option to buy. If she had, she wouldn't have been calling us. She would have been on her way back to Queens, without having to worry about selling a home she had just bought months before.

HOW DO YOU FIND A HOME WHICH YOU CAN
LEASE WITH AN OPTION TO BUY?

□ □ □

As we have already mentioned, builders of new homes and condominiums are excellent prospects for leases with options to buy. Real estate agents can be another good source for finding lease option agreements. Some newspaper listings specifically directed toward rentals of single-family homes and condominiums may contain the words "lease option possible." As we move on to the next step, you might note that any traditional purchase can be a prime candidate for conversion from a "normal sale" to a lease option.

JOINT OWNERSHIP

□ □ □

Another alternative is joint ownership. With joint ownership a homebuyer and a friend, relative, or investor pool their efforts to purchase a home in a manner similar to equity sharing, but quite different in purpose. The homebuyer and investor enter into a partnership agreement to purchase a home as tenants in common for the sole purpose of making and sharing a profit. The homebuyer does the work of finding the investment home; the investor then uses his financial strength to purchase the home. The homebuyer occupies and improves the home while immediately putting the home up for sale at a profit. When the home is sold, the investor receives an immediate return of all monies invested, and the investor and homebuyer share equally in any profits.

While not suited for all homebuyers, joint ownership can provide an immediate solution to the problem of "no money for a down payment." Unlike equity sharing and leasing with an option to buy, joint ownership does not offer a longterm housing situation for you as a homebuyer. I would recommend joint ownership for the single adult, or for a couple with no children attending school. The pressure of such a rapid move can prove too much of a strain on a child. But, for those who are willing, joint ownership can bring to you an equal share of the profits that an investor makes, without having to invest anything but your time in finding, fixing up, and showing the property to the next buyer.

My wife and I have seen profits from such arrangements range from $10,000 to $35,000, with an average of $15,000. For those of you with poor credit, imagine being able to use your half of that money to clear up your credit problems or apply to toward the down payment on your own home (or even toward an investment property of your own!). If, after your first joint ownership transaction, you find that you need more money, you might consider another such financial arrangement with your investor/ partner.

YOUR FIRST JOINT OWNERSHIP TRANSACTION

□ □ □

As in the two other forms of alternative ownership, you are going to have to go out and find an investor. Also as in equity sharing, your partner could be a parent, relative, friend at work, a professional you work with, or even someone whom you advertise for and meet through a classified ad.

Your advertisement for joint ownership could be exactly like the one we showed for attracting an equity-sharing partner. The differences would come out as you told the person responding to your ad that you are interested in a simple investment transaction. Be honest with that person and let him know that your assets are time and desire, while his may well be financial strength and an established credit rating. The synergy that could come with both of you working together is what will help you buy your first or next home.

To write up a joint ownership agreement, you simply need a local lawyer to write up the terms to which you and your partner will agree. I would suggest that the contract should, at minimum, include exactly what you are going to do and what your investor is going to do. Specify who is going to find the property, and, once it is found, who is going to pay for the down payment, closing costs, and so forth. Once the property is purchased, you are going to need to assure your investor, in writing, that you are going to occupy the home and make all agreed-upon repairs in a timely manner. Then, specify your responsibilities in terms of how the property is going to be resold and what will happen if, after six months or so, the property hasn't been sold. You should also address the question of who's going to pay the mortgage payment and utilities while you live in and improve the property, and who will pay for the ad.

With these three tools, you don't have to sit around and wait for that "someday" when you can buy your own home. Take the bull by the horns and choose one of these tools that fits your needs, so you can lock in that price now and begin cleaning up and improving your credit rating.

I read recently that, since 1900, there have only been four known years in which real estate did not post a noticeable increase in value. I can guarantee you that, without a doubt, ownership of a single-family home has brought more family stability, greater assistance in credit qualifying, and more security for retirement than any other single investment. Just look at your own parents and their friends. The person who has vision prepares for the future. I know you have the dream of homeownership. Please use these tools and make it come true.

FIND THE RIGHT HOME

☐   ☐   ☐

Having narrowed down your housing needs and wants, your financing options, and, if necessary, having employed one of the alternative owner-ship techniques discussed, you're now ready to find the right home. For many, this may mean taking the best of the less-than-best houses in the area. Still, that's much better than giving the same money to a landlord. After only one year of house payments, any ex-renter will agree that the reward is worth the sacrifice.

In this step I will teach you how to sort through the mass of homes available and find the best one you can realistically afford, or the one that would fit into a planned equity-sharing, lease option, or joint ownership agreement. Instead of spending weeks teaching you about the housing market, I am simply going to give you a list of assignments. I would like you to perform each one as best you can.

The proper completion of these assignments is what will make or break you in your housing search. You have got to put every bit of time, effort, and concern possible into these assignments so you can find your first or next home. I will do my best to show you every trick in the book that I know to help you find the best home at the best price for you right now. When you're through with this section, the hard work will have been completed. All that will be left is to complete the sections on inspecting the property to make sure it's what you want, financing, negotiating, making the offer, and closing the transaction. (That's not too bad, is it?)

Imagine right now that just for fun you charter a small private plane, one of those miniature Cessnas, and had the pilot fly you over the area where you live. After getting used to the bumpy ride and the fact that cars look like little toys and full-grown trees look like toothpicks, you might look around at how many thousands of homes are in your neighborhood. As you continued to fly around, you might notice that all these houses basically look the same. If you were to drop a sack of flour out the plane's window and buy the house that it most closely landed to or on, you might be using as much common sense as most people exhibit when choosing a house.

We have already developed a picture of how much you can afford for a home, what type of home you want to buy, and where you want that home to be. Instead of shotgunning your efforts around town and buying whatever home happens to fit your price and terms, let's focus our efforts on the areas in which you want to buy and on the potential homes that would work for you.

□   □   □

WORKING WITH YOUR REAL ESTATE AGENT

□ □ □

Before we go any farther, pull out a copy of your area worksheets and highlight on your map, in a nice bright color, the three areas you are going to concentrate on in finding your home. After you've done that, pull out your homebuying team directory and start sorting through the housing jungle by calling the real estate agent who's at the top of your list.

Back in Step #3, as you did an area analysis, one of your assignments was to sift out, from all the available agents in your area, three agents with whom you would like to work. You personally met with each agent and, with their help, chose three areas that you would like your home to be in. Now, as you recall each agent, I want you to follow up on your first conversation with them and ask them if they have found anything in which you might be interested. If they say they haven't, you might reexplain your situation to refresh their memory, and then commit them to a specific plan of action. At minimum, tell them that you will call them back in three days.

If the real estate agent has something for you to look at, then, by all means, verify with your homebuyer's checklist part 2 if it has the items you seek while he is still on the phone. If it measures up, make an appointment either to meet the agent at the property or to have him or her pick you up at your home right now. Repeat this procedure with the two other real estate agents you found back in Step #3. If one of the agents doesn't seem interested in helping you, don't worry. That's why I asked you to write their names in pencil. Erase that name and find another to replace him or her.

Make a point of calling one agent a day, each and every day of the week. This type of serious effort is what it is going to take. I recently read in *The Wall Street Journal* about a young lady in Southern California who bought a bank-repossessed condominium for thousands of dollars below its appraised value. The day she moved in, her net worth increased immensely.

The article told how the only way she was able to negotiate the purchase on her own terms was by calling the banker each day until he finally said yes. As long as you're friendly, no one is ever going to be offended by your persistence. It will only earn their respect.

THE CLASSIFIED ADS

□   □   □

As an investor, I have found that classified ads are an "Old Faithful" source of bargains. To make money as an investor, I can't buy homes at retail, fix them up, and then resell them at retail. I need to consistently be able to buy homes anywhere from 10 to 30 percent below market value, cosmetically improve their appearance, and then resell them at retail. Finding people who would be willing to sell their homes at a deep discount is not impossible. For the last ten years, I have been able to develop several tools which have helped me to be able to do just that on a consistent basis. Classified ads are one of those tools.

As you look at the map with the three areas that you have chosen, find out what major and local papers cover each of the areas. Call each of those sources and get a subscription to each paper, both the local one and major one. Commit a few minutes each day to reviewing each of these sources of homes. Your consistent efforts and meticulous reading of each ad will bring you your first or next home at your price and terms.

You can save yourself a lot of time and energy if you sift through the mass of black and white and spot the hidden clues that often lead you to a real bargain property. As the saying goes, you have to kiss a few frogs to find your prince. This next section will help you learn to recognize those hidden clues and allow you to keep your frog-kissing to a minimum. First, let's look at a couple of typical "Homes for Sale" ads.

By Owner. Lovely 3 bdrm brick 2 bath
w/Frplc, dbl gar, $20,000 down. Assume
FHA 10% Loan. Call 555-1234.

What information did you get from that ad? The owner is attempting to sell it himself (as opposed to using a realtor). It's a lovely (aren't they all?) three-bedroom brick home with two bathrooms, a fireplace, and a two-car garage. The owner wants $20,000 for a down payment, and there is a FHA loan on the house at 10-percent interest that can be assumed by the buyer. (We'll take a closer look at loans later.) With a down payment that high, this one goes in our reject pile. Now look at this next ad:

Desperate. Must sell before foreclosure.
Neg. down.
Assume FHA 10%. Present all offers.
Call 555-1234.

You can hear that one screaming at you. This guy is letting you know that he's in trouble and will consider any offer as a way out of it. What else did you notice? Look at the phone numbers in both ads. Same guy, right? Now, if you were keeping track of the ads you go through, and you noticed the first ad on July 1 and the second one on August 1, what would you conclude? You've got a desperate seller and the makings of a bargain property on your hands!

Using the classified ads is both challenging and fun. I came across an ad recently that began with "Illness forces sale." When I made the call, I asked the seller what type of illness was forcing him to sell. He replied that he was just sick of the property.

With a little practice, you'll be able to read between the black and white and spot hidden clues. As you read and make calls on ads, you'll develop a knack for preevaluating a house. Make sure to keep track of the ads you respond to, and you'll find that after several weeks of reading the classified ads and calling in response to the most promising ones, you will develop an excellent feel for values.

Here are some key phrases you should look for when looking through the classified ads:

MUST SELL
TRANSFERRED
OWNER WILL CARRY
FORECLOSURE
LOW DOWN
DEATH IN FAMILY
WILL TRADE
DESPERATE
NOTHING DOWN
ANXIOUS
FLEXIBLE TERMS
KICK ME, I'M DOWN

Phrases like these and others should immediately tickle your clue-finder. Also, look for the more subtle messages that are often contained in the ads. As you scan the classifieds, here are some other tips to keep in mind:

- Be a little wary of ads that are heavy on the adjectives or use a lot of flowery speech. These don't usually lead to a flexible or motivated seller.

- Look for long-distance phone numbers. When you call on these ads (collect!), you'll more than likely find someone who has recently been transferred or has inherited a house or is the trustee for an estate. Whatever the situation, a long-distance number will usually lead you to a motivated seller.

- Don't rush out to look at every house that appears to be a great bargain. Make a phone call first and check it out against your homebuyer's checklist. Flexible terms or a low price do not necessarily mean that the house is a great deal or that it is what you're looking for.

- Remember that newspaper ads are printed on paper, not carved in granite. The price listed in the ad is what the seller would like, not necessarily what he would settle for.

• Be aware that if a realtor is involved, he or she will be getting a commission of 6–8 percent of the selling price.

AD-SCANNING EXERCISE

□   □   □

The following is an exercise to help you learn to read between the lines of classified ads. Read through each of the ads, and then rate them on a scale of 1 to 4, as follows:

1. Excellent possibility; call this one immediately. Probably includes key phrases, such as "seller anxious" or "nothing down."
2. Definitely worth calling, but possibly not a great bargain. The seller appears anxious, but the price or the down payment is a little too high.
3. Probably worth following up on, but unlikely to be a good deal. The price is too high or the terms too inflexible. Homes handled by realty companies often fall in this category.
4. Don't bother. The seller is obviously expecting top dollar and is not motivated, as yet, to consider anything else.

Sample Ads

1. ____ **Anxious** owner. 6-plex, $89,000, $8,000 down. Owner will carry contract. 888-9090.

2. ____ **Desperate** owner facing foreclosure. Make up back payments, take over loan. 777-8080.

3. ____ **For sale** by owner. 2 bdrm 2 bth. $69,000 firm, $20,000 down. 666-7070.

4. ____ **Lease option.** 3-year option, $1,000 down. Payments $600 555-6060.

5. ____ **Nice** 3 bdrm, 2 bth in good location. $68,000, $20,000 down. 444-5050.

6. ____ **4 bdrm**—Will trade equity, possible no down. Willing to consider all offers. 333-4040.

7. ____ **Low down,** assumable loan, 3 bdrm, 2 bath, $68,000. 222-3030.

8. ____ **9% assumable** loan, 2 bdrm. $59,000 firm, $7,000 down. 111-2020.

9. ____ **Beautiful** 3 bdrm $87,000, $12,000 down. Owner/Agent. 222-1010.

10. ____ **Townhome** for sale. Excellent tax shelter. $93,000 firm. Mtn. View Realty 333-2020.

11. ____ **For sale** by owner. 4 bdrm, 3 bth. $95,000, $10,000 down. Will carry contract. 444-3030.

12. ____ **Nice** 3 brm in exc cond. $88,000, $8,000 down, $850 mo. Will consider all offers. 555-4040.

Here is how I would rate these ads:

#1—2	#2—4	#3—1	#4—1
#5—4	#6—1	#7—1	#8—2
#9—4	#10—4	#11—3	#12—2

Here's your score:

12 correct:	Outstanding—start calling
9–11 correct:	Very good
6–8 correct:	Pretty good; you'll get much better with practice.
less than 5:	Practice makes perfect. Make some phone calls and you'll get a better picture quickly.

Remember, persistence is the key to success. Don't give up if you're having trouble identifying the good ads right now. Pick up your own newspaper and scan the ads. Start making those phone calls; your first or next home may be hidden in one of those obscure little ads. As a side benefit, it may just be thousands below market value.

USING THE HOMEBUYER'S CHECKLIST AS YOU CALL ON PROSPECTIVE HOMES

□   □   □

I can't imagine a worse way to waste your homebuying time than to call in response to a classified ad, get only some basic information from the seller, and then spend an hour driving out to see it only to find that the property didn't have the minimum requirements which you listed on your home-buyer's checklist. As you begin using classified ads, and any other of the home-finding tools, screen each prospective property through your home-buyer's checklist. Before you visit anything, double-check to make sure that it has your "absolute must have's" and doesn't have your "I can't live with's." This screening process will save you and the sellers literally hundreds of hours of wasted time.

Remember, one of your greatest assets in your search for your first or next home is educated persistence. Each frustration or disappointment brings you that much closer to your goal. Don't be discouraged if, after three weeks of scouring the classifieds and beating the streets, you still seem no closer to finding that home you can call your own. It's just around the corner, and, when you find it, it will be well worth all of your efforts.

FOR-RENT ADS

□   □   □

Another way the classified ads can work for you is through the "Houses for Rent" section. Many owners who advertise their homes for rent would like nothing better than to sell the property but have just not been successful in finding a buyer. Perhaps they have had the house listed with a realtor, whose commission forced them to raise the down payment so high that it couldn't sell. Or possibly, they tried to sell the house themselves but had no success, either because of lack of knowledge or lack of luck. Some will simply be rental property owners who are weary of the headaches and hassles.

You should set aside at least one day a week when you can spend an hour going over the "Houses for Rent" section in your local classified ads. Call the homes which look attractive to you and ask the person who responds if he or she is the owner. If they are not, ask for the owner's telephone number. You don't want to waste time talking to someone who can't tell you what you need to know.

When you reach the owner, tell him that you are interested in possibly buying a property like the one they have for rent. Ask the owner whether or not they have ever thought of putting the property up for sale. The worst you will get is a "no," and the best response I've had was an owner who said, "I'm so glad you called—I've been trying to sell that house for months."

When you look through the ads, here are a few key phrases that may point to a landlord who is motivated to sell:

"Must rent quick."

"Available now."

"Rent to own."

"Lease with option to buy."

A long-distance phone number is also a good sign.

If the owner expresses interest in selling his home, immediately pull out a copy of your homebuyer's checklist and go over with him the features of the home. You may have to call a few before you find a gem, but don't worry, they are out there. Calling up "for rent" ads will connect you with a source of sellers who, for the most part, own their homes outright and are more highly motivated than most. They are perfect candidates for lease options or total owner financing.

□   □   □

ADVERTISING FOR SELLERS

□   □   □

Yes, there is yet another way you can use the classified ads to your advantage. Place your own ad in the paper, expressing your desire to buy your first or next home right away. What's good for the goose ought to be good for the gander, right?

When I first came across the idea several years ago, I was amazed at how simple and how obvious it was. I saw a small ad in which a man was advertising that he wanted to buy a home for his family in a certain area for a certain price. As an investor, I created my own ad, which I ran in a local newspaper:

Young family man seeks to buy single-
family home or smaller rental
unit in need of repair with
a low down payment. Call Marc at
(801) 225-8777.

As a potential homebuyer, you should create your own ad today and immediately have it run in all the papers which cover the areas that you want to buy a home in. Your ad might say something like this:

I would like to buy my first home right
away. I can afford up to $700 per month
PITI. East Side locations preferred.
Call Marc at (801) 225-8777.

It's exciting to come home to your answering machine each day and find messages from several people wanting you to call them about buying their properties. Have the paper run your ad in the "Real Estate Wanted Section." Customize the ad to fit your own situation. If you have a wife and three kids, say so. If you are buying your first home, say so. If you can afford only $700 a month, admit it. If you can't buy right now but would like to use a lease option, then say so.

TARGETING YOUR HOMEBUYING AREAS

□   □   □

Once you've put your ad in the paper, make up a flier similar to the ones that follow and pass it out yourself or hire someone to hang one on every doorknob in the neighborhoods where you want to buy. Our goal is to get every homeowner in your neighborhoods to know that you want to buy their house. Simply insert your name in one of the following ads and have copies printed at a local copy shop. The few dollars and the little time you spend will reap great rewards when you get your new home.

ATTENTION: PROPERTY OWNERS

**I am a family man
who is interested in buying
your home or smaller rental unit as
a personal residence. We love your area. Please
help us out. If you have something for sale or know
of someone else who does, please give us a call.**

Name:
Phone:

PROPERTY OWNERS

WE NEED YOUR HELP!!

My wife and I would like to
buy a home for our family in
your neighborhood.

We have excellent references
and would like to move in right away.
If you have something for sale or know
of someone else who does, please give us a call.

Name:
Phone:

DON'T THROW THIS AD AWAY!

**I am not selling anything. I am
someone who is doing everything in his
power to buy a home in your neighborhood.
I love it here!
If you have a home for sale or know of one that
might be, please give me a call.**

Thanks for your help!

Name:
Phone:

VACANT HOMES

□ □ □

Another house-finding tool that has become one of my favorites over the years is locating vacant houses. You've seen them: the overgrown lawn, no curtains in the windows, last month's newspapers rolled up and strewn about the front porch. You probably just kept on driving without giving it a thought, but from now on, I want you not only to notice but to take a particular interest in that house.

There are many reasons why a house may be vacant, but you can bet that whatever the reason, there's an owner out there somewhere who's not happy about it. He's either been transferred and hasn't been successful in selling it yet, or he was forced to leave because of dire financial straits and is facing probable foreclosure. It's possible that there's an out-of-state land-lord who is not able to keep tenants and has become exasperated at the financial black hole that has developed.

Whatever the reason, someone is losing money and is faced with the reality of losing even more unless the situation changes soon. What you, as a prospective homebuyer, want to find is a motivated seller. Can you think of better motivation to sell quickly than a monthly mortgage payment that does nothing for you but allow you to keep a house you don't want for another month, just so you can make another payment next month?

After talking to many homeowners and bank officers on the subject of vacant houses, I have found that most owners will continue to make the payments on a house for about eight months before giving up in despair and letting the bank foreclose. Chances are, by the time you get to him, the owner will have long since stopped advertising and is just struggling to keep the day-to-day ends met in his new location. You may just be the miracle he's been praying for. Not only will he be extremely receptive to your advances as a buyer, but you will most likely be the only suitor.

I related a story in my last book, *Financially Free*, about how I recently bought a home from a man who was transferred to Southern California.

His move was extremely sudden, and he left his home for a neighbor to watch over and a friend to sell. The neighbor did the best he could, the friend tried a little bit, and seven months later the man was still paying his monthly mortgage payment on a vacant house. He tried selling long distance, but he had little control over a situation from 750 miles away. He was having difficulty paying the minimum on his bills in California, and a new house there was out of the question until his old home was sold. Does this sound like an opportunity for a good deal?

One of the neighbors who knew I'd be interested gave me a call and suggested that I look into this deal. The neighbor even gave me the name and telephone number of the homeowner in California.

In this case, success was only a phone call away. I called the owner and established his needs. He wanted only enough out of his house to get into another house. He was willing to take $2,000 cash and let me assume his 11.5-percent VA loan. So I was able to pick up a $63,000 home for only $53,000 with $2,000 down. The owner was ecstatic at having sold his ball and chain; now he could get on with his life. I too was ecstatic; with very little effort I had been handed a golden opportunity on a silver platter.

Finding empties simply requires some perseverance and a good eye. Set aside some time on a Saturday or Sunday afternoon and go for a drive through the areas you've marked on your map. Here are some things to keep an eye out for:

- Any signs of general neglect—an overgrown or dying lawn, broken windows, trash or tree limbs scattered in the yard.

- A conspicuous absence of cars, bicycles, flower pots, and so forth.

- A pile of yellowing newspapers on the front porch and a few pounds of junk mail stuffed in the mailbox.

- No curtains in the windows.

Any combination of these signs would warrant a closer look.

Many vacant houses will have a for-sale or for-rent sign posted, but some won't. The last thing you want to do, however, is to give up and keep driving when there is no sign in the yard. This is where the real fun begins. Finding a vacant house is often the easy part, but how do you find an owner who seems to have disappeared? The Sherlock Holmes in you is going to have to do some sleuthing.

First, look around and see if there are any kids playing nearby. The neighborhood kids will usually know who lived there, when they moved, and where they moved to. You'll at least get a name to go on.

Next, knock on the houses next door and across the street from the vacant house. It's very probable that they'll have an address or phone number for you. When you introduce yourself, make sure you let them know that you're interested in buying the house. Close neighbors would be especially happy to have the vacant house occupied.

If you can't find out anything from the neighbors, go to the nearest post office and fill out a "Change of Address Information Request" form. For a fee of around $1.00, the post office will gladly provide you with the new address of the former occupant.

At this point, it's still possible to have run into nothing but dead ends. The owner may not have left a forwarding address, or the previous occupant may have been a renter and not the owner. You're a resourceful detective, though, and Magnum P.I. sure wouldn't give up this easily.

So, what next? Elementary, my dear Watson. Head down to the county courthouse. There you'll find two sources of almost surefire leads. First, look up the property and find out the name of the lender who holds the mortgage. The bank will usually be more than happy to help you get in touch with the owner, because they know that vacant houses often lead to undesirable foreclosures. Also, while you're at the courthouse, look at the tax rolls in the assessor's office and see who's paying the property tax. Ask for a copy of that property's tax assessment, which will have the most current billing name and address.

If all else fails, go back to the house and leave a note taped to the door with the words ATTENTION OWNER marked in bold letters. You'll be surprised at how successful this method can be. If the owner himself isn't close enough to come back and check on the place or collect the mail, then often he has asked someone else to look after it. I have heard from owners as long as eight weeks after leaving a note on their door.

This unusual method of looking for bargain properties has really been a gold mine for me. I enjoy the detective work and the fun in finding out who the owner is. And, even better, when you do find the owner, you will find someone who will bless you forever. You came in when hope was lost and took a white elephant off his hands.

FORECLOSURES

□   □   □

When a seller is facing foreclosure, he is usually desperate. He needs a buyer for his house immediately if he is going to avoid the long-term damaging effects of foreclosure proceedings. A seller this motivated is exactly what you've been looking for. What's more, this can easily become a win/win situation in which both of you get what you want. By offering to take the problem off his hands, you are like the cavalry coming to the rescue, instead of an opportunistic vulture preying on his misfortune.

There are two different types of foreclosures on a mortgage or a trust deed in the United States: judicial and nonjudicial. The basic difference between the two is that a judicial foreclosure takes place as a legal action resulting from a court judgment and a nonjudicial foreclosure is an action provided for in the original trust-deed in the event of nonpayment on the part of the trustee. Foreclosure procedures differ slightly from state to state, so I would suggest that you consult with an attorney familiar with your state's foreclosure laws before you attempt to buy a foreclosure property. In general, though, the time frame for foreclosures goes something like this:

Month	Action by homeowner	Action by lender
1	Misses a payment	A late fee is charged
2	"	"
3	"	Personal phone calls and

Month	Action by homeowner	Action by lender
		a visit from the lender. Notice of default is filed.
4	"	Letters from attorney.
5	"	"
6	Usually owners have moved out by now.	Posting and publishing a notice of sale on the property.
7	Generally the home is vacant.	"
8	"	"
9	"	The sale.

Whatever the reasons that led to foreclosure proceedings, once the owner has missed a few payments, he needs your help. There are three phases of a foreclosure during which you can buy the property: before the actual foreclosure sale, from the owner; at the foreclosure sale, from the trustee; or after the foreclosure sale, from the bank. For our purposes, your best bet is to contact the lending institutions in your area about the properties they have recently been stuck with after foreclosure sales.

THE CURE DATE

□   □   □

Between the date when the notice of default is filed and the foreclosure sale takes place, a date is set according to local state law, known as the "cure date." This date is, in most states, the point of no return for the homeowner. On or before this cure date the loan must be brought current either by the homeowner or the party to whom they sell the home. Bringing the loan current means paying all the delinquent payments, late fees, and usually the legal fees incurred by the lender for the foreclosure proceedings. You should check with the bank or lending institution holding the loan, but usually a loan brought current before the cure date will not suffer any further penalty. The homeowner or the new owner will simply continue making payments to the lending institution as if nothing had ever happened.

Having established the basic mechanics of a foreclosure, we are now ready to look at your next tools for finding your home.

AFTER THE FORECLOSURE SALE

☐ ☐ ☐

More often than not, the bank is the only one that bids on a foreclosure property at the auction. Today, because of the increasing numbers of fore-closures, banks and loan institutions are flooded with properties that they have been forced to take back. Banks refer to these properties as REOs ("real estate owned").

The bank now has the unwanted task of having to advertise, fix up, and sell these properties. To relieve this headache, banks will often find a real estate agent to do it all for them. Large banks may even have an entire division set up to dispose of these properties. Regardless of how they handle it, each bank will have an officer who is in charge of these REOs. You can personally meet with the officer in charge of the REOs at the bank and not only buy your first or next home, but also negotiate some excellent terms.

I have never found an officer in charge of a bank's REO portfolio to be anything but helpful, friendly, and eager to get rid of these properties. They are doing a good job for the bank if they don't have any properties to work with. You as a homebuyer can help them out. I would like you to call every bank in your area and make an appointment with the officer in charge of the bank's REOs. Show up at each appointment and bring a copy of your complete homebuying package. Show the officer your net worth, your income, what kind of home you like, and what areas you have been looking at. Describe to the banking officer how much you would like to get your own home. Describe the items from your homebuyer's check-list detailing your minimum requirements. Ask the banking officer if they have anything at all which might fit your circumstances.

Buying REOs through banks and having them finance the transaction can be a great help to a young homebuyer without established credit. The bank is in the position where they might overlook a lot of things in giving you the loan. To succeed in getting the loans, I have found that a professional, honest attitude is essential. They may overlook a lot of things, but they aren't going to go out on a limb with a slick or dangerously naive homebuyer. The last thing they want is to have to foreclose on the property again.

FHA AND VA FORECLOSURES

□   □   □

A common misconception most homeowners have when they get an FHA or VA loan is that the government agency is actually lending them the money. The truth of the matter is that FHA or VA in almost all situations is only guaranteeing the loan. The way that a typical FHA/VA loan works is that the buyer first applies for the FHA/VA loan through a local bank or savings and loan. The loan institution does all the checks and qualifying, then sends the completed loan application to the regional FHA/VA office for approval. Once the loan is approved, the closing is done through the lending institution.

In computing the interest, prior to 1984, one-half point extra interest was charged on your loan to insure your lender against the possibility that you might default and force the bank to repossess the home, and cause the government agency to *buy* the home from the lender. (This insurance charge is referred to as the loan's MIP, or mortgage insurance premium.) If you assume a pre-1984 FHA, your monthly payment will include this charge.

Beginning in 1984, the Federal Housing Administration changed the rules concerning the payment of the insurance premium for new FHA loans. Instead of paying an extra one-half point interest, you borrow, on closing, a prepaid insurance fee. This insurance fee varies according to loan amount. On a $43,000 loan this fee is over $1,200. So under the new program you would borrow on your loan $44,200 instead of $43,000. Under this method your interest rate would not be raised by one-half point.

Thus, the protection offered through these government loans ensures the private lender that in the event of the necessary foreclosure of a government-insured property, the government agency will buy the property from the lender. The private lender with this type of loan will not be stuck with another property to fix up, advertise, and sell; the government will.

In most major areas there are dozens of government (FHA, HUD, and VA) foreclosure properties available for sale. It is staggering to see what good deals there are. These government agencies offer these properties for sale to the general public. Usually every two weeks a list of the homes they have for sale is sent out by mail to investors and realtors or inserted into a major Sunday paper. Some real "diamonds in the rough" are hidden in these government repossessions.

Let me explain the major differences between the VA and the FHA programs. In both, the homes are initially put up for sale on a bid basis. These properties are listed for sale with a bid date given. If you are interested in bidding on the property, you fill out one of the government purchase forms (available from the government offices or through your local real estate agents that are listed with the government agencies). Along with this purchase form you must give a refundable earnest money deposit. On the specified date all offers are opened, and the best offer is the one accepted. If there are no offers made, or if none is acceptable, this process is repeated, or the property is put on a first come first served basis, in which case they will accept the first acceptable offer.

The big differences between the VA and the FHA loans come in the form of qualification and financing. The HUD program, which covers the FHA repossessions, requires that purchasers obtain their own outside financing. This means that you would have to go out and qualify for a standard FHA or conventional loan and put up with the standard qualifying process.

The VA program offers purchasers long-term thirty-year financing at competitive market rates in most cases. These loans, or "contracts," usually do not contain due-on-sale clauses. They are really a very attractive loan instrument. The qualifying is easier than the typical "pound of flesh and quart of blood" loan applications that FHA requires.

There are loans available from time to time that offer special financing for homebuyers and investors, and even money beyond the purchase amount which allows the investor the necessary cash to "rehab" a property back into condition so that it may be occupied.

For more information on FHA, HUD and VA repossessions in your area, contact your state's FHA or VA housing offices. These government offices can provide you with full information on the dates of sales and any special local restrictions.

If you notice that in your area these FHA/VA repossessions are selling above market value due to a high demand, I want to share a secret that I have learned as an investor. Think back on the foreclosure process. These homes went through a typical foreclosure and were taken back at the sale by the bank. The bank was then faced with the decision to sell the home to someone like you for the value of the loan, or *give it* to the insuring agency (FHA/VA) and *not make a dime more*. The insuring agency then has the hassle of marketing the home and selling it. You as a homebuyer can go to the bank repossesser officers and let them know that you are interested in knowing about every home they take back before they sell it back to the FHA/VA or other insuring agency such as FNMA. You have a chance through this procedure to not only get a home, but to save thousands of dollars on the purchase price.

I have no doubt that if you explore this specific area of foreclosures you will not only come across some excellent deals, but you'll also start to get excited about the idea of investing in real estate after you get settled into your first or next home. When you do get settled in, you might want to take a look at some books on investing. In my last book, *Financially Free,* I not only detail the process of investing after the sales but I also show you how you can buy homes directly from the owners before the foreclosure and how you can buy them at the foreclosure sale itself for pennies on the dollar. But be forewarned, those tools are a lot of work and are not suited at all for the more inexperienced buyer who is buying a home for a personal residence.

□   □   □

IF ALL ELSE HAS FAILED

☐ ☐ ☐

We have a lot of things going on now. You are calling at least one of your three agents each day. You are reading through the classified ads daily, and you have inserted your own ad in the papers which cover your target homebuying areas. You also have made up a flyer which advertises your desire to buy a home and have distributed it in each of your target areas. As if you're not busy enough already, you also are calling once a week on all the homes in your target areas which are listed for rent in your local papers. You also have learned about the foreclosure process and have started working with several foreclosure officers at local banks and are checking into FHA/VA and even FNMA foreclosures with your real estate agents.

If you have done all that but still want to use even more tools for finding your home, let me share a few that might help you out. First, ask your real estate agents to research and furnish as soon as possible a list of all people with homes in your target areas that have expired sales listings. (If you've developed a solid relationship with them, agents will most likely be glad to help in this way.) These people had listed their home with a real estate agency but for some reason or other canceled their listing. They are now prime candidates for you. You might consider sending each person a letter which describes your situation after checking out the property. The letter could read as follows:

April 11, 1992

Mr. Fred Jones
1811 Apple Pie Way
Hometown, NY 00874

Dear Mr. Jones,

My name is Bob Jones. My wife and I and our three children are doing everything we can to find a home we can buy in your area. I have worked at the Johnson Brickyard as station manager since I graduated from New York Tech in 1987. My wife works at the County Hospital part time as a registered nurse. We have saved up $5,000 for a down payment and can handle as much as $800 per month in house payments.

We heard that you recently canceled the real estate listing on your home. If you would still like to sell your home, please give us a call at (717) 668-9900. We are both home every evening after 5:00 p.m.

We hope we can work something out.

> Our best,
> Bob and Sharla Jones
> 11621 Apartment Row #20,023
> Hometown, NY 00874

Well, what else can I say? If you do what I have shown you here, you are going to be busy. But I have no doubt that you will come up with at least a dozen or more good leads. If you don't get any, go back to the beginning and make sure you are following each step the way I described. If you are still drawing a blank, then I would suggest you go out and contact every real estate agency in your area and broaden your search beyond the initial three areas you chose.

When you have a few leads in hand, let's proceed to the next step and make sure that what you're buying is worth it.

GET YOUR MONEY'S WORTH:
PROPERTY INSPECTION

☐   ☐   ☐

Once the house has been found, it must pass through another funnel: the inspection. This should occur in two phases: the buyer's inspection and the professional inspection. Years ago, homebuyers had to rely on their Uncle Bernie and a whole lot of luck to make sure they weren't getting a bad deal when they signed a real estate contract. Today, a lot has changed. Many states are instituting disclosure laws that require a seller to inform the buyer of any known defects in the home and its operating systems. Many states have also enacted laws requiring that a seller be responsible for any major repairs that are needed during the first ninety days after a sale.

With today's more complicated, energy-efficient homes, such protections for the buyer are only fair. After struggling to buy and finance your first home, would you like to be stuck with a furnace that blows up the second night after you move in?

After you find a home that you are interested in, I want you to go through a simple, step-by-step inspection sheet. I have provided special sheets for a typical single-family home, a condominium, and a co-op apartment at the end of this chapter. These inspection sheets are divided into two areas, the first of which is annual costs. Make sure you fully understand how much this home is going to cost you in terms of maintenance and perhaps increased utility expenses. Then go through a quick fifteen-minute physical inspection of the home. You should do your best to evaluate this home as unemotionally as possible.

Look for its flaws as well as its good points. Are there squeaky floorboards? Do the doors hang properly? Are any of the faucets dripping? Do the ceilings have strange dips? Is there a part of the house the seller doesn't let you see? How is the house positioned on the lot? Is drainage away from the foundation? Are there any visible signs of damage to the foundation, roof, or outside walls? Well, you get the picture. Just follow the inspection sheets and you will do a thorough job in a relatively short amount of time.

If the home still looks good after the inspection, proceed with negotiating and writing the purchase offer. As you write a purchase offer, include a building inspection clause. This clause will make your purchase contingent upon satisfactory inspection by a professional building inspector of your choosing. The clause will actually let you back out of the deal if you are not satisfied with the inspector's report, and it will require the seller to be responsible for correcting any defects uncovered during the inspection. I will give you that clause in Step #9.

In the meantime, select a professional home-inspection service in your area. Let me give you some tips in finding a good property inspector. Take out your home buying team directory and call the names of the inspectors your agents recommended. If your agents didn't furnish you with any recommendation, then look in your local phone book.

One of the largest national homebuying services is HouseMaster of America, with corporate offices located at 421 West Union Avenue, Bound Brook, New Jersey 08805. They have hundreds of local, independent representatives throughout the country. If you are interested in finding the HouseMaster location nearest you, call them toll free at (800) 526-3939. Tell them that you read about their service in this book, and they will furnish you with a discount coupon toward the purchase of an inspection warranty.

Whoever you use, make sure that their home inspection service meets the following minimum standards:

- *Impartiality.* Is home inspection the firm's only business? Or are they also contractors who might have a conflict of interest?

- *Experience.* How long has the firm been in business? How many inspections have they performed? Could they let you talk with a satisfied customer?

- *Reputation.* Does the firm have an unblemished reputation? Are they recognized as professionals? Call your local Better Business Bureau and ask about this company.

- *Credibility.* Will they stand behind their inspection report? Many major companies, such as HouseMaster, offer, as part of their service, a twelve-month limited inspection warranty on resale homes, based upon their reported condition.

The reason I insist that you use an inspection service is that not all of us are experts. And even if we are expert in one area, it is unlikely that we are expert in all areas. While I may have a good grasp of the electrical system and know how to make sure it's functioning properly, I may not be an expert in determining the structural soundness of the siding, roof, plumbing system, cooling system, heating system, appliances in the kitchen, basement, and foundation, or the ceilings, walls, and the floors.

Review the inspection sheets on the following pages. Choose the one that is appropriate to the property you are interested in. Fill in as much of the sheet as you can before you drive out to the property. Take this book (or at least a copy of the inspection sheet) with you when you go to do the inspection. Make written notes; don't rely on remembering details after

Single-Family Home Inspection Sheet

Property Information

Owner's Name_____   Phone_____

Property Address_____

City_____

Financial Information

Asking Price   _____

Required Down Payment   _____

Financing Options and Terms_____

_____

Estimated Monthly Payment After Purchase

Property Taxes Last Year (Annual)   _____ ÷ 12 = _____ ①

Special Local Assessment (Annual)   _____ ÷ 12 = _____ ②

Utilities Last Year (Annual):
- Electricity   _____
- Gas   _____
- Oil   _____
- Coal   _____
- Water   _____
- Sewer and Garbage   _____
- Other   _____

Total Annual Utilities   _____ ÷ 12 = _____ ③

Estimated Monthly Payment (①+②+③)   _____

Property Inspection

		Good	Fair	Poor
Exterior:	Yard			
	Proper Drainage			
	Unusual Odors			
	Paint			
	Overall Appearance			
	Siding			
Foundation:	Wall Cracks			
	Water Seepage			
	Cement/Brick			
	Wood Condition			
Roof:	Gutters			
	Downspouts			
	Shingles			
	Chimney			
Interior:	Ceilings			
	Doors			
	Floors			
	Walls			
	Adequate Lighting			
	Water Damage			
Appliances: (test operation)	Dishwasher			
	Disposal			
	Range/Stove			
	Microwave			

Property Inspection (continued)

		Good	Fair	Poor
Plumbing:	Drainage			
	Leakage			
	Shower/Sink/Toilet			
	Overall Appearance			
Electrical:	Adequate Outlets			
	Minimum 100 Amp			
	Breakers that Trip			
	Replaceable Fuses			
	Test All Switches			
	Overall Appearance			
Heating:	Age			
	Type			
	Overall Appearance			
	Test Operation			
Cooling:	Age			
	Type			
	Overall Appearance			
	Test Operation			
Insulation:	Attic Type			
	Wall Type			
Water Heater:	Capacity			
	Quick Recovery			
	Overall Condition			

Termites/Ants: Date of Last Inspection_____ Inspected by_____

Warranty Valid Until_____ Phone # of Inspector_____

Condominium Inspection Sheet

Property Information

Owner's Name_____   Phone_____

Property Address_____

City_____

Financial Information

Asking Price   _____

Required Down Payment   _____

Financing Options and Terms_____

_____

Estimated Monthly Payment After Purchase

Property Taxes Last Year (Annual)   _____ ÷ 12 = _____ ①

Special Condo Assessment (Annual)   _____ ÷ 12 = _____ ②

Annual Association Fee   _____ ÷ 12 = _____ ③

Utilities Last Year (Annual):
- Electricity   _____
- Gas   _____
- Oil   _____
- Coal   _____
- Water   _____
- Sewer and Garbage   _____
- Other   _____

Total Annual Utilities   _____ ÷ 12 = _____ ④

Annual Condo Maintenance Fee   _____ ÷ 12 = _____ ⑤

Estimated Monthly Payment (①+②+③+④+⑤)   _____

Property Inspection

		Good	Fair	Poor
Common Yard:	Proper Drainage			
	Unusual Odors			
	Paint			
	Overall Appearance			
	Siding			
Common Facilities:	Swimming Pool			
	Health Club			
	Tennis Courts			
	Putting Range			
	Parking Facilities			
	Clubhouse			
Foundation:	Wall Cracks			
	Water Leakage			
	Cement/Brick			
Roof:	Gutters			
	Downspouts			
	Shingles			
	Chimney			
Interior:	Ceilings			
	Doors			
	Floors			
	Walls			
	Adequate Lighting			
	Water Damage			
Appliances:	Dishwasher			

Property Inspection (continued)

		Good	Fair	Poor
Appliances:	Disposal			
	Range/Stove			
	Microwave			
Plumbing:	Water Pressure			
	Drainage			
	Leakage			
	Shower/Sink/Toilet			
	Overall Appearance			
Electrical:	Adequate Outlets			
	Minimum 100 Amp			
	Breakers That Trip			
	Replaceable Fuses			
	Test All Switches			
	Overall Appearance			
Heating:	Age			
	Type			
	Overall Appearance			
	Test Operation			
Cooling:	Age			
	Type			
	Overall Appearance			
	Test Operation			
Insulation:	Attic Type			
	Wall Type			
Water Heater:	Capacity			

Property Inspection (continued)

		Good	Fair	Poor
Water Heater:	Quick Recovery			
	Overall Condition			

Termites/Ants: Date of Last Inspection_____ Inspected by_____

Warranty Valid Until_____ Phone # of Inspector_____

Co-Op Inspection Sheet

Property Information

Owner's Name_____ Phone_____

Property Address_____

City_____

Financial Information

Asking Price   _____

Required Down Payment   _____

Financing Options and Terms_____

_____

Estimated Monthly Payment After Purchase

Property Taxes Last Year (Annual)   _____ ÷ 12 = _____ ①

Special Co-Op Assessment (Annual)   _____ ÷ 12 = _____ ②

Annual Co-Op Association Fee   _____ ÷ 12 = _____ ③

Utilities Last Year (Annual):
- Electricity   _____
- Gas   _____
- Oil   _____
- Coal   _____
- Water   _____
- Sewer and Garbage   _____
- Other   _____

Total Annual Utilities   _____ ÷ 12 = _____ ④

Annual Co-Op Maintenance Fee   _____ ÷ 12 = _____ ⑤

Estimated Monthly Payment (①+②+③+④+⑤)   _____

Property Inspection

		Good	Fair	Poor
Exterior:	Yard			
	Proper Drainage			
	Unusual Odors			
	Paint			
	Overall Appearance			
	Siding			
Foundation:	Wall Cracks			
	Water Seepage			
	Cement/Brick			
	Wood Condition			
Roof:	Gutters			
	Downspouts			
	Shingles			
	Chimney			
Interior:	Ceilings			
	Doors			
	Floors			
	Walls			
	Adequate Lighting			
	Water Damage			
Appliances: (test operation)	Dishwasher			
	Disposal			
	Range/Stove			
	Microwave			

Property Inspection (continued)

		Good	Fair	Poor
Appliances:	Range/Stove			
	Microwave			
Plumbing:	Water Pressure			
	Drainage			
	Leakage			
	Shower/Sink/Toilet			
	Overall Appearance			
Electrical:	Adequate Outlets			
	Minimum 100 Amp			
	Breakers That Trip			
	Replaceable Fuses			
	Test All Switches			
	Overall Appearance			
Heating:	Age			
	Type			
	Overall Appearance			
	Test Operation			
Cooling:	Age			
	Type			
	Overall Appearance			
	Test Operation			
Insulation:	Attic Type			
	Wall Type			
Water Heater:	Capacity			
	Quick Recovery			

Property Inspection (continued)

	Good	Fair	Poor
Water Heater: Overall Condition			

Termites/Ants: Date of Last Inspection_____ Inspected by_____

Warranty Valid Until_____ Phone # of Inspector_____

you leave the property. The property owner will appreciate your organized and efficient approach to viewing his property, especially if you are friendly and objective as you ask questions about his place.

Try to do your inspection quickly. As I suggested earlier, fifteen minutes is the ideal length of time. You can see the major concerns in that time, and the owner is more likely to stay cooperative if you don't take too much of his time.

Once you have completed your inspection, call in the professional inspection service you have chosen. They will either verify your findings or uncover flaws you missed. Either way, their inspection is vital before you begin negotiating for the property.

Please make sure to go through each of these items as carefully as you can. If you don't know how to answer a question, circle it and save it for your property inspector. But do the best you can to evaluate the property's condition before you call in the professional inspectors and before spending the time to negotiate the purchase, arrange the financing, and make a written offer.

FINANCE THE PURCHASE

☐   ☐   ☐

Imagine saving up and planning for years to buy your first bicycle, a big, red, shiny one with every feature you've ever dreamed of. You've compared prices on your bike for months at every store in the county and, despite your monklike thrift, you are still $50 shy of the purchase price. On a beautiful spring Saturday morning, your alarm clock wakes you from your slumber for another fun day of slave labor on other people's yards at 50 cents per hour. As your feet hit the cold floor, you can't help thinking of all your friends who are sleeping right now while you're having to go to work. It doesn't bother you so much that they're going to be playing baseball today or hanging out at the mall later this afternoon; what really irks you is that they get to sleep in. Oh, well, after all, you are working for a purpose.

As you sit down in your dimly lit kitchen to another bowl of Wheaties, you flick on your family's radio to catch the weather report. After all, if it's going to rain, you might as well know right now that you're going to be soaked pulling Mrs. Jensen's weeds. As you sit down for your first crunchy bite, you hear the radio announcer give a special bulletin—the first person to arrive at Dunlop bike shop to buy a bike that morning can take $50 off the price of any bike in the store.

The words are like thunder, you're temporarily paralyzed. Did you hear right? Listen again. Yeah, he did say that. Like a bolt of lightning, the most truly unbelievable luck has transformed your whole world. You are only a few miles away from Dunlop's bikes.

As you round the corner, your breath is like fire, your legs like rubber, but you'll make it—you'll be first, there's the shop right ahead and no one's there yet. As you reach the shop door, the owner flips over the CLOSED sign to OPEN. Hurrah!!! With one stride, you fling open the door and grab the handles of your dream bike. You wheel it to the owner's desk and say in a loud, mature, commanding voice (as best as you can manage), "I want this one." The owner smiles and says, "Well, only one person gets the $50 off, and that's the first bike that anyone wanted to buy today. How do you want to pay, son?" You proudly answer "Cash" and reach automatically for your empty pocket.

At that moment, your stomach sinks as your mind races and remembers instantly every detail of the Ovaltine can stuffed behind your dirty socks in the back of your closet where you hid your money. That's exactly where it is still sitting right now, behind the socks which no burglar would even dare to look behind.

Your mind reels. There's still hope—run home, get the Ovaltine can, be back in minutes. You tell the shop clerk, "I'll be back in a minute." As you turn to go, the bell on the shop door rings. A young couple comes in with their young daughter and says brightly, "We're here to buy that bike for $50 off; has anyone else bought it?" Your voice starts to say yes, but the shopkeeper beats you to it with a loud "No." You mind swims as the shopkeeper loads the shiny new bike into the family's car trunk. You feel like crying as you learn your first lesson in finance: "The person with the funds in hand gets the deal."

In Steps #1 and #3 you figured out your net worth, learned what loans were available, and determined what financing you could afford. Step #7 goes even further; in this step you will actually line up the needed financing for your target house. We will attempt to review all relevant conventional and creative financing techniques. After each area has been explored, we will put together a workable financing package for buying the property.

The area of financing a project can be one of the most difficult. I am going to spend more time than you might expect discussing the concepts which lie behind real estate finance. I am then going to explain the specific financing options that you have and help you put together a good deal. If you already know a FNMA insured loan from an FHA 203K loan, you might want to skim through this preliminary material and jump into putting together a financing package with me later in this chapter. If you are a little shaky on just how real estate finance works, stick with me. I'll remove the mysterious veil which surrounds borrowing money for buying real estate.

THE IMPORTANCE OF REAL ESTATE FINANCE

☐ ☐ ☐

Anyone contemplating future homeownership should have a clear, basic understanding of real estate finance and how it works as an investment. As an individual grows into maturity and considers the need for appropriate housing for his family or commercial property for a business, it soon becomes apparent that there will be a large financial commitment involved in the purchase. However, with the proper understanding and management of one's own personal and investment income stream, real estate ownership and successful investment are possible.

Financing is one of the most important aspects of the real estate transaction. It doesn't matter how much time and effort has gone into making the sale, because the bottom line is that the prospective borrower must have the cash or the purchasing power to obtain the property. If cash is not available, and in most circumstances it is not, the buyer must qualify for or *create* the necessary financing.

The financing process in our free economy is vital. Indeed, our entire economy revolves around it. If the lender runs out of funds, a chain reaction of economic chaos develops. The borrowers will be unable to acquire the funds to purchase, the builders will stop building, the banks will quit lending, the lumber industry will quit cutting, and millions are without jobs. Others affected by these financing problems include real estate agents, appraisers, surveyors, and title companies, followed by a drastic decline in retail sales of furniture, carpeting, and lighting. The list goes on and on to unbelievable lengths. With our economy so closely tied to the housing industry, you can be sure the government will do all it can to make sure that there is a continuous flow of activity.

Perhaps the easiest way to illustrate the importance of real estate finance is with a case study showing the effects of a variety of possible decisions. Let us consider a home that has caught the eye of Jeff and Cindy. The target home is located in a nice, well-developed area of the city and has all of the physical characteristics that Jeff and Cindy determined they wanted in Step #2. In short, they have fallen in love with the home and have resolved to make it their future abode. After all, the price seems reasonable and, with both of them working, the payments seem within their reach. The owner, Mr. Sanders, is asking $72,000. There is an assumable first mortgage with a balance of $45,000 with twenty-four years of monthly payments left at 14 percent. Payments on the assumable first are $544.28, which represents principal and interest only. The current rates on new loans are at 12 percent. Mr. Sanders must have $5,000 cash down and will carry the balance of his equity at 10 percent for ten years ($72,000 sales price — $45,000 loan balance — $5,000 down payment = $22,000 equity). In Step #1, John and Cindy determined that they have $15,000 total cash. They are faced with two options: assume the existing 14-percent interest mortgage and create a second mortgage with the seller, or refinance the property at today's lower interest rates and pay off the seller totally.

The question is, what is the more advantageous financial decision this young couple can make? Let's look at their situation a little more closely. Here are some figures for their two choices:

1. Completely refinance, getting a lower rate of interest. With the points and loan origination costs estimated at around $3,000, this leaves $10,000 toward a down payment and $2,000 to move and fix up their new home.
2. Assume the existing mortgage and put $5,000 down, with the owner carrying a second mortgage in the amount of $22,000. Since there would be no loan origination fees or points to pay, the buyers would be left with $10,000 to move and fix up their home.

An experienced investment acquisition team could come up with at least a dozen other possibilities, but let us consider just these two, since they are the most common and the most helpful for our purposes.

OPTION 1—REFINANCE THE HOME

$ 72,000	Sales price
$ 10,000	Down payment
$ 3,000	Points and loan origination fees
$ 62,000	Amount financed
12%	Interest rate
$ 637.74	Estimated P&I monthly payment for 30 years
$167,586.33	Total interest paid at the end of the 30 years
$242,586.33	Total principal and interest payments that are paid, providing no prepayments are made

□   □   □

OPTION 2—ASSUMPTION AND OWNER FINANCING

$ 72,000	Sales price
$ 5,000	Down payment
$ 45,000	Assumption of a current loan with a payment of $544.28 P&I
$ 22,000	Owner financing at 10 percent for 10 years, with monthly payments at $290.73
$ 835.01	Estimated P&I monthly payments for years 1–10
$ 544.28	Estimated P&I monthly payments for years 11–24
$124,640.24	Total interest paid at the end of the 24 years
$196,640.24	Total principal and interest payments that are paid to the bank and the owner, providing no prepayments are made

As you can see, Option 1 will cost nearly $50,000 (not considering tax implications) more in the long run of the loan. Option 1 also requires you to spend nearly your entire down payment of $15,000. That sure makes Option 2 sound great, but wait . . . Option 2 carries with it higher payments than Option 1 in the first ten years (higher by $197.27 a month).

If we were to look at this strictly in the harsh light of dollars and cents (as all investors should), it really comes down to this: Is paying an extra $197 a month for the first ten years worth saving $93.46 a month for the next fourteen years and then having your payment end in year 24 as opposed to Option 1's six more years of payments of over $600 dollars a month ending in year 30.

Now throw in the benefit of having to spend $8,000 less on your down payment with Option 2 and you are ready to make your decision. Would you rather take Option 1 or Option 2? A basic knowledge of real estate finance sure opens up some intriguing possibilities. In fact, it can save you up to $50,000 on a purchase such as this one.

□ □ □

THE ECONOMIC MAGIC OF OWNING REAL ESTATE

□   □   □

Owning has many different advantages over renting. Six major advantages come easily to mind: cash flow, appreciation, tax benefits, equity increase, hedged inflation, and emotional security.

Is your home purchase an investment? The answers to this question are often confusing. But, if pressed I'd have to say that owning a home should be an investment. The first and primary goal of any investment is to make a profit at some future date. If making a profit is not realistic to a particular investment, then one should quickly abandon the idea or be in the personal financial position that money thrown away is of no concern. In light of our subject, if you can't see your home being a wise financial and emotional decision, then you'd be better off renting.

The opportunities to invest your hard-earned dollar are as vast as the sands of the sea; the problem is that many of these investments come and go almost as quickly as beach sand, leaving few that can stand the test of time. Before making any decisions, you need to consider factors such as opportunity cost (what might your dollar do in some other investment?), control (how secure is your investment?), time (how much time are you going to have to spend managing your investment?), barriers to entry (do I have to have a special license or degree to participate?), and your own personality (will I be able to mentally handle this type of investment?). People who find that they can no longer sleep at night because of their pork-belly futures should seek profits in some other, more secure form of investing.

Success in buying your first or next home requires constant attention to details and an understanding of value. A working knowledge of real estate finance is invaluable to avoid getting burned on a real estate deal, regardless of whether it's your first or your twentieth home. Be careful, learn before you leap. Let's now start homing in on the individual areas of real estate finance that you need to become familiar with.

REAL ESTATE LOANS

□   □   □

We will begin the discussion of real estate loans by exploring the most common sources of funds and loans. You might have already heard about the conventional, FHA, and VA (or GI) loans. These loans have been available for quite some time, and they are familiar to almost anyone who has had any exposure to real estate. We will take some time to go into a little depth on each of them, so that a clearer understanding of each may be realized. It is very important to understand these loans, because you will be faced with them when looking at existing financing.

SOURCES OF MORTGAGE MONEY

□   □   □

There are basically two sources of funds for residential mortgage money. The first is the primary market, where the bank or mortgage company actually makes the mortgage loan from their funds. They collect the funds themselves and administer the loan. Examples of primary lenders are commercial banks, life insurance companies, savings and loans, mortgage companies, and credit unions.

The other source is the secondary market, which supplies mortgage money to primary lenders by purchasing loans from them. These mortgage loans are often pooled and sold to investors. Quite often, in this case, the original lender services the loan (collects payments). The original, or primary, lender makes his profit by charging "points" (points are a percentage of the total loan value you have to pay up front to borrow money from a lender), an origination fee, and loan service fees. Examples of the secondary market are the Federal National Mortgage Association (FNMA is the largest supplier of home mortgage funds), Federal Home Loan Mortgage Corporation (FHLMC), Government National Mortgage Association (GNMA), General Electric Credit Corporation (GECC), and Residential Funding Corporation (RFC).

There are advantages for a mortgage company to sell its loans in the secondary market. For example, selling loans could help to replenish the company's limited supply of mortgage money, making the money for loans in a growing area easier to get.

THE CONVENTIONAL HOME LOAN

□   □   □

The conventional loan is typified by a loan which has a fixed payment with a fixed interest rate over a fixed number of years. It has not had any type of government involvement in the form of insurance or guarantees, but has been left to the full risk of the lender making the loan or his underwriter (investor). At one time, this loan was so common that it represented nearly 75 percent of all home loans that were issued.

Once the bread and butter of most lending institutions, the conventional mortgage soon backfired and became a curse for many of these thriving institutions. The problem came when inflation rose and the cost of the money that the bank borrowed from the secondary market to lend to home buyers was greater than the mortgages they had on their books. You can't borrow money at 12-percent interest and have 80 percent of your loans written at under 8 percent interest, at least not if you want to make money. The banks found themselves losing money on the residential loans they were carrying.

This brought many of these big banks to their knees, scurrying for ways to offset their mistake. As it turned out, they did find some rather creative ways. Necessity is often the mother of invention, and banks aren't dumb. During the ensuing period of the inflated dollar, many of these institutions became greedy and tried to make up for their past mistakes by devising a system of variable rates that would allow them to lower their risk and ensure a more stable income.

In a nutshell, what happens is that, while the economy is in a stabilized position, the lender can give a fixed-rate loan, but if high inflation hits, he loses. Again, borrowing current funds at 12-percent interest or more today while servicing loans with 8-percent interest or less is financial suicide. By giving a fixed-rate loan, the investor of that money takes the risk. (Inflation may hit and create these enormous losses.) Because of this risk, the borrower usually pays a premium (called points) for the benefit of having the risk shifted to the lender.

The risk is not solely the lender's, however; this benefit can be reversed on the borrower if rates go down during the period of his loan. When this happens, all of the bankers who wrote the loans begin their Caribbean cruise celebration on the tears of the unlucky borrowers who lost in the casino game of interest rates. Since most bankers don't anticipate a sustained rollback in interest rates, the fixed-rate conventional mortgage is becoming increasingly difficult to buy.

Other measures have been taken by the lenders to overcome the risk of fixed-rate conventional loans. One of these is the "due-on-sale clause." This clause allows the lender to call the entire amount of the loan due in the event that the home is ever sold (the lender may also, at his option, raise the interest to the prevailing rate, along with requiring full qualification of the new buyer). It is not wise to underestimate all of the ways the lender has to keep tabs on such sales. Of course, if present rates are below what the loan was written for, it's hard to believe that the lender will ever call the loan due. Given that premise, thousands of owners of homes with such notes sold their loans to unwary buyers who were caught off guard when interest rates increased, and the lenders went back into the files and started doing a little homework at the courthouse. When they found a home whose title had been transferred or sold, they started calling all of these "illegally" sold notes due. The due-on-sale clause is now considered akin to a lien on the property and must be fully disclosed to the buyer before closing.

There are advantages to a fixed-rate mortgage. One is that the borrower can budget easily because he will always know what his house payment is going to be. The second and probably greatest advantage is that, as time goes on, the cost of money generally goes up. This "long run approach" has had very few lasting exceptions, making the original money borrowed more and more valuable to the owner of the note (why pay off a 6-percent loan when you'd have to borrow money at 13 percent?).

GOVERNMENT-INSURED LOANS

□ □ □

The two major types of government-secured loans are Federal Housing Administration (FHA) and Veterans Administration (VA) loans. The FHA loan has been the most popular nationwide because it provides attractive benefits for buyers, sellers, and investors. The FHA is not the one who actually loans the money; they merely insure the investor that the loan amount will be repaid. This means that if the borrower defaults on the loan, the lender will be repaid his invested funds by the FHA.

What makes this loan so attractive to the buyer is the fact that he starts by making a low cash down payment and, in some situations, the cash for the down payment can even be a gift from his parents. For example, an FHA loan in the amount of $65,000 would require a down payment of approximately $2,250. That is substantially less than the $6,500 down which would be required by most conventional institutions.

Another benefit to the FHA loan is its resalability. When an owner with an FHA loan sells his home to a prospective buyer, the existing FHA loan is fully assumable, with very little or no qualification. The qualification restrictions depend on the issue of the loan.

Many FHA issues have been put on the market, so many that it's a little hard to tell a 235 from a 245. It would be worth your while to learn a little bit about these government loans. FHA loans vary from state to state and location to location. One area in the state of Utah has a loan amount that cannot exceed $67,500, while sixty miles away they are allowed $72,000. This means that a buyer who wants to use an FHA loan in either of those areas for an $80,000 home must come up with additional cash to pay off the difference.

Another negative factor is that not all lenders are willing to work with FHA loans because of the immense amount of paperwork the government requires. A borrower interested in receiving an FHA loan must first locate a lending institution that works with these loans. This has been a little more of a hassle in the past, but it is presently estimated that 33 percent of the mortgage loans written have some type of government insurance like that found on the FHA loans.

When you attempt to qualify for an FHA loan, the loan officer will first do a prequalification. Don't get too worried; they don't do chromosome checks or take blood samples yet. With the lender's help, you will fill out a fairly simple worksheet. The purpose of the worksheet is to give you an indication of how much of a loan you can qualify for. You will also review the different loan programs that are presently available and which ones you can qualify for. If the prequalification sheet passes, then an estimation of closing documents can be worked up. This information tells you how much cash money will be required at closing. After the preliminary information is complete, the lender will ask for a commitment from the potential borrower, which at this point involves some money. This money is to cover the lender's expenses for a required appraisal of the property in question, a current credit report on you, verification of deposits and employment, and other miscellaneous expenses. These up-front expenses are generally nonrefundable.

If all this information is within the guidelines set by the FHA, the lender will then submit all of the information to the FHA for approval. At this time, the lender will set the closing date for all funds and titled names to be transferred and entered in at the courthouse.

The cost of closing a loan can be astronomical. If you are planning to seek outside financing, it is critical that these costs be narrowed down so you won't get a big surprise when the loan officer informs you of the amount of the cashier's check you need to bring to the closing. One thing to keep in mind is that if the points relative to a specific interest rate are something that you feel you can live with, you may want to consider a lock-in. This is a legal form of gambling in which if the points go up, you win, and if they go down, you lose. This is most difficult to analyze; no one has come up with an easy way to second-guess the money market, and the points can change every hour. So, consider the fact of whether the home you are buying is worth the one-half point of insurance usually charged to lock you in at the current number of points. Once you lock in, there is usually no backing out, since the loan institution simultaneously obtains a commitment from a secondary market investor for a block of money at terms relative to your lock-in. When you lock in, both you and the mortgage company become committed.

For those who don't fully understand points, it would be well worth our time to give a brief explanation. Points are used in loans in several applications. First, a point is equal to one percentage point of the loan amount. So, for example, if you are obtaining a loan for $60,000, one point would be $600. It is as simple as that. What gets confusing are the reasons they charge points. We have already mentioned that points are an inducement for lenders to lend money at a given percentage rate in relation to possible future changes in the interest rates. There are also other reasons. Points are used to pay the lender for his overhead that allows him to set up loans —namely, the office and all it takes to furnish it and keep it going. Points are not to be confused with the setup fee. The setup fee is traditionally one and one half percent. The setup fee is also known in some areas as the "origination fee."

Points are also used to help the lender increase his yield on the money he is lending. For example, if the lender can make 12 percent on his money in the private market and the current FHA rate is at 10 percent, he would be foolish to invest his money in such an venture. However, if he was to get some of his interest up front, that could boost his overall yield up to the current private amount. That's what points are for: They are a hidden interest rate! It is estimated that approximately 2 points are equal to one and one quarter percent interest over the life of the loan.

It is advantageous for the buyer to pay the points only because they can be deducted as interest expense at tax time. In light of the frequent changes in tax laws, you should seek advice from a competent CPA or call the IRS and ask them what the current status is on the deductibility of points. Usually, the seller who pays points can deduct points as a cost of selling his home or property, but, again, check; this is subject to change.

One last thing to remember about the FHA loan is that the original borrower is responsible for the repayment of the loan amount. Even though the loans are fully assumable by another buyer and foreclosure proceedings can be brought against this new assuming borrower, the lender still reserves the right to hold the original borrower responsible for the amount due. Let me give the exception, though: If your seller had you formally assume (an assumption through the original lender with you being qualified by the lending institution), the seller is off the hook in the event of foreclosure.

VETERANS ADMINISTRATION LOANS

☐ ☐ ☐

This loan, in almost all instances, can only be originated by a veteran of the U.S. armed forces. A veteran is eligible for his entire life. The Veterans Administration does not loan the money. Like the FHA loan, it is only guaranteeing the loan. The loan amount guaranteed by the VA is set according to several evaluations. The first of these evaluations is the property itself, which is appraised by an appraiser designated by the VA. The loan amount cannot exceed the value of the property as evaluated by the appraiser or the owner. This does not mean you can't pay more for the property than is evaluated by the appraiser, but you must make up the difference with your own funds.

Like the FHA loan, the VA loan is fully assumable, but it is very important to the buyer and the seller that the VA is notified and a release is signed so that the obligation of the veteran is released. If the release is not completed, the veteran may be held liable for outstanding funds in the event the buyer defaults on the loan. To assume a VA loan, you need not be a veteran, but to qualify for a new loan, it is a must.

Please note that the amount of money that you can borrow on both FHA and VA loans varies from region to region. To determine these limits you should contact your local FHA or VA offices.

To conclude this section, let's review the basic types of residential real estate loans:

CONVENTIONAL LOANS

Program	Maximum Term	Maximum Loan	Down Payment	Miscellaneous Information
80% Conventional	30 years	Varies	20%	Nonowner Occupied
90% Conventional	30 years	Varies	10%	Owner Occupied
95% Conventional	30 years	Varies	5%	Owner Occupied Highest Interest Rates

FHA GUARANTEED LOANS

FHA 203B	30 years	$67,500 to $93,420*	2–5%	FHA Inspection Required
FHA 245A	30 years	''	3–12%	Negative Amortization (loan value increases for the first five years)

* Check with local FHA offices concerning specific loan amounts. Many loan amounts are higher for multifamily homes.

VA GUARANTEED LOANS

VA	30 years	$110,000 with no down payment†	0%	Vet must meet eligibility requirements
VA Graduated Payment	30 years	''	2–5%	Negative Amortization

† Check with local VA officers concerning your eligibility and current loan program specifics. Generally, to be eligible for a program, a veteran must have honorably served 181 days of active duty. During wartime, only 90 days of active duty is required. These time requirements do not include training time.

ALTERNATIVE FINANCING

□   □   □

Next to location, financing a home is the single most important aspect in a purchase. An individual or family can always live with a poor floor plan, hot pink carpets, or a rundown house, but to have to live with payments that make life unbearable or the house impossible to resell can be devastating. The old adage "location, location, location" as the three keys in purchasing a property has been expanded to include "terms, terms, terms." For myself, I prefer to say "location, terms, price."

Terms, location, and price are three very important words for a personal financial portfolio. Can you imagine working for years, slaving your life away to build equity in your home, only to find that the negative amortization (the loan balance is *increasing)* of an adjustable-rate mortgage has secretly robbed you and your loved ones of any monetary rewards. Always remember, in many cases the financing you sign for today will follow you for the next thirty years. So make sure you become knowledgeable before making your decision.

Shopping around is most important. Interest rates and points will vary from bank to bank, and all will offer their own special benefits. For example, one institution may offer fewer points and charge more for their closing costs. Look at the entire package an institution offers, including the penalties for backing out and not closing on a loan and also the terms for prepayment and assumptions. In other words, always ask for the bottom line figures before the smoke finally clears at the closing table. Know, before you even apply, what actual costs, expenses, and responsibilities you will incur. If the company is not interested in providing such early information, take your business elsewhere.

In the beginning of this chapter, we talked about the young boy who lost out on the bike. Imagine if, when he had reached down and found his pockets empty, he had been immediately open with the bike owner and said, "I left my money in the Ovaltine can behind my dirty socks in my closet at home. If you let me leave my Boy Scout knife, lucky rabbit's foot, secret decoder ring, and the 'choose the right' ring from my Sunday school class here as a deposit, I'll run home and be back with the money for you in five minutes." Then, pausing a second for breath, he blurts out the clincher, "To make it really worth your while, I'll stay here all day and wash every window and sweep out your store."

I have no doubt that, with that kind of approach, the owner would have agreed. That kind of creative gumption just could have saved his bike. That kind of bargaining is just what creative real estate financing is all about.

Because of volatile interest rates and the shake-up among lenders, individuals have increasingly turned to methods of home financing that could be termed alternative, or creative. Alternative financing is not always easy. No matter how experienced you are, it feels a little as if you're wading in unknown water. You become, in essence, the bank officer who sets up and arranges the loan. Depending upon which side of the fence you're on, there are many things to consider, from how to set up the loan to qualifying yourself as a borrower. You will also hear a lot of terms that many times will be hard to understand, let alone pronounce. But don't let this intimidate you. No matter how ridiculous you think you may seem or how many times it has been explained to you, keep asking questions until you fully understand. By simply forcing the issue and having your questions exposed to the light of day, you could make the difference of several thousand dollars in or out of your pocket.

When financing a property, there are several areas to look into. We have already discussed the conventional method of going to an institution that provides mortgage services, but this only scratches the surface of all of the many possibilities that are available. Now we will explore some unconventional methods, beginning with those areas where the seller can become involved with the financing of a property to help expedite a sale. These concepts are as useful to the seller as they are to the buyer. In many situations the seller can make the necessary concessions to close the deal.

The owner of a real estate property usually has a full deck of cards that can be used in a variety of ways to make him a winner. The fun and exciting aspect of this real estate game is that both buyer and seller can be winners and everyone can leave the closing with smiles on their faces. You have a very desirable product that others want and are willing to pay for, and all you have to do is make your product competitive with other similar products on the market.

The owner, in most circumstances, has built up a certain amount of equity in his property. That is, the loans currently against the property are less than what the house will sell for. (Sales price would be the property's current market value, in relationship to the amount of time and exposure to buyers that the property has had.) The seller can use this equity as bargaining power, which can be far more valuable than the initial equity amount shows. The equity can be seller-financed over a mutually agreed (between the buyer and the seller) period of time. This alternative financing would allow the buyer to get into the home with a lower amount down than would normally be required. Also, the seller can enjoy additional interest income on the amount being financed. (Generally, the interest that a seller can charge on his equity is several points over what he might receive from a bank certificate of deposit for a similar period of time. In addition, the owner will be able to sell his home with alternative financing, whereas in many cases the buyer might have passed it by for more attractive terms elsewhere.)

It is estimated that about half of the homes sold on today's market have some type of owner financing in one form or another. This happens because of the equity we have talked about and also because the interest rates on the existing loans are generally lower than what can be found in current mortgage rates. The seller financing usually is a very small amount. But it is, in most cases, the difference between the existing loan amounts plus the down payment and the purchase price.

For example, a transaction is made in which the buyer is going to assume a current mortgage of $55,000, the owner is willing to sell the property for $65,000, and the buyer has $5,000 to put toward the down payment. The seller agrees to finance the remaining $5,000 of equity for five years. This transaction has met the needs of both parties in a legal and most effective way. As security, the seller retains a lien against the home until the $5,000 plus interest is paid in full. If payments aren't made on the $5,000, then the seller forecloses. If payments are made on a timely basis and are paid off in full, the note is reconveyed and recorded as having been paid in full.

Many homeowners are more than willing to become involved in private lending because good terms can usually command a higher sales price. In a day and age in which total closing costs easily run to several thousands of dollars, alternative financing terms can sidestep these enormous costs and benefit both buyer and seller. The buyer has to come up with less money to buy the property with, and the seller gets more profit from the sale. While terms sound like the answer to all problems, they can also create new ones. While it is true that a buyer and seller can write their own deals, it is advisable for both the novice and experienced investor to use professionals to both close and record all financial transactions.

Working with professionals, including real estate attorneys, selling or buying agents, title companies, and paid consultants, can in the long run save you thousands. A few hundred dollars of savings at the outset of a transaction does not compensate for the legal nightmares of faulty or inaccurate documents down the road. Play it safe and keep some of that quiet peace of mind that allows you a good night's rest.

One more note: when considering seller financing you should check with the IRS to determine the *minimum* mandatory interest rate your seller can charge you. In other words, the IRS can fine your seller if he doesn't charge you enough interest.

THE WRAPAROUND LOAN

□   □   □

The wraparound loan is used when the seller has an attractive first mortgage in which the interest rate is significantly lower than what can be found at current market rates. However, the down payment that the buyer is willing to invest may not cover the additional amount needed to cash out the seller after the loans are assumed. The seller can "wrap" the first by financing the remainder of the cash needed. It is called a wrap because the first mortgage stays in the seller's name, so that one payment on both the first and the new second are paid to the seller, or a mutually designated trust company, by the buyer. The seller or the trust company then pays the first mortgage payment, with the remainder of the payment going to the seller as monthly income. The new mortgage is said to envelope, or wrap, the original mortgage.

To use a wrap, the seller's original mortgage must not contain an acceleration or due-on-sale clause. In such cases (usually with a conventional mortgage) the lender would require immediate payoff, or an increase in interest rates. Usually a seller or investor will wrap a VA or FHA loan.

The advantage to the buyer is a lower payment and more control. When the buyer uses a wraparound, the title is actually passed from the seller to the buyer upon purchase rather than somewhere down the road as in a contract for deed. This solves a lot of problems of having a titled clouded, or encumbered, from an unknown lien. The advantages to the seller are being able to sell the property more quickly, plus realizing an increase in profits. The seller not only makes money from the sales price, but also from the interest rate differential. The seller may have an 8-percent first mortgage for $40,000. He sells his home on a wrap for $60,000 with $5,000 down, the balance to be financed on a wrap at 12 percent. The seller receives $565.74 each month P&I, and each month makes the first mortgage payment of only $292.51. The seller nets $272.23. The $272.23 represents not only his profit from the sale but the 4-percent profit of selling his $40,000 first at 12-percent interest and paying only 8-percent interest on it.

The wrap has also been used on loans that were not assumable, called a "blind wrap," in which the lender is never notified of the sale, thus avoiding a potential due-on-sale clause. I have seen real estate agents and title companies and even bank officers encourage people to do these. *Be careful!!!* Blind wraps can be very risky, and care should be taken before entering into one no matter what side of the negotiating table you sit on.

Wraps aren't just limited to owner financing. An increasing number of institutions are becoming involved in the wraparound mortgage. The banking institution assumes the first; then, depending on what interest rate it requires (blended rate), it charges an appropriate rate on your bridge financing, or second. The bank simply finances the second at a rate that will give it the yield it desires.

These institutions look at all the areas of creditworthiness of the buyer as well as property location to make sure that the loan is basically risk-free. In dealing with wraparounds you too should be cautious. It is advisable to use the wrap only on assumable loans. As a buyer or as a seller, you should always seek competent legal counsel when developing such loans. A trust or a escrow account is very important when using a wrap. The way an escrow works is that at closing all of your documents are kept by an independent bank or mortgage office in trust. They figure what the amount and time of distribution of your payments should be. At closing, both you and your seller sign the trust agreement. For a nominal fee the trust will collect your payments and disperse the required amounts (first mortgage payment, insurance, tax, owner's equity payment, and so forth) to all the right parties. This relieves you as a buyer of the potential problem that might occur when your payment to a seller on a wrap never makes its way to the first mortgage holder. I've heard too many stories of people who've bought homes on wraps or land contracts who suddenly got a knock one day on their door from the sheriff serving them with a repossession notice. These people never missed making even one payment to the seller, but their seller had missed the last sixteen payments to the mortgage company. And since the mortgage had remained in the seller's name, the buyer received no notices of missed payments—until the sheriff came to call.

In other words, without a competent escrow company, the buyer is at risk because he has no guarantee that the seller won't pocket all the cash that should go to the first mortgage holder. If that happens, a foreclosure can occur in circumstances where the buyer will receive his first notice that the mortgage is in trouble when the sheriff shows up on the doorstep announcing that the property must be vacated immediately. (It has happened before, so don't fall prey to such stupidity when you buy your home.)

□   □   □

WRAPAROUND MORTGAGE EXAMPLE

□   □   □

A seller, who wants to sell his home for $120,000, has an existing FHA loan for $50,000 at 8-percent interest. This loan could be assumed by the buyer, but he has only $10,000 available for the down payment. This would leave $60,000 in equity still unpaid by the buyer. Current market rates are 13 percent, making qualifying for a full refinance out of the question for the buyer.

Solution

The seller agrees to help the buyer by using a wrap. The entire first mortgage of $50,000 and the seller's equity are bundled into a wrap for $110,000 at 12-percent interest. The buyer pays the seller $10,000 down and monthly payments of $1,131.47 (P&I) each month for thirty years on the $110,000/12-percent wrap. The seller or designated trustee then pays the existing first mortgage payment of $366.88 (P&I). The net of $764.59, which would be applied to the remaining equity, is the seller's net monthly profit.

LAND CONTRACTS

□   □   □

The land contract (also called contract for deed, installment contract, and contract for sale) is perhaps one of the oldest methods of buying and selling properties. It was used extensively in the several decades when home sales were easy and appreciation was high. The land contract allows the seller to hold the legal title to the property until the amount is paid in full. In this situation, the seller will keep paying the mortgage obligations

Wraparound Loan

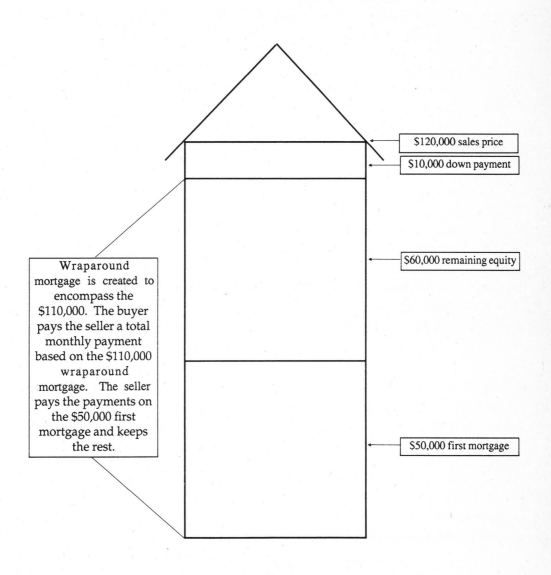

$120,000 sales price

$10,000 down payment

$60,000 remaining equity

Wraparound mortgage is created to encompass the $110,000. The buyer pays the seller a total monthly payment based on the $110,000 wraparound mortgage. The seller pays the payments on the $50,000 first mortgage and keeps the rest.

$50,000 first mortgage

while the buyer continues to make payments directly to him. This type of financing activity has resulted in numerous multiple ownership claims because, without a properly recorded claim, a property may be resold many times to different people. The original owner retains the title to the property.

The land contract was to be an answer for the buyer who was short on cash, who might have had bad credit, and who couldn't qualify for a loan, or to those who believe that interest rates will decline in the future. Sellers liked the land contract because, if the buyer did not keep current on the payments due, the property could be taken back very easily since the traditional long foreclosure process associated with a conventional home sale was eliminated. The seller retained the title, so he merely evicted the buyer as he would an unwanted tenant. This rule was challenged, however, in the courts and found to be overly severe. Now most courts will not allow the seller to simply take over the property without allowing a fair and equitable amount of time to elapse. With such rulings most land contracts have been much more difficult to foreclose on, making this method of home sale less popular.

The benefit of the land contract is that the buyer and seller do all the negotiating and the only requirement that is regulated is the imputed interest rate that was discussed previously. Also, the buyer avoids paying closing costs while locking in the price and still leaving open the option of future refinancing. All contracts for deed should be recorded in the county courthouse for the protection of the buyer, in addition to having a title check.

Contract-for-Deed Example

A buyer wants to buy a home for $120,000. He has $10,000 to put down and is unwilling or unable to obtain a new mortgage loan of $110,000 at the current market rate of 13 percent. The seller has an existing mortgage of $50,000 at 8-percent interest with no due-on-sale clause and payment of $366.88 (P&I).

The seller agrees to take back a $110,000 land contract at 12-percent interest with payment of $1,131.47 (P&I). The seller also agrees to continue making the $366.88 first mortgage from the $1,131.47 he will receive from the buyer. In five years time a balloon (or lump sum) payment will be due for the balance owned on the $120,000 sales price, and the seller will deliver the deed or title at that time.

ADJUSTABLE RATE LOANS

□ □ □

The adjustable rate mortgage is one of the newest marketplace breeds of nontraditional financing. The adjustable rate mortgage, or the ARM, was instituted to help the future homeowner in a variety of ways. Since the fixed rate loan is a higher risk for the money investor, the interest percentage rate is increased to compensate for the risk that interest rates may go up (and the investor would consequently realize a smaller return). As a result of these higher interest rates, many people have been turned away and denied the opportunity to borrow money because they did not qualify for the monthly payment with traditional financing methods.

The solution is to lower the sales price, lower the interest rate, or extend the life of the loan (imagine a sixty-five-year mortgage). The price has always been the first place to turn, since it is a negotiable item between the buyer and the seller. While the banker had no power to change this figure, eager buyers and sellers have been able to work this out. The lender did regulate the life of the loan, but thirty years was a long time, and since most people buy their homes in their late twenties to early thirties, it did not seem practical to extend the loan period beyond most life expectancies. The interest rate charged seemed a little flexible, but with increased competition and sources of information there is a great deal of competition in this area and less and less leeway.

The lender is given the rate by the investment company so that its individual investors will be guaranteed a certain amount of return on their money invested. The ARM came about to allow more flexibility for the lending institutions. The idea was again to shift the risk from the investor to the borrower. (Is this starting to sound familiar?) This flexibility was achieved by basing the interest rate on a loan on the prime rate (prime is the rate at which banks borrow their money) plus a small profit figure. This profit figure was usually 2–3 percent. The catch was that the rate would then fluctuate with the prime rate. This was attached to one of several market indicators, such as the treasury bills and the market index. These loans have caps (or limits) and some ceilings so that the rate can only increase so many points in a given amount of time.

The beauty of the ARM is that a young couple that fails to qualify for a fixed rate mortgage at, let's say, 12 percent, might pass with flying colors at 9 percent. Their initial monthly payment with an ARM is drastically reduced from the level required through the current rates of conventional financing.

This loan seemed like the answer to everyone's problem, and there were many who took advantage of this new creative technique. However, because this was a new invention, all of the possible bugs never were totally worked out. For example, some borrowers noticed that even though the rate had gone down from the initial amount, the balance of the loan was increasing (negative amortization). This is the stuff nightmares are made of. This negative amortization occurred because the computer was recording a shortfall in monthly payments and was adding the difference onto the loan amount, as happens in a negative amortization loan or deferred interest. There were additional problems with payments that were set too high because of improper rounding procedures on the interest rate.

Other clients complained because the period of adjustment was too short. They said changes in payments seemed to crop up without warning, leaving them with impossibly high payments and a loan that was almost impossible to pass to another buyer. With all of this in mind, the lending institutions have gone to work to tailor an ARM that would meet the needs of the average borrower and would be more fair in regulating their effects.

It is true that many ARMs are just too sophisticated for the lenders who use them. You'd have to be a genius to keep track of all the variables. Many lenders were caught in a variety of mistakes, such as using wrong indexes to calculate adjustments, the wrong index date, the wrong interest equation in calculating the monthly payment, unfair rounding procedures, and the wrong payment amount with the proper rate.

Negative Amortization with ARM (and 3% Inflation)

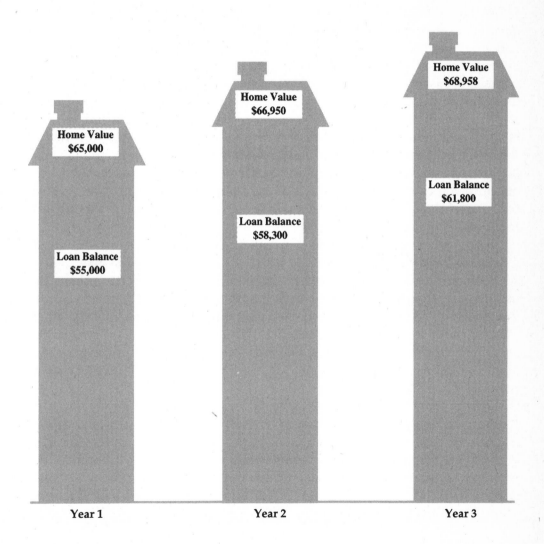

Before you take on an adjustable rate mortgage, be sure you know all the facts. Review several possible scenarios with the lender to make sure you understand how the payment will change given a change in the index to which the loan is pegged. If you feel a little uneasy, seek competent help from a certified public accountant or other financial manager. Doing your homework at the beginning will save many sleepless nights caused by an unanticipated giant monthly payment.

I would strongly suggest that, before you take on an ARM, you ask the questions, shown on the ARM Information Sheet on page 153.

If you don't ask these questions about an ARM, you run the risk of finding yourself in a bad situation.

Let's discuss some additional facts about the ARM. The federal government now requires the lender to notify the borrower 30–120 days before any change of payment begins; make sure you understand when you are notified what the new rate is going to be, when it will take effect, and what the new payment amount will be. Know what index your particular loan is attached to so that you can follow the trend. It is important that you find out how you can watch these indexes for yourself. The institution you are working with will be able to track this information for you, if you only ask them to.

If you want to check the bank's calculations, you should first find out at what date the lender tracks the index rate. This is usually forty-five days in advance of the anniversary date of your first payment. When you have the index value, then you add the lender's margin (a percentage which can be found in your contract). This will either be like Christmas in July when you see the rate going down, or hell in January when you see you're not only have to finish paying off Christmas but have to pay another $125 a month in house payments as well. Surprise! But you asked for it when you signed up for the loan.

When you do check the indexes, make sure you read to see what figure the amount rounds out to. For example, most will round to the nearest one eighth of a percent. It is very important to know if this figure is rounded to the nearest eighth or always rounded up. (It makes a big difference; ask yourself, "If I were the bank, which way would I do it?") Though it may not seem like very much, it can be substantial when you look over the entire life of the loan. If your figures don't correspond correctly to that of

ARM Information Sheet

Name_____ Date_____

Loan Company_____ Contact_____

Loan Type_____

Amount Expected to Borrow   _____

Interest Rate   _____

Closing Costs (including points, etc.)   _____

Beginning Monthly Payment   _____

Questions to Ask the Lender

- On what financial index are changes in
  payments based?   _____

- Can this index be changed during the
  course of the loan?   _____

- Does the loan have a cap (maximum
  amount of interest or highest payment that
  can be charged)?   _____

- If this cap is on the payment, how is the
  negative amortization handled?   _____

- Is this cap for the life of the loan?   _____

- Is there an annual cap?   _____

- What happens if the index decreases?   _____

- What are the reverse caps (lower limits for
  interest)?   _____

- How often is the index reviewed and the
  payment adjusted?   _____

- How much more would this ARM cost
  than a fixed-rate loan under a
  worst-case scenario?   _____

- Can this loan be assumed?   _____

- Can the loan be refinanced?   _____

- Are there any prepayment penalties?   _____

the lender, don't let yourself be intimidated into assuming that the bank is right and that you would only be a fool to question them. Always seek outside advice to double-check yourself.

The ARM is a valuable tool for selling real estate; it allows those who are starting out in life, and will have larger incomes in the future, to get into some real estate today. It allows investors to purchase properties with lower initial cash flows. Many of the loans allow for ARMs to be converted to fixed rates at a charge and within specific periods of time. These facts should be thoroughly understood so that the future risk of the beast can be minimized. These precautions in no way diminish the value of these loans. In my opinion, the ARM is the loan of the future. When you consider the beating that the banks took in the seventies and early eighties, the ARM is one of the only practical solutions to protect the banks from unfavorable interest rate swings in the future.

OTHER ALTERNATIVE FINANCING METHODS

□   □   □

Other alternative financing methods include loan assumptions, second mortgages, and lease purchase agreements.

Loan Assumptions

In a typical assumption, the buyer takes over the responsibility for making payments on the current mortgage held by a seller. The buyer then pays, or creatively finances, the owner's remaining equity. Assumptions are excellent, safe financing methods for everyone from a first-time home buyer to the advanced investor. The advantage is that a buyer may avoid the time and expense of qualifying for and securing a new loan while being able to "inherit" a lower interest rate. The disadvantage is that the owner loses control over his loan and remains liable in most cases in the event of a default from the person who assumes the loan, since he was the originator of the loan. The assumption today is mainly used with the VA and FHA loan varieties.

Please note that as of today many of the loan assumption rules are changing. In fact, many loans now require some qualifying.

Second Mortgages

Second mortgages are made behind the first mortgage of a property to provide additional financing for a purchase when the buyer is short of cash or seeks to increase his return through increased leverage. The second mortgage can be provided by either the seller or a conventional bank or finance company.

By providing a seller-financed second mortgage, a seller can substantially increase his sales price. He also can make his property more attractive to a potential buyer. In many cases, the buyer's payments may be higher by using a second mortgage than they might be with a total refinance, but the advantage is a lower down payment with easier qualification.

Lease Purchase Agreement

In a lease purchase a buyer signs a lease and a sales contract simultaneously. The lease is used first, and the sales contract becomes effective at some future date. As noted in Step #4, many investors are turning to lease options in selling their properties to give the future buyer a chance to qualify himself for the purchase of a home. By giving a buyer a one-year lease, the seller can test the waters to see how the lessee will make the payments and in what condition he will maintain the property. This is done without the risk of a typical sale.

As we previously discussed, lease options are also used by buyers who cannot qualify or who don't have the money to finance the purchase today. The advantages for the buyer are that the price is locked in and he gets a period, such as one year (determined by mutual agreement and written into the lease option by the buyer and seller), to see if he likes the home and the neighborhood. If he doesn't, then he isn't required to purchase the home. Other advantages of the lease option for the seller are that the owner has a cash flow from renting the property, additional funds commensurate with an option consideration, and extra money each month that you can justifiably charge for the option in addition to the monthly rent.

CASE STUDY

□ □ □

Sarah and John have found the home that they want to buy. It is a three-bedroom, one-bath located in a nice suburb about thirty-five minutes away from where they work. Even though it's a big commitment, they are excited about the tax benefits and investment potential that buying a home has for them. The owner is asking $92,000, but Sarah and John feel positive that the owner would accept an offer of $85,000. Sarah and John are prepared to put down as much as $5,000. That would leave them with $80,000 to finance. The seller has an assumable FHA loan at 8-percent interest with payments of $418.22 (principal and interest). There are twenty years left on the assumable balance of $50,000.

Sarah and John have several alternatives: Assume the loan and get their own second mortgage on the remaining $30,000 equity; assume the loan and get the seller to take back his equity in the form of a second mortgage at 10-percent interest over the next ten years; or simply refinance the whole thing.

If current interest rates are higher than 8 percent, I would suggest, without exception, assuming the underlying low interest first mortgage and opting first for the seller financing on the remaining $30,000. As a last resort, I would seek a regular commercial loan to buy the seller out of his second.

If the seller is willing to take his equity as a note (it's very common), the biggest fear people have is that they won't be able to figure out what the payments will be. For that purpose I have included a complete monthly amortization schedule with the payment required to amortize (pay off) a loan at the indicated interest rates. I include the most common loan durations (one to thirty years) and interest rates (9 percent to 13 percent) in these loan amortization schedules. (See Appendix C.)

Using our example, take a minute to calculate what your payment would be if you were to have the owner take back his remaining equity over ten years at 9 percent. Simply turn to the 9-percent-interest section of the amortization tables, locate the ten-year column, then run your finger down until you bisect the $30,000 line. You will see that your payment under those terms would be $316.69.

Great! Now, let's see how much the payment would be if you were to give your seller 13-percent interest on the note. Got it? That's right: $447.94. A whopping $131.25 more per month for the next ten years, or a total extra payment of $15,750 because of the 4-percent difference in interest.

Which would you rather pay? Now you see the importance of finance. The person who knows the numbers wins the game. To ensure that you get the loan at 9 percent, you need to sharpen your negotiation skills. With that in mind, let's move on to the next step and finalize your preparation to making the offer on your home.

NEGOTIATE THE PRICE

☐   ☐   ☐

Now is the moment for you to pull together everything you have learned in this book about how to find and purchase your first or next home. All your hard work is about to pay off. You have found the house you want to buy and can afford; it is in the area of town you find most acceptable. You have had a professional inspection service evaluate the home after your own quick inspection. You have either prequalified for a conventional mortgage loan or you have worked out one of the creative-financing methods discussed in Step #7. Now, at last, you are ready to negotiate the price and the terms of the purchase.

Are you excited? Good, you should be. But don't let your excitement over the thought of actually owning the home of your (even modified) dreams keep you from acting carefully and objectively at this step, because negotiating may well be the most crucial step of all in the process of buying your home.

Actually, you began negotiating (or at least storing ammunition for negotiating) when you first said "Hello" to the seller. Every word you and the seller have said after that has become a bargaining chip for the negotiating process. Comments, good and bad, made about the house are later translated into dollars. How much down, how much per month, how much period. When you oohed and aahed over the bay window in the living room, you were letting the seller know that you were willing to pay for that feature. When you pointed out the awkwardness of the kitchen arrangement and indicated that remodeling would be necessary to make the kitchen one you could live with, you were sending the seller a signal: The price of the house must be lower to allow for that defect. In other words, a lot of informal negotiating has already been done.

Now let's talk about the formal negotiating, when you and the seller actually determine the price of the house, the terms (how much down, what percent of interest will be charged on any seller financing, how soon you can close the deal), and who will be responsible for what repairs needed to get the house into acceptable condition for you.

The first lesson in negotiating is this: Everything in a deal is negotiable, but not everything is worth negotiating. You must decide what the most important issues are ahead of time, so you don't lose sight of them during the actual negotiation. You don't want to let garish orange paint on the living room walls (a superficial defect that can easily be corrected) become a major issue. Zero in instead on big-ticket repairs, such as foundation damage or termite problems. Get the seller to stand the cost of such repairs if they have turned up in one of the inspections. Try to get the seller to pay for any costs that you won't be able to recoup should you decide to sell the house later on.

This is the stage at which you will be glad you had that professional inspection done. Before you go to the seller to negotiate, itemize all the repairs you or the inspector anticipate. Put them into categories—structural repairs and other less costly repairs—so you will know exactly what to bargain for. Keep in mind that the house is a financial investment even if it is to be your home. Make sure that the seller, not you, pays for any structural repairs necessary to make the house safe and sturdy.

You should insist that the seller make (and pay for) the structural repairs. Those are the most important items on your negotiating list. Structural repairs must be done, but they will not net you any additional money if you sell the house later on. The key thing to watch for is that the seller doesn't agree to the repairs and then pass them along to you by raising the price of the house or altering the terms of any seller financing to recoup these costs with a higher interest rate or longer payoff period. To avoid low-quality work, your purchase offer should also be contingent on your approval of the repairs.

The remodeling costs you will have to bear yourself. If you want to make that large bedroom upstairs into one smaller bedroom and a sewing room, you will have to pay for those changes. Don't expect the seller to foot the bill for that kind of thing. (You may get him to come down a little on the price if he is anxious to sell and realizes that making some concession here will help him make the sale.)

The second lesson is to remember that the purchase (or sale) of real estate—even if it is your dream home—is first of all a business deal which involves a legal contract. Naturally you want to do everything you can to make sure you understand the terms of the contract and that they are as favorable for you as they can be. It is a good idea to have someone who is familiar with the language in such contracts look it over for you before you sign on the dotted line. Having a good real estate attorney review the contract is a good investment. He will know exactly what pitfalls to watch for and can advise you of any possible problems before you get legally locked into a contract. Paying for legal advice to prevent a problem is always better (and cheaper) than paying for legal services once the problem has become real.

Other professionals like real estate brokers and title company officers are also able to help you understand the terms of the contract before you make a commitment. At this step you want someone who is not a party to the deal to be your watchdog; choose someone who doesn't stand to gain by the sale of the property.

The third negotiating lesson is that the written words of the contract, not any verbal discussions or agreements made between you and the seller, are what is legally binding. Don't be fooled into thinking that the contract will necessarily reflect the fact that the seller agreed to have the leaky basement repaired before the sale is final. If the words aren't in the contract, you have no legally binding agreement with the seller. Don't let anyone tell you that his word is as good as law. If you and the seller have agreed to a specific condition to the sale—say he has agreed to have the electrical wiring redone—make sure that this agreement appears in the contract before you sign it.

Fourth, a deal or purchase can be made only when both parties agree to the terms. If you offer to buy the house for $65,000 with a $5,000 down payment and owner-financing for thirty years at 10-percent interest, you don't have a deal unless the seller agrees to your terms. If he counters with a sales price of $67,500, a down payment of $7,500, and an interest rate of 11 percent, your deal is essentially dead unless you accept his terms or you continue to negotiate until you do come to an agreement that is acceptable to both of you. Only when the seller accepts your offer or you agree to compromise and accept his terms, do you have a deal.

The fifth negotiating lesson is to be wary of any suggestion on the part of the seller that you can sign an agreement now and then make changes to it later by yourself. Once a contract has been agreed upon, it can be changed only by the mutual consent of both parties—and that can be a difficult, if not impossible, thing to accomplish. The agreement should say what you want the final terms of the deal to be, because that is exactly what a contract holds you to.

Negotiating lesson number six is to remember that most real estate agents and brokers are working for the seller. This is easy to forget when you have "hired" the agent yourself and he is presenting the offer to the seller for you. But the plain truth is the agent or broker is working for the seller, who pays him a commission only if he makes the sale. You must make certain that your written offer, the one presented to the seller by the agent, accurately reflects your preferences and terms. Be sure that the language is clear and specific. And also, see that it includes everything you want. If you know that the cellar leaks, you want the seller to remedy that as part of the terms of the sale. But don't stop there. Instead, make an inspection and any necessary repairs it turns up (including the leak in the cellar) the condition for the sale. That way, any important repairs will become the responsibility of the seller. If he fails to comply, then the deal is off and you are protected.

When it comes to preparing the contract of sale, you (or your real estate agent) can use the basic preprinted contract forms available in many stationery stores for a modest price. To alter the contract to fit the specific terms of your deal, simply cross out any unacceptable language and insert needed changes. To make the changes legal, both you and the seller must initial each change on all copies of the contract. If the changes are long— say you want to leave out or rewrite an entire section of the contract—it is best to write these changes on a separate sheet of paper and attach them to the contract. These additions, known as "addenda," must be signed by both the buyer and the seller to be valid. As a further precaution, make sure that the original contract makes written reference to the addenda, so an accidental detachment of these sheets from the contract won't leave you with the wrong contract.

You, the seller, your real estate agent, or an attorney representing either you or the seller all can make changes to the contract. The limitations that are placed on an agent's or broker's right to make contract changes varies from locality to locality, so check to see what is acceptable. In any event, be certain that you understand what the changes are and how they affect the contract before initialing them or signing the contract. Don't be embarrassed to ask for explanations for anything you don't understand or want clarified. Don't let the seller, the agent, or even an attorney intimidate you. You have a right to protect yourself by asking questions, and you should do so if there is anything at all that is unclear to you.

Every real estate deal is unique, so each contract must be unique also. Take the time to be certain that the contract reflects the exact terms of the deal you think you are making.

One of the terms of your deal to buy that dream home, which can make a big difference in what mortgage payment you pay per month (and also what you pay in total for the home if you remain in it long enough to pay off the mortgage), is the interest rate. Even a small change in the percentage rate on your mortgage can make a big difference overall. Often the contract will spell out the interest rate, say 10.5 percent. Others will call for "10.5 percent or the best available rate." If the contract you are about to sign includes the phrase "or the best available rate," you will want to protect yourself by limiting what kind of interest rate is acceptable to you. Stipulate the maximum rate you are willing to pay and, if that agreed-upon rate is not available, the deal is off and you are to have all of your deposit returned to you.

Another area that you want to negotiate is what fixtures come with the home purchase. You can pretty much count on the stoves, furnaces, bathroom fixtures, and fences to remain with the property (but it won't hurt to double-check even on these items). There are some items that may or may not be included and should be part of the negotiation. If you want the microwave in the kitchen to be part of the deal, make that clear. And don't just tell the seller you expect to have it included. List it in the contract with other items that are to remain with the property.

The list should include items such as curtains, drapes, indoor shutters (as well as the drapery rods and so forth), window air-conditioners, chandeliers, portable appliances like dishwashers, the washer and dryer, movable outdoor sheds, and even the children's swing set in the backyard. Perhaps even the adorable mailbox at the curb that has been custom-designed to match the house should be included in your list.

In addition to the interest maximum that we discussed earlier, include also the stipulation that the entire transaction is contingent upon your getting the financing outlined in the contract. If such financing is not available, then the deal is off and all of your deposit is to be returned. This kind of clause is a key protection to you, the buyer, and no contract should be signed if such a clause is not included.

Now that you have prepared your checklist of items to negotiate, you are ready to come to terms with what you and the seller agree upon. The next step is to present an offer that reflects the negotiating you have done and the terms of the deal that you wish to make.

MAKE THE OFFER

☐　☐　☐

This is the top of the mountain. You have climbed all this way from knowing little or nothing about purchasing your home to knowing how to actually make an offer on that dream house (or the next best thing). This step isn't—or shouldn't be—difficult. Don't be so frightened of a single sheet of paper that you are willing to waste everything that you have learned so far. Now is the time for you to sit down with the seller to work out the details of the sale and fill in the blanks on the standard real estate sales contract. If outside help is needed, there are real estate agents, title officers, or attorneys who will gladly help. This step will help the buyer find those sources of help and comfort.

In this section I will also include actual clauses that can be inserted into any standard contract to protect the buyer. These clauses will allow the buyer to back out of the deal before closing without penalty.

THE SALES CONTRACT

□   □   □

Once you have found the home that meets your needs (and even some of your wants) and the decision to buy has been made, you are ready to prepare a sales contract. Sometimes this is referred to as "the offer." It is a formal presentation of your bid to buy the house that the seller has up for sale.

We mentioned the standard (or basic) real estate contract briefly in Step #8. What I didn't tell you was how many provisions such contracts usually contain, although I did mention many of them as we discussed negotiating techniques. You are aware that most of the provisions of the sales contract are negotiable. As long as you were negotiating verbally, the terms of the contract weren't set in concrete. But once all parties have signed the contract and the buyer has given his deposit (or earnest money), both the buyer and the seller are legally committed to the sales agreement.

You must be aware of every provision in the contract you are offering to the seller, and you want to be sure that each item appears exactly as you want the deal to be structured. Let's review the possible provisions that you will be dealing with, so you can feel comfortable with each one and so you can protect yourself at each step along the way. As was mentioned before, the exact sales contract in your area may differ somewhat from the one presented here, but they are all complex and take time and effort to understand. The time you spend reading this chapter of the book will pay good dividends to you in the understanding you will gain in how to read and understand such contracts and how to write them when you are ready to make your offer.

It might be useful to go to your local stationery store or a real estate office and obtain a copy of the real estate sales contract form that is used in your area before continuing this chapter. That way you can follow this discussion by referring to the actual contract you will use to make your offer. In case you don't have time to locate a contract, you'll find a sample on pages 168–69.

I hope you are feeling the excitement of what you are about to do. You are almost ready to make the offer on your dream home, and if you pay attention to the help I will give you in this chapter, you should be able to feel confident about the offer that you make.

Sales Price

Okay, got the local sales contract in hand? Then let's get started. The first item you will want to consider is the agreed-upon sales price. During the negotiating session with the seller you should have arrived at this figure. Now you are ready to fill in the blank on the contract form. (Do this practice form in pencil. You will probably need to make some revisions before you arrive at the perfect product.) If the price you and the seller agreed on was $62,500, then that is what you should put in this blank.

Address or Legal Description

The second item to fill in is a street address or description of the boundaries of the property. Often this is stated in terms of the legal description of the property as it is recorded in the courthouse. You may wish to include both the street address by which the property is commonly known and the legal description just for clarity. You don't want to accidentally buy the house next door to your dream home!

Earnest Money Deposit

Now you are ready to fill in the blank which tells how much earnest money deposit you are willing to make initially and the terms for the payment of the remainder of it. There is some flexibility here, but you should make the earnest money amount enough to indicate that you have a

Earnest Money Receipt and Offer to Purchase

"This is a legally-binding contract; if not understood, seek competent advice."

1. Date and Place of Offer:_____ 19____ _____
_____(city)_____ _____(state)_____

2. Principals: The undersigned Buyer_____ _____ _____
agrees to buy and Seller agrees to sell, according to the indicated terms and conditions, the property described as follows:

3. Property: located at _____
_____(street address)_____ _____(city)_____ _____(state)_____

with the following legal description: _____
including any of the following items if at present attached to the premises: plumbing, heating, and cooling equipment, including stoker and oil tanks, burners, water heaters, electric light fixtures, bathroom fixtures, roller shades, curtain rods and fixtures, draperies, venetian blinds, window and door screens, towel racks, linoleum and other attached floor coverings, including carpeting, attached television antennas, mail-

boxes, all trees and shrubs, and any other fixtures, EXCEPT _____

The following personal property shall also be included as part of the purchase: _____
At the close of the transaction, the Seller, at his expense, shall provide the Buyer with a Bill Of Sale containing a detailed inventory of the personal property included.

4. Earnest Money Deposit: Agent (or Seller) acknowledges receipt from Buyer of _____ dollars

$_____ in the form of ( ) cash; ( ) personal check; ( ) cashier's check; ( ) promissory note at _____ % interest per annum due _____ 19_____,

or other _____
as earnest money deposit to secure and apply on this purchase. Upon acceptance of this agreement in writing and delivery of same to Buyer, the earnest money deposit shall be assigned to and deposited in the

listing Realtor's trust account or _____ to apply on the purchase price at the time of closing.

5. Purchase Price: The total purchase price of the property shall be _____ dollars $_____

6. Payment: Purchase price is to be paid by Buyer as follows: Aforedescribed earnest money deposit....... .... $_____

Additional payment due upon accept~ .... $_____

Additional payment due at cl~ .... $_____

Balance to be paid as follows: _____

_____

_____

_____

_____

7. Title: Seller agrees to furnish good and marketable title free of all encumbrances and defects, except mortgage liens and encumbrances as set forth in this agreement, and to make conveyance by Warranty

Deed or _____.Seller shall furnish in due course to the Buyer a title insurance policy insuring the Buyer of a good and marketable title in keeping with the terms and conditions of this agreement. Prior to the closing of this transaction, the Seller, upon request, will furnish to the Buyer a preliminary title report made by a title insurance company showing the condition of the title to said property. If the Seller cannot furnish marketable title within thirty days after receipt of the notice to the Buyer containing a written statement of the defects, the earnest money deposit herein receipted shall be refunded to the Buyer and this agreement shall be null and void. The following shall not be deemed encumbrances or defects: building and use restrictions general to the area; utility easements; other easements not inconsistent with Buyer's intended use; zoning or subdivision laws, covenants, conditions, restrictions, or reservations of record; tenancies of record. In the event of sale of other than real property relating to this transaction, Seller will provide evidence of title or right to sell or lease such personal property.
8. Special Representations: Seller warrants and represents to Buyer (1) that the subject property is connected to ( ) public sewer system, ( ) cesspool or septic tank, ( ) sewer system available but not connected, ( ) city water system, ( ) private water system, and that the following special improvements are included in the sale: ( ) sidewalk, ( ) curb and gutter, ( ) special street paving, ( ) special street lighting; (2) that the Seller knows of no material structural defects; (3) that all electrical wiring, heating, cooling, and plumbing systems are free of material defects and will be in good working order at the time the Buyer is entitled to possession; (4) that the Seller has no notice from any government agency of any violation or knowledge of probable violations of the law relating to the subject property; (5) that the Seller has no notice or knowledge of planned or commenced public improvements which may result in special assessments or otherwise directly and materially affect the property; and (6) that the Seller has no notice or

knowledge of any liens to be assessed against the property, EXCEPT _____

9. Escrow Instructions: This sale shall be closed on or before_____ 19_____ by _____
or such other closing agent as mutually agreed upon by Buyer and Seller. Buyer and Seller will, immediately on demand, deposit with closing agent all instruments and monies required to complete the purchase in

accordance with the provisions of this agreement. Contract of Sale or Instrument of Conveyance to be made in the name of _____

10. Closing Costs and Pro-Ration: Seller agrees to pay for title insurance policy, preliminary title report (if requested), termite inspection as set forth below, real estate commission, cost of preparing and recording any corrective instruments, and one-half of the escrow fees. Buyer agrees to pay for recording fees for mortgages and deeds of conveyance, all costs or expenses in securing new financing or assuming existing financing, and one-half of the escrow fees. Taxes for the current year, insurance acceptable to the Buyer, rents, interest, mortgage reserves, maintenance fees, and water and other utilities constituting liens, shall be pro-rated as of closing. Renters' security deposits shall accrue to Buyer at closing. Seller to provide Buyer with current rental or lease agreements prior to closing.

11. Termite Inspection: Seller agrees, at his expense, to provide written certification by a reputable licenced pest control firm that the property is free of termite infestation. In the event termites are found, the Seller shall have the property treated at his expense and provide acceptable certification that treatment has been rendered. If any structural repairs are required by reason of termite damage as established by acceptable certification, Seller agrees to make necessary repairs not to exceed $500. If repairs exceed $500, Buyer shall first have the right to accept the property "as is" with a credit of $500 to the Buyer at closing, or the Buyer may terminate this agreement with the earnest money deposit being promptly returned to the Buyer if the Seller does not agree to pay all costs of treatment and repair.

12. Conditions of Sale: The following conditions shall also apply, and shall, if conflicting with the printed portions of this agreement, prevail and control:

_____
_____
_____
_____
_____
_____
_____

13. Liability and Maintenance: Seller shall maintain subject property, including landscaping, in good condition until the date of transfer of title or possession by Buyer, whichever occurs first. All risk of loss and destruction of property, and all expenses of insurance, shall be borne by the Seller until the date of possession. If the improvements on the property are destroyed or materially damaged prior to closing, then the Buyer shall have the right to declare this agreement null and void, and the earnest money deposit and all other sums paid by Buyer toward the purchase price shall be returned to the Buyer forthwith.

14. Possession: The Buyer shall be entitled to possession of property upon closing or _____, 19_____

15. Default: In the event the Buyer fails to complete the purchase as herein provided, the earnest money deposit shall be ret___ ___ the Seller as the total and entire liquidated damages. In the event the Seller fails to perform any condition of the sale as herein provided, then the Buyer, may, at his option, treat the contract as termin___ ___ments made by the Buyer hereunder shall be returned to the Buyer forthwith, provided the Buyer may, at his option, treat this agreement as being in full force and effect with the right to actio___ ___ance and damages. In the event that either Buyer, Seller, or Agent shall institute suit to enforce any rights hereunder, the prevailing party shall be entitled to court costs and a reason___

16. Time Limit of Offer: The Seller shall have until _____, 19_____

    (hour)   (date)

to accept this offer by delivering a signed copy hereof to the Buyer. If this offer is not so acce___ ___gent (or Seller) shall refund the earnest money deposit to the Buyer forthwith.

17. General Agreements: (1) Both parties to this purchase reserve their rights to assign ___ ___o cooperate in effecting an Internal Revenue Code 1031 exchange or similar tax-related arrangement prior to close of escrow, upon either party's written notice of intention to d___ ___offer by the Seller, this agreement shall become a contract between Buyer and Seller and shall inure to the benefit of the heirs, administrators, executors, successors, personal r___ ___of said parties. (3) Time is of the essence and an essential part of this agreement. (4) This contract constitutes the sole and entire agreement between the parties hereto and n___ ___ shall be binding unless attached hereto and signed by all parties to the contract. No representations, promises, or inducements not included in this contract shall be binding___

18. Buyer's Statement and Receipt: "I/we hereby agree to purch___ ___ordance with the terms and conditions above stated and acknowledge receipt of a completed copy of this agreement, which I/we have fully read and understand." Dated _____ _____ 19_____ _____

                                               (hour)

Address _____   _____Buyer

_____   _____Buyer

Phone No: Home (_____)_____ Business (_____)_____

19. Seller's Statement and Response: "I/we approve and accept the above offer, which I/we have fully read and understand, and agree to the above terms and conditions this day of _____, 19_____

                          (hour)   _____Seller

Address _____   _____Seller

_____   Phone No: Home (_____)_____ Business (_____)_____

20. Commission Agreement: Seller agrees to pay a commission of_____% of the gross sales price to _____ for services in this transaction, and agrees that, in the event of forfeiture of the earnest money deposit by the Buyer, said deposit shall be divided between the Seller's broker and the Seller (one half to each party), the Broker's part not to exceed the amount of the commission.

21. Buyer's Receipt for Signed Offer: The Buyer hereby acknowledges receipt of a copy of the above agreement bearing the Seller's signature in acceptance of this offer.

Dated _____ _____, 19_____   _____Buyer

_____Buyer

©1983 The Allen Group, Inc. Form B82GL

serious interest in the property. You will want to complete the payment of the earnest money amount in a relatively short period of time. The terms here could indicate $500 for the initial payment and the final $1,000 when the contract is accepted and signed.

Down Payment

In addition to the amount of earnest money you are willing to put up, you must also include the total amount of down payment that you are offering to make to secure this deal. The down payment will be, say, $5,000. You will indicate the down payment in three stages: the initial earnest money, the balance of the earnest money, and the balance due after those payments have been made. The time to make the final payment due on the down payment is usually at the closing. (The closing will be discussed in detail in Step #10.) That amount in our example would be $5,000 less the two earnest money payments of $500 and $1,000 respectively, or $3,500.

Mortgage Terms and Rate

The next provision to make is the one discussed in Step #8 which allows you as the buyer to withdraw from the sale if you cannot arrange a mortgage with specified terms and rate. This clause is essential and should always be included in the offer even if you have money to burn. It is one of the great ways for the buyer to protect himself from paying more for the property than he had intended to. A jump in the interest rate can add to both your total price for the home and to the amount of the mortgage payment you will make each month. It could even disqualify you for the loan you have prearranged, forcing you to seek less favorable financing. So by all means put this clause into the contract offer.

Assumption of the Seller's Mortgage

Assumption of the seller's mortgage is another of the advantages you as the buyer want to secure for yourself—especially if the interest rate on the mortgage is favorable. To do this you must include a provision in the offer contract that makes the contract null and void if the mortgage cannot be assumed. You will recall that assuming the seller's mortgage is the process by which you, the buyer, undergo only a brief qualifying procedure and take over the seller's mortgage as it already exists. (This is discussed at length in Step #7.) Often, getting the more favorable interest rate on the mortgage you can assume will be one of the deciding factors in the purchase of a particular home, so don't give up this advantage. Include as one of the conditions for sale the ability to assume the seller's mortgage. If that isn't possible, then the offer is no longer valid.

Seller Financing

Another provision that must be included in your offer, if it is applicable to your deal, is one that spells out any owner financing that is to be part of the transaction. If the seller has agreed to take back a second mortgage for the difference between his equity and the amount of down payment you can make, now is the time to tie down the terms of that financing so both of you understand exactly what the terms are. If he has offered to finance $15,000 for ten years at 10 percent, then those precise figures should be included in this provision. Also, you should indicate the terms of the repayment—whether it is to be made in monthly payments, in semiannual payments, in annual payments, in a balloon (or lump sum) payment at the end of ten years. Also establish when the interest is to be paid, with the principal payments or at some other time. For example, you might make annual interest payments if you are going to pay a balloon at the end of ten years, or you might make monthly interest payments if you make an annual payment on the principle. Whatever you are offering to do in terms of repayment of owner financing, the exact terms should be written out in this provision.

The Closing

Both the date for and the location of the closing of the sale should be included at this step. For the closing to work properly, both you and the buyer need to know the date of the closing and where it is to occur. You will want to choose a date that is near enough to enable you to keep the financing terms you have arranged for, yet you need to allow the title company time to do its work in researching the deed and other pertinent data. (The closing will be discussed in full detail in Step #10.)

Date of Occupancy

You are excited about buying your first or next home. You want to get into it and begin living your dream. So indicate in writing in the offer exactly when you want to take possession of the property. Often occupancy can take place shortly after the closing and as soon as the recording of the deed has taken place. You will want to consider what date of occupancy will help you avoid paying an unnecessary month's rent where you are now, too. You won't want to get stuck with a rent payment and a mortgage payment in the same month. But you will also have to consider the needs of the seller in this matter. Probably during the negotiations you were able to get a pretty good idea of how soon the owner can vacate the house (if he is still living in it). If the house is vacant, an earlier occupancy date may be possible.

Agreement to Offer

To keep this procedure from dragging on too long, indicate a date by which the seller must accept the offer. Let him know that your offer is good for only three days or a week or whatever is appropriate in the circumstances. This will help you retain the financing you have arranged for, and it will also keep you from wasting time on this particular house if the seller is not going to agree to your terms. If he refuses your offer, you must start over in your search for your dream home, so you want to know as soon as possible what his answer to your offer is.

When you are writing this provision for an answer, be sure to include both a date and a time by which his acceptance must be received. Be realistic, but gear this deadline for your own benefit.

Type of Deed

In this provision you will specify a warranty deed, or other deed of your choice, as the type of deed the seller must be willing and able to convey to you at the closing.

Personal Property and Household Fixtures in Deal

In this provision you will be spelling out what you consider to be part of the deal. If you want the living room drapes, the portable dishwasher, and the doghouse in the backyard to be included in the sale, you must state these expectations clearly in this step. Include even those items that you assume will be included, such as the kitchen stove and the electric water heater. After putting up the down payment and the other costs of the purchase, you are not going to want to have to buy household items that you assumed were part of the deal but weren't. If you want something, put it in writing.

Termite and Other Inspections

Following our plan to get the seller to pay for certain kinds of repairs, you need to include a provision for termite inspection and any other inspection that seems warranted. (Remember the professional inspectors.) Include the procedure you want followed if any needed repairs turn up in the inspections. Be very clear about who is to pay for such repairs, when they are to be done, and so forth.

Unless otherwise specified in the contract, the buyer agrees to accept the property in its present condition. This makes the inspections and subsequent negotiations for who is to pay for needed repairs extremely important.

Easement Rights

Easement rights are the right of someone else to legally use your land. If the local utility companies have easement rights on the property or if other property owners in the area have easement rights, this needs to be stated in the contract. Exactly what the rights are, how much of the property is affected, what the access rights are, and so forth needs to be included here.

Payment of the Broker's Fee

This provision should state how much the broker's fee is to be and who is going to pay it. Usually the seller pays this fee, and the payment of it is included in the closing procedure. But it is always wise to put your understanding of this into writing and make it a formal part of the contract, so you don't have any unpleasant surprises later.

Where Earnest Money Will Be Held Until Closing

In many locales the broker has a special bank account in which earnest money funds are kept until the day of the closing. You should know what is acceptable in your locality and specify in this provision where the earnest money is to be kept until the closing and how you can get it refunded if the sale falls through.

Prorating Taxes, Rents, Utilities, and the Like

In the usual course of homeownership, certain expenses such as taxes accrue over a period of time. A decision must be made as to how these expenses will be divided between the buyer and the seller. If the seller occupies the property for seven months and the buyer will have possession for the remaining five months of the year, then the costs are usually divided accordingly, with the seller paying seven twelfths of the debt and the buyer paying the remaining five twelfths. If the tax on your home-to-be is $650 per year, then the seller would pay $379.17 and you would pay $270.83. This is one of the items usually included in the closing settlement.

Obtaining Title Insurance

How the title insurance policy is to be obtained must be included. You need to name the title insurance company that you have chosen to do this work. This provision should also contain the contingency that the sale become invalid if the title to the property is not clear, making it unmarketable. You don't want to buy someone else's IRS liens or a property whose chain of ownership is clouded. You don't want to pay for a home only to discover years down the road that the person who sold it to you wasn't the legal owner. Title insurance companies protect you from this kind of problem. The insurance they give offers you the protection that you need not only from title problems or tax liens, but it also guarantees that you have bought a specified piece of property at a specified location and that the property is of a certain dimension. I know of a retired couple who bought a home in good faith only to discover that the property was ten feet narrower than the title company had attested to prior to the purchase. The title company had to reimburse the couple for the dollar value of the 10′ by 65′ strip they had paid for but not gotten in the purchase of the property.

Who Is Responsible for Damage or Loss Before Closing?

One item that is often overlooked when preparing an offer is the rights and responsibilities of the seller and the buyer in the period between the signing of the sales contract and the closing of the sale. In your offer you need to specify what will happen during this interim. Who is going to be responsible for the yard work, who will pay for damage to the property such as vandalism or flooding caused by a broken pipe? What if the house catches fire and is partially destroyed? Does the buyer still have to honor the contract? These problems should be addressed in the sales contract itself. If the seller is living in the home, then naturally he will be expected to maintain it properly until the time that he vacates it. If, on the other hand, the house is vacant, other provisions must be made for the maintenance of the property.

Whatever you want to include in this clause, be very clear. If you want the seller to maintain the yard as well as the house, say so. If you find it possible to do so in exchange for some of the closing costs, put that in this provision. Every real estate sale is different, so you can tailor this one to your needs and wants insofar as they are reasonable and not likely to discourage the seller from dealing with you.

Unpaid Repairs and Property Liens

If improvements have been made on the house in the last six months, have the seller provide you with the receipts showing the services have been paid for in full. You don't want to end up paying for things that were done to the home before you made an offer on it.

Also have the seller warrant that there are no liens against the property, either tax liens or mechanic's liens. While this warranty is standard terminology in most contracts, it would be worth your while to make sure this point is covered.

Space for Addenda

As mentioned in Step #8, it is sometimes necessary to add rather long sections to the basic contract form. You should leave space to do this wherever you think it is likely to occur. If the provision for inspections and repairs is likely to be lengthy, leave the necessary space for indicating what is wrong and how the problem is to be effectively cured.

City or County Inspection

If a city or county inspection is required to prove that the house meets existing building codes prior to occupancy, include a provision that requires the seller to make the necessary repairs to bring the house up to code (and to pay for them). These codes are usually involved with plumbing, electrical, structural, and other basic areas. You want the assurance that the seller will comply with these codes before you commit to buying the property.

Buyer Financing

An indication that the buyer will do everything in his power to obtain the necessary financing must be included. It should also contain a deadline date by which the buyer must make application for the financing. The seller has the right to be assured that he has a serious buyer on his hands, and settling the financing goes a long way toward reassuring the seller on this point. As the buyer, however, you want to include in this provision that unless suitable financing (at less-than-an-agreed-upon percentage rate) is obtained, the purchase is aborted.

Seller Financing

If the seller is providing all or part of the financing, he has a right to make the contract conditional upon the buyer's supplying him with a satisfactory credit report. Such a report can be obtained from one of the credit-reporting agencies discussed in Step #7 or it can consist of an independent credit report put together by the buyer, with references such as his banker, his landlord, and other persons or firms who are familiar with his credit history.

Number of Person's to Occupy the Dwelling

In some instances the number of persons the buyer intends to have occupy the dwelling is stated. Some houses are in residential areas that limit the occupancy to a single family. Reassurances must be given that such restrictions are not violated, for the protection of the other property owners in the area.

Assignment of the Contract

In certain circumstances it becomes desirable or necessary for the sales contract to be assigned to another individual. If the original buyer is transferred unexpectedly, or his spouse dies, or he becomes disabled, then provisions need to be made for what to do with the contract if he is thus unable to honor it. Exactly what conditions must exist before the sales contract can be assigned and to whom should be included in this provision.

In this section we have tried to help you become familiar with the various kinds of provision you should include in the offer contract you draw up. Be aware that the provisions listed are general ones and that what provisions apply in your specific area of the country need to be determined by you before you make the final draft of the offer to present to the buyer.

Of course, much of the time you will be working with a real estate agent and he or she will then be familiar with what is needed in the offer contract. If you make up the contract yourself, have an attorney or a title company office review it for you before you present it to the seller. These trained professionals are worth their weight in gold because they can keep you from making dreadful errors from lack of knowledge or lack of familiarity with the language of such contracts.

Okay, you are now ready to write up the offer. Once you have done that and had it reviewed by a professional (or reviewed it yourself if an agent or broker writes it for you), you are ready to take it to the seller.

The seller will have just a few days to make his answer. If he agrees to your terms, the final step (except for moving in) is the closing of the sale. For your reference, a sample of a completed copy of an earnest money agreement follows.

□   □   □

Earnest Money Receipt and Offer to Purchase

"This is a legally-binding contract; if not understood, seek competent advice."

1. **Date and Place of Offer:** _6/24_ 19__; _Smithville_ (city) _Conn._ (state)

2. **Principals:** The undersigned Buyer _Marc Stephen Garrison_ agrees to buy and Seller agrees to sell, according to the indicated terms and conditions, the property described as follows:

3. **Property:** located at _1917 Fir Avenue_, (street address) _Smithville_, (city) _Conn._ (state)

with the following legal description: _n/a_

including any of the following items if at present attached to the premises: plumbing, heating, and cooling equipment, including stoker and oil tanks, burners, water heaters, electric light fixtures, bathroom fixtures, roller shades, curtain rods and fixtures, draperies, venetian blinds, window and door screens, towel racks, linoleum and other attached floor coverings, including carpeting, attached television antennas, mailboxes, all trees and shrubs, and any other fixtures, EXCEPT _no exceptions_

The following personal property shall also be included as part of the purchase: _19 cu. ft. Amana almond-colored refrigerator_
At the close of the transaction, the Seller, at his expense, shall provide the Buyer with a Bill Of Sale containing a detailed inventory of the personal property included.

4. **Earnest Money Deposit:** Agent (or Seller) acknowledges receipt from Buyer of _Five hundred and 0/100_ dollars
$ _500.00_ in the form of ( ) cash; ( ) personal check; ( ) cashier's check; (X) promissory note at _0_ % interest per annum due _on closing_ 19__;
or other _n/a_
as earnest money deposit to secure and apply on this purchase. Upon acceptance of this agreement in writing and delivery of same to Buyer, the earnest money deposit shall be assigned to and deposited in the
listing Realtor's trust account or _n/a_ , to apply on the purchase price at the time of closing.

5. **Purchase Price:** The total purchase price of the property shall be _Seventy thousand and 0/100_ dollars $ _70,000.00_

6. **Payment:** Purchase price is to be paid by Buyer as follows: Aforedescribed earnest money deposit..$ _500.00_

Additional payment due upon acceptance of this offer...$ _0_

Additional payment due at closing...$ _4,500.00_

Balance to be paid as follows: _Seller to take back second mortgage for $7,000.00._ _This second mortgage is to be paid as follows: 120 equal monthly_ _payments at 11% interest. There will be no pre-payment_ _penalty charged if buyer decides to pay this off early._

7. **Title:** Seller agrees to furnish good and marketable title free of all encumbrances and defects, except mortgage liens and encumbrances as set forth in this agreement, and to make conveyance by Warranty
Deed or _n/a_ Seller shall furnish in due course to the Buyer a title insurance policy insuring
the Buyer of a good and marketable title in keeping with the terms and conditions of this agreement. Prior to the closing of this transaction, the Seller, upon request, will furnish to the Buyer a preliminary title report made by a title insurance company showing the condition of the title to said property. If the Seller cannot furnish marketable title within thirty days after receipt of the notice to the Buyer containing a written statement of the defects, the earnest money deposit herein receipted shall be refunded to the Buyer and this agreement shall be null and void. The following shall not be deemed encumbrances or defects: building and use restrictions general to the area; utility easements; other easements not inconsistent with Buyer's intended use; zoning or subdivision laws, covenants, conditions, restrictions, or reservations of record; tenancies of record. In the event of sale of other than real property relating to this transaction, Seller will provide evidence of title or right to sell or lease such personal property.

8. **Special Representations:** Seller warrants and represents to Buyer (1) that the subject property is connected to (✓) public sewer system, ( ) cesspool or septic tank, ( ) sewer system available but not connected, ( ) city water system, ( ) private water system, and that the following special improvements are included in the sale: (✓) sidewalk, (✓) curb and gutter, (✓) special street paving, ( ) special street lighting; (2) that the Seller knows of no material structural defects; (3) that all electrical wiring, heating, cooling, and plumbing systems are free of material defects and will be in good working order at the time the Buyer is entitled to possession; (4) that the Seller has no notice from any government agency of any violation or knowledge of probable violations of the law relating to the subject property; (5) that the Seller has no notice or knowledge of planned or commenced public improvements which may result in special assessments or otherwise directly and materially affect the property; and (6) that the Seller has no notice or
knowledge of any liens to be assessed against the property, EXCEPT _n/a_

9. **Escrow instructions:** This sale shall be closed on or before _7/16_ 19__ by _Action Title Company_
or such other closing agent as mutually agreed upon by Buyer and Seller. Buyer and Seller will, immediately on demand, deposit with closing agent all instruments and monies required to complete the purchase in
accordance with the provisions of this agreement. Contract of Sale or Instrument of Conveyance to be made in the name of _Marc S. Garrison and or_
assigns

180

10. Closing Costs and Pro-Ration: Seller agrees to pay for title insurance policy, preliminary title report (if requested), termite inspection as set forth below, real estate commission, cost of preparing and recording any corrective instruments, and one-half of the escrow fees. Buyer agrees to pay for recording fees for mortgages and deeds of conveyance, all costs or expenses in securing new financing or assuming existing financing, and one-half of the escrow fees. Taxes for the current year, insurance acceptable to the Buyer, rents, interest, mortgage reserves, maintenance fees, and water and other utilities constituting liens, shall be pro-rated as of closing. Renters' security deposits shall accrue to Buyer at closing. Seller to provide Buyer with current rental or lease agreements prior to closing.

11. Termite Inspection: Seller agrees, at his expense, to provide written certification by a reputable licenced pest control firm that the property is free of termite infestation. In the event termites are found, the Seller shall have the property treated at his expense and provide acceptable certification that treatment has been rendered. If any structural repairs are required by reason of termite damage as established by acceptable certification, Seller agrees to make necessary repairs not to exceed $500. If repairs exceed $500, Buyer shall first have the right to accept the property "as is" with a credit of $500 to the Buyer at closing, or the Buyer may terminate this agreement with the earnest money deposit being promptly returned to the Buyer if the Seller does not agree to pay all costs of treatment and repair.

12. Conditions of Sale: The following conditions shall also apply, and shall, if conflicting with the printed portions of this agreement, prevail and control:

Offer subject to partner's approval. Offer subject to satisfactory inspection of the property by a building contractor and a termite inspector.

13. Liability and Maintenance: Seller shall maintain subject property, including landscaping, in good condition until the date of transfer of title or possession by Buyer, whichever occurs first. All risk of loss and destruction of property, and all expenses of insurance, shall be borne by the Seller until the date of possession. If the improvements on the property are destroyed or materially damaged prior to closing, then the Buyer shall have the right to declare this agreement null and void, and the earnest money deposit and all other sums paid by Buyer toward the purchase price shall be returned to the Buyer forthwith.

14. Possession: The Buyer shall be entitled to possession of property upon closing or _____n/a_____, 19____.

15. Default: In the event the Buyer fails to complete the purchase as herein provided, the earnest money deposit shall be retained by the Seller as the total and entire liquidated damages. In the event the Seller fails to perform any condition of the sale as herein provided, then the Buyer, may, at his option, treat the contract as terminated, and all payments made by the Buyer hereunder shall be returned to the Buyer forthwith, provided the Buyer may, at his option, treat this agreement as being in full force and effect with the right to action for specific performance and damages. In the event that either Buyer, Seller, or Agent shall institute suit to enforce any rights hereunder, the prevailing party shall be entitled to court costs and a reasonable attorney's fee.

16. Time Limit of Offer: The Seller shall have until _____5:00 pm_____ (hour) _____6/25_____ (date), 19____

to accept this offer by delivering a signed copy hereof to the Buyer. If this offer is not so accepted, it shall lapse and the agent (or Seller) shall refund the earnest money deposit to the Buyer forthwith.

17. General Agreements: (1) Both parties to this purchase reserve their rights to assign and hereby otherwise agree to cooperate in effecting an Internal Revenue Code 1031 exchange or similar tax-related arrangement prior to close of escrow, upon either party's written notice of intention to do so. (2) Upon approval of this offer by the Seller, this agreement shall become a contract between Buyer and Seller and shall inure to the benefit of the heirs, administrators, executors, successors, personal representatives, and assigns of said parties. (3) Time is of the essence and an essential part of this agreement. (4) This contract constitutes the sole and entire agreement between the parties hereto and no modification of this contract shall be binding unless attached hereto and signed by all parties to the contract. No representations, promises, or inducements not included in this contract shall be binding upon any party hereto.

18. Buyer's Statement and Receipt: "I/we hereby agree to purchase the above property in accordance with the terms and conditions above stated and acknowledge receipt of a completed copy of this agreement, which I/we have fully read and understand." Dated _____6/24_____, 19____. _____8:00 am_____ (hour)

Address _____P.O. Box 1096_____ _____Marc Stephen Garrison_____ Buyer

_____Orem, Utah   84057_____ _____ Buyer

Phone No: Home (_801_) _225-8777_ Business (____) _(same)_

19. Seller's Statement and Response: "I/we approve and accept the above offer, which I/we have fully read and understand, and agree to the above terms and conditions this day of

_____, 19____. _____ Seller
(hour)

Address _____ _____ Seller

Phone No: Home (____) _____ Business (____) _____

20. Commission Agreement: Seller agrees to pay a commission of____% of the gross sales price to _____ for services in this transaction, and agrees that, in the event of forfeiture of the earnest money deposit by the Buyer, said deposit shall be divided between the Seller's broker and the Seller (one half to each party), the Broker's part not to exceed the amount of the commission.

21. Buyer's Receipt for Signed Offer: The Buyer hereby acknowledges receipt of a copy of the above agreement bearing the Seller's signature in acceptance of this offer.

Dated _____, 19____ _____ Buyer

_____ Buyer

©1983 The Allen Group, Inc. Form B82GL

181

CLOSE THE TRANSACTION

☐　　☐　　☐

The closing (known in some states as closing the escrow) is relatively simple. It is handled by a real estate attorney, a mortgage officer, or a title
officer, depending on locale.

Many first-time homebuyers are unaware that they must pay a number
of expenses in addition to the down payment at the time of the closing of
the sale. To acquaint you with the kinds of costs you can expect at the
closing, a checklist of closing costs appears on page 194. Since every real
estate transaction is unique, not all these costs will be incurred at your
closing. Your actual costs at closing will vary according to the home you
buy, how you have arranged your financing, and what you were able to
negotiate with the seller when you made your offer.

For many people, buying a home is the most significant financial step in their lifetime. Especially if this is the first home you have purchased, you need several pieces of information to help you make this crucial financial step to your best advantage. Let's look at some of this information now. Take a deep breath, relax, and just read through these pages. Become familiar with the information, but don't try to memorize it. It will always be right here in the book whenever you need a refresher course.

SETTLEMENT COSTS

□   □   □

Settlement is the formal process by which ownership of real property passes from seller to buyer. It is the last step in the home-buying process, the point at which title to the property is transferred from the seller to the buyer. Because of the significance of the financial commitment made in buying a home, there is a federal statute which helps to protect you in the settlement process. It is known as the Real Estate Settlement Procedures Act (RESPA).

RESPA covers most residential mortgage loans used to finance the purchase of one- to four-family properties: houses, condominiums or cooperative apartment units, a lot with a mobile home, or a lot on which you will build a house or place a mobile home using the proceeds of the loan. While RESPA does not set the prices of the settlement services, it does take the mystery out of the settlement process. Knowing in advance what occurs during settlement allows you to shop for settlement services and make informed decisions about the process.

□   □   □

SHOPPING FOR SETTLEMENT SERVICES

□   □   □

Once you have found the home of your choice, reached an agreement with the seller, and signed a sales contract, you are ready to find the necessary financing—either a conventional mortgage or one of the creative solutions discussed in earlier steps.

Between the time you make a loan application and the closing, you have time to begin shopping for settlement services. Doing this will ensure that you obtain good value for your money. Settlement services include such professionals as your agent or broker, an attorney, a lender, a settlement agent, and a title company, which is often the closing agent, too.

By this point you have made a partial payment for the property by making an earnest money deposit and you have signed a contract binding you to the deal. Next several settlement services will be performed on your behalf, for which you are expected to pay. The costs of the services can vary, so you want to take some time now to find the most efficient and economical ways to arrange for these services to take place.

You can negotiate with the seller to determine who pays what costs that arise prior to and during the closing. There are generally no fixed rules about who pays for what; however, in some locales custom dictates which party to the transaction pays for what settlement services. Usually the negotiations are concluded by the time the sales contract is signed, but you can actually negotiate with the seller right up to the actual closing over the settlement costs. The various professionals and organizations whose services you may require during the course of closing your deal include the following: the real estate agent or broker, the attorney, the lender, the settlement agent, the title service, and the escrow agent.

□   □   □

THE REAL ESTATE AGENT OR BROKER

□ □ □

As stated earlier, the agent or broker is really working on the seller's behalf. Although the law requires him to deal fairly with all parties to the transaction, speak up if you feel you are being treated unfairly.

A broker may recommend a particular lender, title company, attorney, and so forth. If he does, ask him why he is making that particular recommendation. A broker should have good experience with these providers of settlement services and may be recommending the ones who have shown good results in the past. On the other hand, the broker may have another motive for suggesting a particular service, so let him know that while you welcome his suggestions, you reserve the right to make the final choice.

THE ATTORNEY

□ □ □

Before you commit to an attorney, ask how much experience he has had with real estate deals and what services he will perform for what fee. Minimum fees cannot be established by bar associations (the U.S. Supreme Court has declared this practice illegal), so feel comfortable about discussing fees and shopping for an attorney whose fees you can afford.

Some questions you may wish to ask the attorney include: What is the charge for reading documents and giving advice concerning them? For being present at settlement? Will the attorney represent any other party in the transaction except you? In some areas the attorney can act as the settlement officer. If he does, he will be representing the interests of others, too, and he may not represent your interest fully as a result.

□ □ □

THE LENDER

□   □   □

Choose the lender on the basis not only of the kind of mortgage you can arrange but also on the basis of what kind of settlement costs will be required of you. Lending institutions all require some settlement costs, but the number of costs (and therefore the total expense) vary from lender to lender, so do shop for the best deal.

The kinds of costs likely to be incurred include a new survey of the property, title insurance, appraisal of the property, and a credit report on you.

Often lending institutions prefer to arrange for the closing with title companies, attorneys, appraisers, and surveyors that they have a history with and have confidence in. If the lender makes such a requirement of you, you have certain rights under RESPA. Under these circumstances the lender must provide you with, as part of the good faith estimates, a statement in which he sets forth the name, address, and telephone number of each settlement provider that he has designated. In addition, he must provide you with a statement of the specific services each provider is to perform, as well as an estimate of the cost of the service based on the lender's prior experience with the provider. (If the services or charges are not clear to you, ask questions before committing.) The lender must also state whether the firms designated to perform these services for you have a business relationship with the lender. A business relationship may not be a problem; the designated firms often provide the services needed. However, a conflict of interest may exist if a settlement provider has a business relationship with the lender; sometimes a choice will have to be made as to whether the provider should protect your interests or those of the lender.

Where legal services are involved, it is always wise to hire your own attorney to ensure that your interests are protected. As for the other services, you should contact other firms to see if their costs are competitive and their services comparable.

If your lender allows you to choose the settlement service providers, you should do some comparison shopping before designating which firms are to provide the services for the closing.

Questions you want to ask the lender include the following:

- If you are required to carry life or disability insurance, must you obtain it from a particular company?

- Is there a late payment charge? How much is it? How late may your payment be before the charge is imposed?

- If you wish to pay off the loan in advance of maturity (if you sell the house to someone who wishes different financing or your Aunt Agatha dies and leaves you a fortune), must you pay a prepayment penalty? How much?

- Will the lender release you from personal liability if your loan is assumed by someone else when you sell your house?

- If you sell your house and the buyer assumes your loan, will the lender have the right to charge an assumption fee, raise the rate of interest, or require payment in full of the mortgage?

- If you have a financial emergency, will the terms of the loan include a future advances clause, permitting you to borrow additional money on the mortgage after you have paid off part of the original loan?

- Will you be required to pay monies into a special reserve (escrow or impound) account to cover taxes or insurance? If so, how large a deposit will be required at the closing of the sale? (The amount of reserve deposits required is limited under RESPA. Some recent state laws have required that these accounts bear interest to the borrower—the buyer. Check to see if you have such laws in your state.) If reserve requirements

can be waived, you will be responsible for paying the tax col-
lector and the insurance company yourself.

- What can you offer in the way of FHA, VA, and Farmers
  Home Administration loans? How do their terms and requirements differ from conventional loans?

THE SETTLEMENT AGENT

☐ ☐ ☐

Settlement practices vary from community to community, even within
the same county or city. Settlement services are offered, variously, by lending institutions, title insurance companies, escrow companies, real estate
brokers, and attorneys. Take the initiative; don't just settle for the first
such service that is recommended to you. Do some investigating; compare
fees and services; check out the business reputation of the different firms.
Some effort on your part here can benefit you in two ways: You can save
money and you can be sure you are dealing with a reliable settlement
service.

THE TITLE SERVICE

☐ ☐ ☐

Having a clear title to the property is absolutely essential, so you want to
choose a reliable firm to perform this service. In some areas both title
insurance companies and attorneys perform this function; check to see
what is done in your locale. Basically, a title search may take the form of
an abstract, which is a compilation of pertinent legal documents which
provides a condensed history of the property ownership and related matters. Sometimes title searches are performed by extracting information
from public records without assembling abstracts. Either method requires

an expert examination to determine the status of a particular title. Compare the options in your area to get the best buy.

In some areas a few days or weeks before the settlement the title insurance company will issue a binder (sometimes called a commitment to insure), or preliminary report, a summary of findings based on the search or abstract. The binders lists all the defects in and liens against (if any) the title identified by the search. You should arrange to have a copy sent to you (or to an attorney who is representing you) so that you can raise an objection if there are matters affecting the title which you did not agree to accept when you signed the contract of sale.

Title insurance is often required to protect the lender against loss if a flaw in title is not found by the title search made when the house is purchased. You may also get an owner's title policy to protect yourself.

Keep in mind that a title insurance policy issued to the lender does not protect you, nor does a policy issued to the prior owners. To protect yourself from a loss because of a mistake made by the title searcher, or because of a legal defect of a type which does not appear on the public records, you will need an owner's policy. While such mistakes rarely occur, when they do it can be financially disastrous to the uninsured. If you buy an owner's policy, it is usually much less expensive if purchased simultaneously with a lender's policy.

Depending on the general practice in your area, there may be no need for a full historical title search each time a home's title is transferred. If you are buying a home which has changed hands in the last several years, inquire at the title company which issued the previous title insurance policy about a "reissue rate," which would be lower in cost than a new policy. If the title insurance policy of the previous owner is available, take it to the title insurer or lawyer whom you have selected to do your search.

To mark the boundaries of the property as set out in the title, lenders may require a survey. A home buyer may be able to avoid the cost of a repetitive complete survey of the property if he can locate the surveyor who previously surveyed the project, which he can just update. However, the requirements of investors who buy loans originated by your lender may limit the lender's discretion to negotiate this point. Check with the lender or the title company about this.

THE ESCROW CLOSING

□   □   □

As stated earlier, settlement practices differ from state to state. In some parts of the country, settlement may be conducted by an escrow agent, which may be a lender, real estate agent, title company representative, attorney, or an escrow company. After entering into a contract of sale, the parties sign an escrow agreement which requires them to deposit specified documents and funds with the agent. Unlike other types of closing, there is no meeting of interested parties to sign documents. The escrow agent may request a title report and policy, draft a deed or other documents, obtain rent statements, pay off existing loans, adjust taxes, rents, insurance between the buyer and seller, compute interest on loans, and acquire hazard (homeowner's) insurance. All of this may be authorized in the escrow agreement.

If all the required papers and monies are deposited with the escrow agent within the agreed time, the escrow is "complete." The escrow agent then records the appropriate documents and gives each party the documents and money each is entitled to receive, including the Uniform Settlement Statement.

If one party has failed to fulfill his agreement, the escrow is not closed and legal complications may follow.

HOMEBUYER'S OBLIGATIONS

□   □   □

As the homebuyer you make certain legally binding commitments during the closing process. You sign papers legally obligating you to pay the mortgage loan financing the purchase of your home for openers. Once you have signed the papers, you must pay according to the terms of the loan interest rate, amount and due date of each monthly payment, repayment period—all of which are specified in the documents signed by you. A note or bond signed by you at the settlement is your promise to repay the loan for the unpaid balance of the purchase price. You will also sign a mortgage or deed of trust which pledges your home as security for repayment of the loan.

Failure to make monthly mortgage payments on time may lead to a late payment charge, if provided for in the documents. If you default on the loan by missing payments altogether and do not make them up within a period of time usually set by state law, the documents also specify certain actions which the lender may take to recover the amount owed. Ultimately, after required notice to you, a default could lead to foreclosure and sale of the home which secures your loan.

Because your home is the security for your loan (and for your own satisfaction and comfort), you should maintain it in a proper state of repair. The mortgage or deed of trust may in fact specifically obligate you to keep the property in good repair and not allow deterioration.

Read the documents carefully at or before closing so you can be fully aware of your obligations as a homeowner. Until you have paid that final mortgage payment and own the home free and clear, you have to answer to other people for how you take care of the property.

Use the following Closing Costs Checklist to estimate the closing costs for each house that you seriously consider buying; it is possible that the closing costs could be a factor in your final decision of which home to buy. Closing costs are those costs that you will pay at the closing in addition to the balance due on the down payment. This is a generic checklist; as stated earlier, the actual costs you will pay at closing will depend on what home you buy.

The earnest money is the first installment of the down payment. What the difference is between the earnest money paid and the total down payment required is only one of the costs you must be prepared to pay at closing. When you apply for a loan, federal law requires the lender to give you a "good faith" estimate of the closing costs in connection with the mortgage. And the estimate must be in the mail within three days after you apply for the mortgage loan.

In addition there are such costs as the fee to the title company, the cost of the credit report, prepaid homeowner's insurance, the cost of having the property surveyed and inspected, loan origination fee, loan discount points, prorated property taxes, attorney's fees, and so on.

Use the checklist on the next page to help you get a close estimate as to how much money you will need to come up with in addition to the down payment. Shortly before the closing, the title company (or whoever is doing the actual closing for you) will notify you of the exact amount of the cashier's check you will need to bring with you to the closing. In the meantime, it is wise for you to work out this estimate so you can arrange for the necessary cash to be available when you need it.

You will enjoy the peace of mind of knowing in advance what is expected of you financially at the closing.

Now sharpen your pencil and get to work on the Closing Costs Checklist.

On the page immediately following the Closing Costs Checklist is a checklist to help you prepare for the closing. Many of the items on this checklist will be done by your real estate agent or the closing company but some of the items are yours alone. You should check off each item as it is completed, regardless of who does the preparation.

Closing Costs Checklist

Initial Mortgage Payment   _____

Loan Origination Fee (charged by the lender)   _____

Loan Discount Fee (points charged by the lender)   _____

Loan Assumption Fee (if applicable)   _____

Prepaid Mortgage Insurance (if required)   _____

Credit Report   _____

Property Survey   _____

Inspections of Property   _____

Recording Deed   _____

Prepaid Homeowner's Insurance for First Year   _____

Prorated Property Taxes for Current Year   _____

Attorney's Fees   _____

Closing Company's Fees   _____

Title Search and Insurance (usually paid by seller)   _____

Credit Life Insurance   _____

Other Closing Costs   _____

Down Payment (down payment less earnest money paid)   _____

Amount Needed at Closing   _____

Checklist for Closing

❏ 1. Hire an attorney, if necessary.

❏ 2. Make financial arrangements (mortgage or creative finance).

❏ 3. Insure the mortgage, if appropriate.

❏ 4. Arrange for homeowner's insurance.

❏ 5. Have property surveyed and appraised. (If you go through a lending institution for a mortgage, it should handle these details.)

❏ 6. Arrange for general building inspection.

❏ 7. Arrange for termite inspection.

❏ 8. Do your own inspection of home before closing.

❏ 9. Ask about warranty deed.

❏ 10. Know your closing costs.

❏ 11. Have cashier's check prepared for closing.

❏ 12. Have the deed recorded after closing.

Well, that's it. You've got your home. Let me be the first to congratulate you. My hope is that it will be a source of personal and financial strength for both you and your family. As a personal favor to me, I would appreciate it if you would jot me a quick note about the process of getting a new home. If you could, I would appreciate receiving with that note a photograph of your new home.

Thanks again. I look forward to hearing from you.

My best,

Marc Stephen Garrison
M. S. Garrison and Company
P.O. Box 1096
Orem, Utah 84057
(801) 225-8777

SAMPLE AGREEMENTS FOR EQUITY SHARING

☐ ☐ ☐

**AGREEMENT OF
LIMITED PARTNERSHIP OF
A CALIFORNIA LIMITED PARTNERSHIP**

1. FORMATION

1.1 *Date of Agreement:*

1.2 *Name of Partnership:* A California Limited Partnership

1.3 *Place of Business:* The address of the partnership is 1935 East Beech Avenue, Visalia, California 93277. It may be changed by the general partner by giving at least ten (10) days prior written notice to the limited partner.

1.4 *General Partners:*

1.5 *Limited Partners:* See Exhibit "A."

1.6 *Applicable Law:* This partnership is formed under the part of the California Corporations Code known as the California Revised Limited Partnership Act.

1.7 *No Permits Obtained:* The partnership interests have not been registered with any governmental agency, and no permits have been obtained.

1.8 *Certificate of Limited Partnership:* The general partner shall file a Certificate of Limited Partnership with the office of the California Secretary of State and may record a certified copy in any necessary counties.

1.9 *Purpose:* The partnership's purpose is to buy and hold as an equity sharing investment under Internal Revenue Code Section 280A, the property described in Exhibit "B".

    1.9(1) The class "B" limited partner(s) shall lease the property from the partnership for use as a residence under the terms of the lease attached as Exhibit "D".

1.10 *Term of Partnership:* The partnership starts on the date of this agreement and will end three (3) years from that date unless sooner terminated as provided for below.

    1.10(1) The partnership term may be extended for a total of four (4) consecutive six (6) month periods upon written notice from any limited partner of each such extension being delivered to the general partner and each limited partner at least 30 days before expiration of the initial term or preceding extension.

1.11 *Limited Liability:* No limited partner is liable for any partnership losses greater than his capital contribution.

2. CAPITAL CONTRIBUTIONS AND DISTRIBUTIONS OF FUNDS

2.1 *Capital Contributions:* The partnership's capital will be _____ _____ ($_____), set forth in Exhibit "A".

2.2 *Loans to Partnership:* A partner may only lend money to the partnership with the general partner's approval. The loan shall be kept in a separate account.

2.3 *Definition of "Spendable Income":* "Spendable Income" means net receipts remaining from ownership of the partnership's assets after deductions for all expenditures on expenses, reserves and loan reduction, excluding depreciation schedules.

2.4 *Distribution of Spendable Income:* Spendable income is first distributed to the limited partners in a sum equal to ten percent (10%) a year, cumulative, on their original contributions; then any remaining spendable income is distributed pro rata to all limited partners on their ownership interest.

2.5 *Participation in Proceeds of Refinance/Sale:* Net proceeds from the sale or refinance of all or some of the partnership property are distributed as follows:

    2.5(1) First, to the limited partners, until they receive their capital contributions plus ten percent (10%) a year since the date of contribution, less any disbursement received;

    2.5(2) Then, all remaining funds shall be distributed to the limited partners to be shared in accordance with their ownership ratio.

2.6 *Depreciation Allocation:* Depreciation shall be taken on a straight-line method and allocated to the partners proportionately to their initial capital investments.

    2.6(1) Only the Class "A" limited partners shall be entitled to deduct their share of the depreciation allocation.

2.7 *Tax and Interest Allocation:* Deductions for property tax and interest payments shall be allocated to the limited partners pro rata on their initial capital investments.

3. MANAGEMENT, COMPENSATION, DUTIES AND POWERS

3.1 *Management of Partnership Property:* The general partner has full charge of the management of the partnership business.

3.2 *Compensation:* No partner shall be paid for working for the partnership or for being a partner, except as this section provides.

3.3 *Duties:* The general partner shall do what is needed to conduct the partnership business.

3.4 *Other Ventures:* Any partner may have an interest in any other business venture. Neither the partnership nor the partner has any right, by this agreement, in any such venture or to its income or profits.

4. ACCOUNTS AND ACCOUNTING

4.1 *Inspection of Partnership Records:* The partnership shall maintain accurate books at its principal office. All partners may inspect such books at reasonable times upon reasonable notice. A separate income and capital account shall be maintained for each partner.

4.2 *Annual Audit and Report to Limited Partners:* The general partner shall audit the books and deliver to each limited partner, within sixty (60) days after the end of the partnership year, a balance sheet and profit statement showing each partner's capital account, the distribution to each partner, and the taxable amount of it, and a copy of the partnership income tax return. A majority interest of the limited partners may order an audit of the partnership books, at the partnership's expense, by an accountant named by a majority of limited partners.

5. ASSIGNMENT OF INTEREST, SUBSTITUTED LIMITED PARTNER

5.1 *Assignment of Class "B" Interest:* A Class "B" limited partner may assign his partnership interest to any other limited partner at any time after he has given the general partner ten (10) days notice to buy his interest on the same terms agreed upon with another limited partner.

5.2 *Invalid Assignment of Interest:* All other assignments or transfers of Class "B" limited partners' interest are terminated under Section 6.

5.3 *Assignment of Class "A" Interest:* A Class "A" limited partner may assign his partnership interest to any other person or entity provided written notice of any such assignment is given to the general partner and all remaining limited partners.

6. TERMINATION OF PARTNERSHIP INTERESTS

6.1 *Termination of General Partner:* The termination of the general partner does not terminate any of the general partner's rights as a limited partner.

6.2 *Events Causing Termination of a Limited Partner:* A limited partner may be terminated if any of the following events occur:

6.2(1) He dies;

6.2(2) He is adjudged insane, incompetent or is committed to a mental institution;

6.2(3) He transfers his interest to a non-partner without getting prior consent from each remaining limited partner under Section 6;

6.2(4) He fails to immediately remove a charging order against his interest;

6.2(5) His bankruptcy filing;

6.2(6) His voluntary retirement, withdrawal or resignation as a partner;

6.2(7) His expulsion by court order or by all of the remaining limited partners;

6.2(8) His failure to contribute capital to the partnership agreed to in Section 2.1, Capital Contributions; or

6.2(9) He defaults on the terms of the Lease Agreement described in Section 2.1.

6.3 *Notice of Termination:* Service upon the limited partner to be terminated of a written notice stating the cause for termination and the effective date of termination terminates all of his powers and his right to share in partnership profits as of the effective date. The effective date is thirty (30) days after service of the notice. Each remaining partner shall be served a copy of the notice of termination and notice of his option rights under Section 7.

7. OPTION TO PURCHASE

7.1 *Option to Purchase Upon Termination:* Upon the termination of a limited partner's interest under Section 6, the remaining limited partners may;

7.1(1) Dissolve and liquidate the partnership under Section 10.1; or

7.1(2) Buy the terminated limited partner's entire interest. Where more than one limited partner exercises their option, those exercising shall purchase their pro rata share as among their cumulative ownership interest.

7.2 *Notice of Exercise of Option:*

7.2(1) When a partner dies, notice of the option shall be given to the deceased's representative within one hundred and twenty (120) days after the representative's appointment.

7.2(2) When a limited partner's interest is terminated under Section 6, notice of the exercise of the option shall be given to the terminated partner before the effective date of termination, and in the way notice of termination is given under Section 6.3.

7.3 *Death or Termination Does Not Dissolve Partnership:* A limited partner's death or termination does not automatically dissolve the partnership. The business shall continue unless the majority of the limited partners vote to dissolve.

7.4 *Partnership Name Continues:* If an election is made under Section 8.1(2), the remaining partners may continue to use the partnership name.

8. VALUATION OF PARTNERSHIP INTEREST

8.1 *Dead, Incompetent or Insane Partners:* If an election is made to buy the interest of a limited partner terminated because of death, incompetency, or insanity, the value of the interest shall equal:

8.1(1) The sum of:

    a) The partner's capital contributions less distributions;

    b) The balance of the partner's income account;

8.1(2) Less:

    a) All unpaid assessments due;

    b) All other debts to the partnership;

8.1(3) Plus the partner's interest in the "additional value" of the partnership assets determined as follows:

    a) Each partner has a pro rata ownership share of the additional value;

    b) Within thirty (30) days after the close of each partnership year, the limited partners shall execute an "Agreement of Additional Value" (Exhibit "C"). The "Agreement" shall state an amount set by the limited partners as the increased value of the partnership assets over the partners' invested capital;

    c) The additional value set within two (2) years before the termination of a deceased, insane or incompetent limited partner binds the remaining partners and their successors in interest.

    d) If additional value was not set within two (2) years before termination of the deceased, insane or incompetent limited partner, it shall be set by arbitration under Section 14.5.

8.2 *Other Partners:* If an election is made to buy the interest of a partner who is terminated for reasons other than death, insanity or incompetency, the value of the interest shall equal the amount described in Section 8.1 excluding any "Additional Value."

9. PAYMENT OF PURCHASE PRICE

9.1 *Dead, Incompetent or Insane Partners:* Payment of the amount described in Section 8.1 shall be made in three equal annual installments including interest of ten percent (10%) a year. The first installment is due one hundred eighty (180) days after the death, insanity or incompetency of the partner.

The amount owed shall be evidenced by a promissory note having an acceleration clause and an attorneys' fee clause, which shall be executed by all partners executing the option. The note shall be secured by a pledge of the interest purchased.

9.2 *Other Partners:* The amount described in Section 8.2 shall be due and payable upon the dissolution of the partnership. It shall be evidenced by a promissory note which shall be executed by all partners executing the option, and shall be secured by a pledge of the interest purchased.

10. BUYOUT OPTION

10.1 *Grant of Option:* The Class "A" Limited Partners hereby grant to the Class "B" Limited Partners, the irrevocable option to purchase their interest in the partnership on the following terms:

10.2 *Option Period:* The Class "B" Limited Partners may exercise their buyout option at any time prior to the expiration of three (3) years after the partnership's acquisition of the property, providing the Class "B" Limited Partners are not then in default under this agreement.

    10.2(1) In the event the partnership term is extended as provided in Sections 1.10 and 1.10(1), the buyout option term shall be extended for the same period.

10.3 *Option Price:* The option price shall be determined as follows:

    10.3(1) The Class "B" Limited Partners shall obtain an FHA/VA appraisal of the property's value within three months of exercise of this option, which determination of value shall be deemed the property's fair market value.

    10.3(2) Should any limited partner object to the FHA/VA determination of value, the FHA/VA appraisal shall be disregarded, provided written notice of the objection is given to the general partner and all other limited partners within ten (10) days of the objecting partner's receipt of the FHA/VA appraisal. In the event objection to the FHA/VA appraisal is timely made, then each class of limited partners, on two weeks notice from the optionee, shall name a licensed real estate appraiser, which appraisers shall jointly choose a third appraiser within two weeks after notice of their appointment. Each appraiser shall deliver to the partnership their written opinion of the property's fair market value, and the average of the three appraisals shall be deemed the property's fair market value. Each class of partners shall pay the appraisers they select and one-half the cost of the third appraiser.

10.3(3) The partners may agree to the fair market value of the property.

10.3(4) Then deduct from the fair market value the principal balance(s) remaining on the property's loan encumbrances to determine the property's gross equity.

10.3(5) Then deduct from the property's gross equity all customary closing costs, including a brokerage fee of 6% as though the property had been sold to a third party, to determine the property's net equity.

10.3(6) The option price, in cash, to be the greater of:

1.) The capital contributions of the Class "A" Limited Partners, plus ____% per annum from the date of each capital contribution less any disbursements; or

2.) The Class "A" Limited Partners' pro rata ownership share of the property's net equity under 10.3(5).

10.3(7) Any escrow closing costs actually incurred in the exercise of this option shall be paid by the Class "B" Limited Partners.

10.4 *Exercise of Option:* The Class "B" Limited Partners may exercise the buyout option only by:

10.4(1) Giving written notice of their intent to exercise the option to the general partner and each of the Class "A" limited partners during the option term;

10.4(2) Depositing within ten days of giving the notice of intent to exercise the option signed escrow instructions into an escrow account providing for purchase of the Class "A" ownership interest on the terms stated in this agreement;

10.4(3) Depositing into escrow cash or the cash equivalent of the total option price within 30 days of opening escrow; and

10.4(4) Causing escrow to close on or before its 30th day, time being strictly of the essence.

10.5 *Transfer of Ownership:* Within ten days of the opening of escrow, the Class "A" limited partners shall execute and deposit into escrow all documents and instruments necessary for escrow to close within the escrow period.

10.6 *Expiration of Option:* This option is deemed an irrevocable offer to sell. This offer shall be deemed expired if not accepted by exercise of the option under Section 10.4.

11. SALE OF PARTNERSHIP PROPERTY

11.1 *Marketing of Property:* Upon the expiration of the buyout option in Section 10, the general partner shall cause the property to be sold.

11.2 *Sale Price:* The general partner is authorized to then sell the property for the highest price obtainable in marketing the property for a reasonable period of time. The sale price to be paid by the purchaser shall be all-cash unless the partners unanimously agree to finance a portion of the price.

11.3 *Sale Costs:* The general partner, on behalf of the partnership, is authorized to retain a licensed real estate broker, including himself, at the customary commission rate and to incur such other customary selling costs as are reasonable.

11.4 *Sale Proceeds:* Proceeds from sale of the property shall be distributed as provided in Section 12.4.

12. PARTNERSHIP DISSOLUTION AND DISTRIBUTION OF CAPITAL

12.1 *Dissolution:* The partnership shall be dissolved when all the limited partners agree.

12.2 *Accounting:* Upon dissolution, the partnership shall take account of partnership assets and liabilities. The assets shall be sold quickly and for fair value.

12.3 *Business Ends:* The partnership shall do no further business after dissolution other than that needed to wind up the business and distribute the assets.

12.4 *Distribution of Proceeds:* Proceeds from the liquidation of partnership assets and non-liquidated assets shall be distributed as follows:

12.4(1) All partnership liabilities shall first be paid;

12.4(2) All debts owed to partners shall then be paid;

12.4(3) All remaining funds are to be distributed according to the method described in Section 2.5.

12.5 *After Dissolution:* The limited partners shall continue to divide assets and liabilities after dissolution in the way Section 12.4 provides.

13. LIMITATIONS OF PARTNERS' AUTHORITY

13.1 *General Partner:* Unless all limited partners consent in writing, the general partner may not violate this agreement, make it impossible to perform the partnership's business, or confess to judgment against the partnership.

13.2 *Limited Partners:* No limited partner may engage in the management or control of the partnership business.

13.3 The general partner shall not transfer title prior to expiration of the option period described in Section 10 or encumber the partnership property without the prior written approval of a majority in interest of the limited partners.

14. RIGHTS OF LIMITED PARTNERS

14.1 *Rights of Limited Partners:* A majority in interest of the limited partners may vote upon any matter permitted by California Corporations Code Section 15632.

14.2 *Exercise of Rights:* Each limited partner shall be given seven (7) days' written notice of any proposed act of the partnership concerning the above matters or any proposed sale of the partnership property. The notice shall state that the limited partners may vote on such matters and shall request that those limited partners vote within seven (7) days of mailing the notice or their failure to respond will be counted in favor of the proposal. The terms of any sale shall be set forth in the notice.

    14.2(1) The majority of limited partners may remove the general partner and elect a new general partner or add a new general partner as described in Section 14.2. The notice shall contain the name and address of the existing and proposed general partner and will state that a substitution or addition of a general partner is proposed.

14.3 *Notices:* Any limited partner may ask that the notice be mailed by the general partner, mail it himself, or call a meeting of the limited partners for the above purposes. The costs of mailing notices shall be borne by the partnership if the matter voted upon is approved by the limited partners. If the matter is not approved, the costs shall be borne by the limited partners requesting the meeting. The notice shall be written and sent by registered mail, postage prepaid, return receipt requested. The general partner shall give a list to any partner requesting the same.

14.4 *Exceptions:* No limited partner may withdraw or reduce his contribution to the capital of the partnership except as allowed by the buy and sell provisions of the agreement. No partner may sue the partnership for partition. No limited partner may demand property other than cash or notes in return for his contribution. No limited partner has priority over any other limited partner, except as provided in this agreement. No limited partner shall have the power or right to cause the termination and dissolution of the partnership, except as set forth in this agreement.

14.5 *Partners' Rights Specified:* This agreement contains the entire voting, assignment, withdrawal and miscellaneous rights of the partners. No other such rights are provided to the partners except as specified herein.

15. AMENDING THE AGREEMENT

15.1 *Amendments:* A majority in interest of the limited partners may vote to amend this agreement as follows:

    15.1(1) To change the partnership's name or any limited partner's amount of contribution;

    15.1(2) To substitute a new general partner;

    15.1(3) To substitute a new limited partner;

    15.1(4) To add limited partners;

The agreement shall be amended to reflect any such change.

15.2 *Endorsement:* Any amendment of the agreement must be signed by the general partner, any new partner and the assigning limited partner when a limited partner is to be substituted.

16. MISCELLANEOUS PROVISIONS

16.1 *Validity:* If any part of this agreement is invalid, the validity of the remainder of the agreement will not be affected.

16.2 *Notice:* All notices shall be written and personally delivered or sent by registered or certified mail, return receipt requested, postage prepaid, to the parties and to the partnership at the address stated herein.

16.3 *Survival of Rights:* This agreement binds the parties and their successors in interest.

16.4 *Paragraph Headings:* The paragraph headings do not affect the meaning of this agreement.

16.5 *Arbitration:* Any dispute between any partner and the partnership, or regarding any activities of the general partner that cannot be settled by the general partner shall be arbitrated under the rules of the American Arbitration Association.

SIGNATURE PAGE FOR LIMITED PARTNERSHIP AGREEMENT
BY GENERAL AND/OR LIMITED PARTNERS

I hereby agree to purchase Class "_____" limited partnership interest(s) in _____, a limited partnership, in the sum of _____ ($ _____) Enclosed herewith is my check for the total sum made payable to: _____.

The undersigned hereby executes this page as part of the Agreement of Limited Partnership which consists of _____ pages, not including this page, plus exhibits attached thereto and incorporated therein by reference, and agrees to the terms of the partnership agreement.

METHOD OF TITLE

I desire to hold legal title in the Limited Partnership as:

    /__/ Joint Tenants   /__/ Separate Property
    /__/ Tenants in Common   /__/ Community Property

with _____ whose relationship to me is

_____.

LIMITED PARTNER

Name: _____   _____
                                   Signature

Address:
Telephone Number: (   )
Social Security Number:

STATE OF CALIFORNIA)
COUNTY OF _____) ss

On _____, before me, the undersigned, a Notary Public in and for said County and State, personally appeared _____, known to me to be the person that executed the within instrument and acknowledged to me that he/she executed the same

WITNESS my hand and official seal.

_____

Notary Public in and for said County and State.

ACCEPTED:

_____   _____

                 (General Partner)   (Date)

EXHIBIT "A"

**AGREEMENT OF LIMITED
PARTNERSHIP OF** _____

Amount of Capital Contribution	Nature of Contribution	Percentage of Interest
GENERAL PARTNER:		
_____	_____	_____

CLASS "A" LIMITED PARTNERS:

		PROPERTY	50%
and	_____	INTEREST	
_____	_____	_____	_____
_____	_____	_____	_____
_____	_____	_____	_____
_____	_____	_____	_____
_____	_____	_____	_____
_____	_____	_____	_____
_____	_____	_____	_____
_____	_____	_____	_____
_____	_____	_____	_____

CLASS "B" LIMITED PARTNERS:

		CASH	50%
_____	_____	_____	_____
_____	_____	_____	_____
_____	_____	_____	_____

EXHIBIT "B"
AGREEMENT OF LIMITED PARTNERSHIP

LEGAL DESCRIPTION

The real property in the County of   , State of California,
described as follows:

_____

_____

_____

_____

_____

_____

_____

_____

EXHIBIT "D"
AGREEMENT OF LIMITED
PARTNERSHIP OF _____

ADDENDUM TO LIMITED PARTNERSHIP AGREEMENT
PROVISIONS FOR ADDITIONAL VALUE

The limited Partnership Agreement contains provisions for "Additional Value" and requires, within thirty (30) days after each calendar year, that the parties to the Limited Partnership Agreement agree upon any additional valuation then existing.

It is agreed this _____ day of _____, 19   , as follows:

The Additional Valuation as of this date is $???. This figure is exclusive of loans, if any, which exist against the interest held by the partnership and exclusive of all capital contributions made to date.

This amends the Limited Partnership Agreement to include this Additional Valuation.

IN WITNESS WHEREOF the parties have hereto set their hands the day and year opposite their signature to be effective on the date first above written.

Date: _____   _____
                                                                        PARTNER

Date: _____   _____
                                                                        PARTNER

Date: _____   _____
                                                                        PARTNER

Date: _____   _____
                                                                        PARTNER

Date: _____   _____
                                                                        PARTNER

Date: _____   _____
                                          PARTNER

Date: _____   _____
                                          PARTNER

Date: _____   _____
                                          PARTNER

EXHIBIT "D"
LEASE AGREEMENT

_____, LTD, a California limited partnership (hereafter "lessor") hereby leases to _____, Class "B" limited partners of the partnership (hereafter "lessee") that certain property commonly known as _____, _____, California (hereinafter "the property"), and consisting of a _____-family dwelling, on the following terms and conditions:

1. *Term:* The term of this lease shall be five years, beginning on _____, 19___, and ending on _____, _____, unless sooner terminated as herein provided. In the event the term of _____, a California limited partnership, is not extended to a total of five years as provided in Sections 1.10 and 1.10(1) of the partnership agreement, then this lease shall terminate along with the partnership agreement.

2. *Rent:* Lessee agrees to pay to lessor, as initial rent for the use and occupancy of the property, the sum of $_____.___ per month payable in advance on the first day of each and every month. The initial rent shall be adjusted periodically in an amount equal to any and all increases in monthly payments due from lessor or lessor's existing first trust deed loan of record, including increases of interest rate and impounds for property tax and insurance. Lessee agrees to pay to lessor this increased monthly rental amount upon 30 days written notice of the effective date of the increase.

3. *Condition and Maintenance of Premises:* Lessee acknowledges he has inspected the property, including all utilities and appliances, and accepts the property as being in satisfactory condition at the outset of this lease. Lessee agrees to maintain and perform all necessary repairs to the property during the lease term at his sole expense.

4. *Use of the Property:* The property is to be used only as a private residence by lessee and for no other purpose without the express written consent of lessor. Lessee shall comply with all laws and governmental requirements regarding use of the property, and shall not allow any waste or nuisance to occur on the property.

5. *Utilities:* Lessee shall pay all costs of public utilities to the property, including any required deposits, installation or service fees.

6. *Alterations and Improvements:* Lessee shall make no alterations or improvements to the property without prior express written consent of lessor. Any and all alterations and improvements made to the property by lessee with the consent of lessor, shall become the property of lessor and remain on the property upon termination of this lease.

7. *Insurance:* Lessee shall maintain at his sole expense a fire insurance policy fully covering the replacement cost of all structures on the property during the entire term of the lease.

8. *Waiver of Damage:* Lessee hereby expressly releases lessor from any and all liability for loss or damage to lessee or any property of lessee caused by water leakage, breaking pipes, theft, vandalism, or any other cause beyond the reasonable control of lessor.

9. *Hold-Harmless Clause:* Lessee shall indemnify and hold lessor free and harmless from any and all liability, damages, or expenses, including attorneys' fees and costs, arising from the death or injury of any person, including lessee, or from the damage to or destruction of any property, including property owned by lessee, caused or allegedly caused by some condition of the property, the fault of lessee, or some act or omission, whether negligent or intentional, of lessee or any person in, on, or about the property as a guest, licensee, or invitee of lessee.

10. *Assignment and Subletting:* Lessee shall not assign this lease or sublet all or any portion of the property without the prior written consent of lessor. Any assignment or subletting without the prior written consent of lessor shall be void and shall, at the option of lessor, terminate this lease.

11. *Binding on Heirs and Successors:* This lease shall be binding on and shall inure to the benefit of the heirs, executors, administrators, and successors of lessor and lessee, but nothing in this paragraph shall be construed as a consent by lessor to any assignment of this lease by lessee.

12. *Time of Essence:* Time is expressly deemed to be the essence of this lease.

13. *Waiver:* The waiver of any breach of any of the provisions of this lease by lessor shall not constitute a continuing waiver or a waiver of any subsequent breach by lessee.

EXECUTED on _____, 19___ , at _____ , California.

LESSOR:

By:_____
    General Partner

LESSEE:

_____

SUBSCRIPTION AND AGREEMENT TO INVEST

To: , LTD.
A California Limited Partnership

From: _____
          Subscriber-Investor

SUBSCRIPTION

I hereby offer to invest $_____ as a Class "_____" Limited Partner in the above California Limited Partnership.

Receipt is hereby acknowledged of my deposit in the amount of $_____ toward this investment. Upon presentation to me of the signature page to the partnership agreement for execution, I will deliver up the balance of the purchase price.

· GENERAL REPRESENTATIONS

I represent and warrant as follows:

I am purchasing the Interests for my own account, or in a fiduciary capacity for the account and benefit of a person or entity, for long-term investment, and not to resell or distribute to any person . . . . Yes___ No___

I understand that the Interests have not been registered under the Securities Act of 1933 and have not been qualified nor a permit obtained from the California Department of Corporations nor any other agency of the State of California . . . . Yes___ No___

I have read the Investment Circular and Agreement of Limited Partnership and I understand the speculative nature of the proposed investment . . . . Yes___ No___

I have had unrestricted access to all information concerning the proposed investment and have received no representations or warranties regarding the investment not contained in the investment circular . . . . Yes___ No___

SUITABILITY REPRESENTATIONS

I represent and warrant that:

I have known the following partners personally or in business as follows:

_____

_____

I have a projected adjusted gross income for the taxable year of 19____ of at least $_____;

I have an existing net worth of at least $_____ (net worth to be determined exclusive of home, furnishings and automobiles);

I have had the following experience with investments:

_____

_____

_____

I have had the following occupational experience:

_____

_____

_____

I have achieved the following educational level:

_____

_____

_____

Date: _____   _____

(Signature)

PROMISSORY NOTE SECURED BY ASSIGNMENT
AND SECURITY AGREEMENT

$\$$_____ , California, _____, 19_____

For value received, the undersigned promise to pay   ,
husband and wife as community property, or to order, at _____, California or as designated by holder, the principal sum of _____ Dollars with
interest from the date hereof until paid at the rate of 10 percent (10%), per annum
payable $\$$_____ monthly, all due and payable _____, 19_____.

In the event the partnership term for   , LTD., A California
Limited Partnership, is extended as provided in Sections 1.10 and 1.10(1) of the limited partnership agreement, the due date for all remaining principal and interest on
this note shall be extended for the same period. All other terms of this note shall
remain in force during any such extension.

Should interest not be so paid, it shall thereafter bear like interest as the principal.
Should default be made in the payment of any installment of principal or interest
when due, then the whole sum of principal and interest shall become immediately
due and payable at the option of the holder of this note. The prevailing party in any
litigation involving this agreement shall recover his costs and attorneys' fees.

This note is secured by an Assignment and Security Agreement of same date as this
note.

The entire sum of principal and interest shall become immediately due and payable
if:

1.) The undersigned sells or encumbers or otherwise transfers any portion of his
interest in the limited partnership described in the Assignment and Security Agreement;

2.) The undersigned defaults under the terms of the limited partnership agreement
described in the Assignment and Security Agreement;

3.) The undersigned exercises the Buyout Option stated in Section 10 of the limited
partnership agreement described in the Assignment and Security Agreement; or

4.) Any of the events stated in Section 6.2 of said limited partnership agreement occurs.

In the event of termination of the undersigned's partnership interest under Section 6 of said limited partnership agreement, the total sum due hereunder shall be applied as an offset against any amount to be paid by the holder hereof to the undersigned under Section 9 of said Limited Partnership Agreement.

Sample Residential Lease with Option to Purchase

Received from _____

_____, hereinafter referred to as

Tenant, the sum of $_____ (_____dollars),

evidenced by_____as a deposit

which, upon acceptance of this Lease, the Owner of the premises, herein-

after referred to as Owner, shall apply said deposit as follows:

	Deposit Received	Balance Owing Prior to Occupancy
Nonrefundable option consideration	$_____	$_____
Rent for the period from _____ to _____	$_____	$_____
Security Deposit	$_____	$_____
Other	$_____	$_____
Total	$_____	$_____

   In the event that this agreement is not accepted by the Owner or his/her authorized agent within _____ days, the total deposit received shall be refunded.

   Tenant hereby offers to lease from the Owner the premises situated in the City of _____, State of _____, described as _____

_____ ,

and consisting of _____

upon the following terms and conditions:

1. **Term:** The term hereof shall commence on _____ 19____, and continue for a period of _____ months thereafter.

2. **Rent:** Rent shall be $_____ per month, payable in advance, upon the _____ day of each calendar month to Owner or his/her authorized agent, at the following address: _____

_____, or at such other places as may be designated by Owner from time to time. In the event rent is not paid within five (5) days after due date, Tenant agrees to pay a late charge of $_____ plus interest at _____ percent per year on the delinquent amount. Tenant further agrees to pay $_____ for each dishonored bank check.

Sample Residential Lease with Option to Purchase (continued)

3. **Utilites:** Tenant shall be responsible for the payment of all utilities and services, except _____ , which shall be paid by Owner.

4. **Use:** The premises shall be used as a residence with no more than_____ adults and _____ children, and for no other purpose, without the written prior consent of Owner.

5. **Pets:** No pets shall be brought on the premises without the prior consent of Owner.

6. **Ordinances and Statutes:** Tenant shall comply with all statutes, ordinances and requirements of all municipal, state and federal authorities now in force, or which may hereafter be in force, pertaining to the use of the premises.

7. **Assignment and Subletting:** Tenant shall not assign this agreement or sublet any portion of the premises without prior written consent of the Owner which may not be unreasonably withheld.

8. **Maintenance, Repairs, or Alterations:** Tenant acknowledges that the premises are in good order and repair, unless otherwise indicated herein. Owner may at any time give Tenant a written inventory of furniture and furnishings on the premises and Tenant shall be deemed to have possession of all said furniture and furnishings in good condition and repair, unless he/she objects thereto in writing within five (5) days after receipt of such inventory. Tenant shall, at his/her own expense, and at all times, maintain the premises in a clean and sanitary manner, including all equipment, appliances, furniture and furnishings therein, and shall surrender the same, at termination hereof, in as good condition as received, normal wear and tear excepted. Tenant shall be responsible for damages caused by his/her negligence and that of his/her family or invitees and guests. Tenant shall not paint, paper or otherwise decorate or make alterations to the premises without the prior written consent of Owner. Tenant shall irrigate and maintain any surrounding grounds, including lawns and shrubbery, and keep the same clear of rubbish or weeds, if such grounds are a part of the premises and are exclusively for the use of Tenant.

9. **Entry and Inspection:** Tenant shall permit Owner or Owner's agents to enter the premises at reasonable times and upon reasonable notice for the purpose of making necessary or convenient repairs, or to show the premises to prospective tenants, purchasers, or mortgagees.

Sample Residential Lease with Option to Purchase (continued)

10. **Indemnification:** Owner shall not be liable for any damage or injury to Tenant, or any other person, or to any property, occurring on the premises or any part thereof, or in common areas thereof, unless such damage is the proximate result of the negligence or unlawful act of Owner, his/her agents or his/her employees. Tenant agrees to hold Owner harmless from any claims for damages, no matter how caused, except for injury or damages for which Owner is legally responsible.

11. **Physical Possession:** If Owner is unable to deliver possession of the premises at the commencement hereof, Owner shall not be liable for any damage caused thereby, nor shall this agreement be void or voidable, but Tenant shall not be liable for any rent until possession is delivered. Tenant may terminate this agreement if possession is not delivered within _____ days of the commencement of the term hereof.

12. **Default:** If Tenant shall fail to pay rent when due, or perform any term hereof, after not less than three (3) days' written notice of such default given in the manner required by law, Owner, at his/her option, may terminate all rights of Tenant hereunder, unless Tenant, within said time, shall cure such default. If Tenant abandons or vacates the property, while in default of the payment of rent, Owner may consider any property left on the premises to be abandoned and may dispose of the same in any manner allowed by law. In the event Owner reasonably believes that such abandoned property has no value, it may be discarded. All property on the premises is hereby subject to a lien in favor of Owner for the payment of all sums due hereunder, to the maximum extent allowed by law.

In the event of a default by Tenant, Owner may elect to (a) continue the lease in effect and enforce all his/her rights and remedies hereunder, including the right to recover the rent as it becomes due, or (b) at any time, terminate all of Tenant's rights hereunder and recover from Tenant all damages he/she may incur by reason of the breach of the lease, including the cost of recovering the premises, and including the worth at the time of such termination, or at the time of an award if suit be instituted to enforce this provision, of the amount by which the unpaid rent for the balance of the term exceeds the amount of such rental loss which the Tenant proves could be reasonably avoided.

13. **Security:** The security deposit set forth above, if any, shall secure the per-

Sample Residential Lease with Option to Purchase (continued)

formance of Tenant's obligations hereunder. Owner may, but shall not be obligated to, apply all portions of said deposit on account of Tenant's obligations hereunder. Any balance remaining upon termination shall be returned to Tenant.

14. Deposit Refunds: The balance of all deposits shall be refunded within two weeks from date possession is delivered to Owner or his/her authorized agent, together with a statement showing any charges made against such deposits by Owner.

15. Attorney's Fees: In any legal action brought by either party to enforce the terms hereof or relating to the demised premises, the prevailing party shall be entitled to all costs incurred in connection with such action, including a reasonable attorney's fee.

16. Waivers: No failure of Owner to enforce any term hereof shall be deemed a waiver, nor shall any acceptance of a partial payment of rent be deemed a waiver of Owner's right to the full amount thereof.

17. Notices: Any notice that either party may give or is required to give, may be given by mailing the same, postage prepaid, to Tenant at the premises or to Owner at the address shown below or at such other places as may be designated by the parties from time to time.

18. Heirs, Assigns, Successors: This lease is binding upon and inures to the benefit of the heirs, assigns and successors in interest to the parties.

19. Time: Time is of the essence of this agreement.

20. Holding Over: Any holding-over after expiration hereof, with the consent of Owner, shall be construed as a month-to-month tenancy in accordance with the terms hereof, as applicable. No such holding-over or extension of this lease shall extend the time for the exercise of the option unless agreed upon in writing by Owner.

21. Pest Control Inspection: The main building and all attached structures are to be inspected by a licensed structural pest control operator prior to delivery of physical possession, Owner is to pay (1) for elimination of infestation and/or infection of wood-destroying pests or organisms; (2) for repair of damage caused by such infestation and/or infection or by excessive moisture; (3) for correction of conditions which caused said damage; and (4) for repair

---

Sample Residential Lease with Option to Purchase (continued)

---

of plumbing and other leaks affecting wood members, including repair of leaking stall showers , in accordance with said structural pest control operator's report.

Owner shall not be responsible for any work recommended to correct conditions usually deemed likely to lead to infestation or infection of wood-destroying pests or organisms, but where no evidence of active infestation is found with respect to such conditions.

If the inspecting structural pest control operator shall recommend further inspection of inaccessible areas, Tenant may require that said areas be inspected. If any infestation or infection shall be discovered by such inspection, the additional required work shall be paid by Owner. If no such infestation or infection is discovered, the additional cost of inspection of such inaccessible areas shall be paid by Tenant.

As soon as the same are available, copies of the report and any certification or other proof of completion of the work shall be delivered to the agents of Tenant and Owner who are authorized to receive the same on behalf of their principals.

Funds for work to be done at Owner's expense shall be held in escrow and disbursed by escrow holder to a licensed structural pest control operator upon receipt of Notice of Work Completed, certifying that the property is free of infestation or infection.

22. **Option:** So long as Tenant is not in substantial default in the performance of any term of this lease, Tenant shall have the option to purchase the real property described herein for a **Purchase Price** of $_____ (_____ dollars), upon the following **Terms and Conditions:** _____

_____

_____

_____

_____.

23. **Disclaimer:** The parties acknowledge that speculation of availability of financing, purchase costs and lender's prepayment penalties is impossible. Therefore, the parties agree that these items shall not be conditions of performance of this agreement and the parties agree they have not relied upon any other representations or warranties by brokers, sellers or other parties.

24. **Fixtures:** All improvements, fixtures, attached floor coverings, draperies

---

Sample Residential Lease with Option to Purchase (continued)

including hardware, shades, blinds, window and door screens, storm sashes, combination doors, awnings, outdoor plants, potted or otherwise, trees, and items permanently attached to the real property shall be included, free of liens, unless specifically excluded.

25. **Personal Property:** The following personal property, on the premises when inspected by Tenant, shall be included in the purchase price and shall be transferred by a Warranty Bill of Sale at close of escrow.

26. **Encumbrances:** In addition to any encumbrances referred to above, Tenant shall take title to the property subject to (1) real estate taxes not yet due and (2) covenants, conditions, restrictions, reservations, rights, rights of way and easements of record, if any, that do not materially affect the value or intended use of the property.

The amount of any bond or assessment which is a lien shall be _____ paid, _____ assumed by _____.

27. **Examination of Title:** Fifteen (15) days from date of exercise of this option are allowed the Tenant to examine the title to the property and to report in writing any valid objections thereto. Any exceptions to the title which would be disclosed by examination of the records shall be deemed to have been accepted unless reported in writing within said 15 days. If Tenant objects to any exceptions to the title, Owner shall use all due diligence to remove such exceptions at his own expense within 60 days thereafter. But if such exceptions cannot be removed within 60 days allowed, all rights and obligations hereunder may, at the election of Tenant, terminate and end, unless he/she elects to purchase the property subject to such exceptions.

28. **Evidence of Title:** Evidence of Title shall be in the form of _____ a policy of _____ title insurance, _____ other: _____ _____, be paid for by _____.

29. **Closing Costs:** Escrow fees, if any, and other closing costs shall be paid in accordance with local custom, except as otherwise provided herein.

30. **Close of Escrow:** Within _____ days from exercise of the option, or upon removal of any exceptions to the title by Owner, as provided above, whichever is later, both parties shall deposit with an authorized escrow holder, to be selected by Tenant, all funds and instruments necessary to complete the sale in accordance with the terms and conditions hereof. The representa-

---

Sample Residential Lease with Option to Purchase (continued)

---

tions and warranties herein shall not be terminated by conveyance of the property.

31. **Prorations:** Rent taxes, premiums on insurance acceptable to Tenant, interest and other expenses of the property are to be prorated as of recordation of deed. Security deposits, advance rentals or considerations involving future lease credits shall be credited to Tenant.

32. **Expiration of Option:** This option may be exercised at any time after _____, 19____, and shall expire at midnight, _____,19____, unless exercised prior thereto. Upon expiration Owner shall be released from all obligations hereunder and all of Tenant's rights hereunder, legal or equitable, shall cease.

33. **Exercise of Option:** The option shall be exercised by mailing or delivering written notice to Owner prior to the expiration of this option and by an additional payment, on account of the purchase price, in the amount of $_____ (_____ dollars) for account of Owner to the authorized escrow holder referred to above, prior to the expiration of this option.

Notice, if mailed, shall be by certified mail, postage prepaid, to Owner at the address set forth below, and shall be deemed to have been given upon the day following the day shown on the postmark of the envelope in which such notice is mailed.

In the event the option is exercised, the consideration paid for the option and _____ percent from the rent paid hereunder prior to the exercise of the option shall be credited upon the purchase price.

The undersigned Tenant hereby acknowledges receipt of a copy hereof.

Dated: _____ Time: _____

_____ Tenant's Broker

By: _____ Agent

Broker's Initials _____ Dated: _____

_____ Address and Phone

_____ Name of Tenant

_____ Signature of Tenant

_____ Address and Phone

Sample Residential Lease with Option to Purchase (continued)

Acceptance

The undersigned Owner accepts the foregoing offer.

Brokerage Fee. Upon execution hereof the Owner agrees to pay to _____ , the Agent in this transaction, _____ percent of the option consideration for securing said option plus the sum of $_____ (_____ dollars) for securing said option plus the sum of $_____ (_____ dollars) for leasing services rendered and authorizes Agent to deduct said sum from deposit received from Tenant. In the event the option is exercised, the Owner agrees to pay Agent the additional sum of $_____ (_____ dollars). This agreement shall not limit the rights of Agent provided for in any listing or other agreement which may be in effect between Owner and Agent. In the event legal action is instituted to collect this fee, or any portion thereof, the Owner agrees to pay the Agent a reasonable attorney's fee and all costs in connection with such action.

The undersigned Owner hereby acknowledges receipt of a copy hereof.

Dated: _____ Time: _____

_____ Owner's Broker

By: _____ Agent

_____ Name of Owner

_____ Signature of Owner

[Adapted from Professional Publishing Corp. Form 105. Used with permission.]

AMORTIZATION SCHEDULE

9.00%
MONTHLY

PAYMENT REQUIRED TO AMORTIZE A LOAN

TERM AMOUNT	1 year	2 years	3 years	4 years	5 years	6 years	7 years	8 years	9 years	10 years	11 years	12 years
50	4.38	2.29	1.59	1.25	1.04	.91	.81	.74	.68	.64	.60	.57
100	8.75	4.57	3.18	2.49	2.08	1.81	1.61	1.47	1.36	1.27	1.20	1.14
200	17.50	9.14	6.36	4.98	4.16	3.61	3.22	2.94	2.71	2.54	2.40	2.28
300	26.24	13.71	9.54	7.47	6.23	5.41	4.83	4.40	4.07	3.81	3.59	3.42
400	34.99	18.28	12.72	9.96	8.31	7.22	6.44	5.87	5.42	5.07	4.79	4.56
500	43.73	22.85	15.90	12.45	10.38	9.02	8.05	7.33	6.78	6.34	5.99	5.70
600	52.48	27.42	19.08	14.94	12.46	10.82	9.66	8.80	8.13	7.61	7.18	6.83
700	61.22	31.98	22.26	17.42	14.54	12.62	11.27	10.26	9.49	8.87	8.38	7.97
800	69.97	36.55	25.44	19.91	16.61	14.43	12.88	11.73	10.84	10.14	9.57	9.11
900	78.71	41.12	28.62	22.40	18.69	16.23	14.49	13.19	12.19	11.41	10.77	10.25
1000	87.46	45.69	31.80	24.89	20.76	18.03	16.09	14.66	13.55	12.67	11.97	11.39
2000	174.91	91.37	63.60	49.78	41.52	36.06	32.18	29.31	27.09	25.34	23.93	22.77
3000	262.36	137.06	95.40	74.66	62.28	54.08	48.27	43.96	40.63	38.01	35.89	34.15
4000	349.81	182.74	127.20	99.55	83.04	72.11	64.36	58.61	54.18	50.68	47.85	45.53
5000	437.26	228.43	159.00	124.43	103.80	90.13	80.45	73.26	67.72	63.34	59.81	56.91
6000	524.71	274.11	190.80	149.32	124.56	108.16	96.54	87.91	81.26	76.01	71.77	68.29
7000	612.17	319.80	222.60	174.20	145.31	126.18	112.63	102.56	94.81	88.68	83.73	79.67
8000	699.62	365.48	254.40	199.09	166.07	144.21	128.72	117.21	108.35	101.35	95.69	91.05
9000	787.07	411.17	286.20	223.97	186.83	162.23	144.81	131.86	121.89	114.01	107.65	102.43
10000	874.52	456.85	318.00	248.86	207.59	180.26	160.90	146.51	135.43	126.68	119.61	113.81
11000	961.97	502.54	349.80	273.74	228.35	198.29	176.98	161.16	148.98	139.35	131.57	125.19
12000	1049.42	548.22	381.60	298.63	249.11	216.31	193.07	175.81	162.52	152.02	143.53	136.57
13000	1136.87	593.91	413.40	323.51	269.86	234.34	209.16	190.46	176.06	164.68	155.50	147.95
14000	1224.33	639.59	445.20	348.40	290.62	252.36	225.25	205.11	189.61	177.35	167.46	159.33
15000	1311.78	685.28	477.00	373.28	311.38	270.39	241.34	219.76	203.15	190.02	179.42	170.71
16000	1399.23	730.96	508.80	398.17	332.14	288.41	257.43	234.41	216.69	202.69	191.38	182.09
17000	1486.68	776.65	540.60	423.05	352.90	306.44	273.52	249.06	230.23	215.35	203.34	193.47
18000	1574.13	822.33	572.40	447.94	373.66	324.46	289.61	263.71	243.78	228.02	215.30	204.85
19000	1661.58	868.02	604.20	472.82	394.41	342.49	305.70	278.36	257.32	240.69	227.26	216.23
20000	1749.03	913.70	636.00	497.71	415.17	360.52	321.79	293.01	270.86	253.36	239.22	227.61
21000	1836.49	959.38	667.80	522.59	435.93	378.54	337.88	307.66	284.41	266.02	251.18	238.99
22000	1923.94	1005.07	699.60	547.48	456.69	396.57	353.96	322.31	297.95	278.69	263.14	250.37
23000	2011.39	1050.75	731.40	572.36	477.45	414.59	370.05	336.96	311.49	291.36	275.10	261.75
24000	2098.84	1096.44	763.20	597.25	498.21	432.62	386.14	351.61	325.03	304.03	287.06	273.13
25000	2186.29	1142.12	795.00	622.13	518.96	450.64	402.23	366.26	338.58	316.69	299.03	284.51
26000	2273.74	1187.81	826.80	647.02	539.72	468.67	418.32	380.91	352.12	329.36	310.99	295.89
27000	2361.19	1233.49	858.60	671.90	560.48	486.69	434.41	395.56	365.66	342.03	322.95	307.27
28000	2448.65	1279.18	890.40	696.79	581.24	504.72	450.50	410.21	379.21	354.70	334.91	318.65
29000	2536.10	1324.86	922.20	721.67	602.00	522.75	466.59	424.86	392.75	367.36	346.87	330.03
30000	2623.55	1370.55	954.00	746.56	622.76	540.77	482.68	439.51	406.29	380.03	358.83	341.41
31000	2711.00	1416.23	985.80	771.44	643.51	558.80	498.77	454.16	419.84	392.70	370.79	352.79
32000	2798.45	1461.92	1017.60	796.33	664.27	576.82	514.86	468.81	433.38	405.37	382.75	364.17
33000	2885.90	1507.60	1049.40	821.21	685.03	594.85	530.94	483.46	446.92	418.04	394.71	375.56
34000	2973.36	1553.29	1081.20	846.10	705.79	612.87	547.03	498.11	460.46	430.70	406.67	386.94
35000	3060.81	1598.97	1113.00	870.98	726.55	630.90	563.12	512.76	474.01	443.37	418.63	398.32
36000	3148.26	1644.66	1144.80	895.87	747.31	648.92	579.21	527.41	487.55	456.04	430.59	409.70
37000	3235.71	1690.34	1176.60	920.75	768.06	666.95	595.30	542.06	501.09	468.71	442.55	421.08
38000	3323.16	1736.03	1208.39	945.64	788.82	684.98	611.39	556.71	514.64	481.37	454.52	432.46
39000	3410.61	1781.71	1240.19	970.52	809.58	703.00	627.48	571.36	528.18	494.04	466.48	443.84
40000	3498.06	1827.39	1271.99	995.41	830.34	721.03	643.57	586.01	541.72	506.71	478.44	455.22
41000	3585.52	1873.08	1303.79	1020.29	851.10	739.05	659.66	600.66	555.26	519.38	490.40	466.60
42000	3672.97	1918.76	1335.59	1045.18	871.86	757.08	675.75	615.31	568.81	532.04	502.36	477.98
43000	3760.42	1964.45	1367.39	1070.06	892.61	775.10	691.84	629.96	582.35	544.71	514.32	489.36
44000	3847.87	2010.13	1399.19	1094.95	913.37	793.13	707.92	644.61	595.89	557.38	526.28	500.74
45000	3935.32	2055.82	1430.99	1119.83	934.13	811.15	724.01	659.26	609.44	570.05	538.24	512.12
46000	4022.77	2101.50	1462.79	1144.72	954.89	829.18	740.10	673.91	622.98	582.71	550.20	523.50
47000	4110.22	2147.19	1494.59	1169.60	975.65	847.21	756.19	688.56	636.52	595.38	562.16	534.88
48000	4197.68	2192.87	1526.39	1194.49	996.41	865.23	772.28	703.21	650.06	608.05	574.12	546.26
49000	4285.13	2238.56	1558.19	1219.37	1017.16	883.26	788.37	717.86	663.61	620.72	586.08	557.64
50000	4372.58	2284.24	1589.99	1244.26	1037.92	901.28	804.46	732.52	677.15	633.38	598.05	569.02
55000	4809.84	2512.67	1748.99	1368.68	1141.71	991.41	884.90	805.77	744.86	696.72	657.85	625.92
60000	5247.09	2741.09	1907.99	1493.11	1245.51	1081.54	965.35	879.02	812.58	760.06	717.65	682.82
65000	5684.35	2969.51	2066.99	1617.53	1349.30	1171.66	1045.80	952.27	880.29	823.40	777.46	739.72
70000	6121.61	3197.94	2225.99	1741.96	1453.09	1261.79	1126.24	1025.52	948.01	886.74	837.26	796.63
75000	6558.87	3426.36	2384.98	1866.38	1556.88	1351.92	1206.69	1098.77	1015.72	950.07	897.07	853.53
80000	6996.12	3654.78	2543.98	1990.81	1660.67	1442.05	1287.13	1172.02	1083.44	1013.41	956.87	910.43
85000	7433.38	3883.21	2702.98	2115.23	1764.47	1532.18	1367.58	1245.27	1151.15	1076.75	1016.67	967.33
90000	7870.64	4111.63	2861.98	2239.66	1868.26	1622.30	1448.02	1318.52	1218.87	1140.09	1076.48	1024.23
95000	8307.90	4340.06	3020.98	2364.08	1972.05	1712.43	1528.47	1391.77	1286.58	1203.42	1136.28	1081.13
100000	8745.15	4568.48	3179.98	2488.51	2075.84	1802.56	1608.91	1465.03	1354.30	1266.76	1196.09	1138.04

MONTHLY 9.00%

PAYMENT REQUIRED TO AMORTIZE A LOAN

TERM AMOUNT	13 year	14 years	15 years	16 years	17 years	18 years	19 years	20 years	25 years	30 years	35 years	40 years
50	.55	.53	.51	.50	.48	.47	.46	.45	.42	.41	.40	.39
100	1.09	1.05	1.02	.99	.96	.94	.92	.90	.84	.81	.79	.78
200	2.18	2.10	2.03	1.97	1.92	1.88	1.84	1.80	1.68	1.61	1.57	1.55
300	3.27	3.15	3.05	2.96	2.88	2.81	2.76	2.70	2.52	2.42	2.36	2.32
400	4.36	4.20	4.06	3.94	3.84	3.75	3.67	3.60	3.36	3.22	3.14	3.09
500	5.45	5.25	5.08	4.93	4.80	4.69	4.59	4.50	4.20	4.03	3.92	3.86
600	6.54	6.30	6.09	5.91	5.76	5.62	5.51	5.40	5.04	4.83	4.71	4.63
700	7.63	7.35	7.10	6.90	6.72	6.56	6.42	6.30	5.88	5.64	5.49	5.40
800	8.72	8.40	8.12	7.88	7.68	7.50	7.34	7.20	6.72	6.44	6.28	6.18
900	9.81	9.45	9.13	8.87	8.63	8.43	8.26	8.10	7.56	7.25	7.06	6.95
1000	10.90	10.49	10.15	9.85	9.59	9.37	9.17	9.00	8.40	8.05	7.84	7.72
2000	21.80	20.98	20.29	19.70	19.18	18.73	18.34	18.00	16.79	16.10	15.68	15.43
3000	32.70	31.47	30.43	29.54	28.77	28.10	27.51	27.00	25.18	24.14	23.52	23.15
4000	43.59	41.96	40.58	39.39	38.36	37.46	36.68	35.99	33.57	32.19	31.36	30.86
5000	54.49	52.45	50.72	49.23	47.95	46.83	45.85	44.99	41.96	40.24	39.20	38.57
6000	65.39	62.94	60.86	59.08	57.53	56.19	55.02	53.99	50.36	48.28	47.04	46.29
7000	76.28	73.43	71.00	68.92	67.12	65.56	64.19	62.99	58.75	56.33	54.88	54.00
8000	87.18	83.92	81.15	78.77	76.71	74.92	73.36	71.98	67.14	64.37	62.72	61.71
9000	98.08	94.41	91.29	88.61	86.30	84.29	82.53	80.98	75.53	72.42	70.56	69.43
10000	108.97	104.90	101.43	98.46	95.89	93.65	91.69	89.98	83.92	80.47	78.40	77.14
11000	119.87	115.39	111.57	108.30	105.47	103.01	100.86	98.97	92.32	88.51	86.24	84.85
12000	130.77	125.88	121.72	118.15	115.06	112.38	110.03	107.97	100.71	96.56	94.08	92.57
13000	141.66	136.37	131.86	127.99	124.65	121.74	119.20	116.97	109.10	104.61	101.92	100.28
14000	152.56	146.86	142.00	137.84	134.24	131.11	128.37	125.97	117.49	112.65	109.76	108.00
15000	163.46	157.35	152.14	147.68	143.83	140.47	137.54	134.96	125.88	120.70	117.60	115.71
16000	174.35	167.84	162.29	157.53	153.41	149.84	146.71	143.96	134.28	128.74	125.44	123.42
17000	185.25	178.32	172.43	167.37	163.00	159.20	155.88	152.96	142.67	136.79	133.28	131.14
18000	196.15	188.81	182.57	177.22	172.59	168.57	165.05	161.96	151.06	144.84	141.12	138.85
19000	207.04	199.30	192.72	187.06	182.18	177.93	174.22	170.95	159.45	152.88	148.96	146.56
20000	217.94	209.79	202.86	196.91	191.77	187.29	183.38	179.95	167.84	160.93	156.80	154.28
21000	228.84	220.28	213.00	206.75	201.35	196.66	192.55	188.95	176.24	168.98	164.64	161.99
22000	239.73	230.77	223.14	216.60	210.94	206.02	201.72	197.94	184.63	177.02	172.48	169.70
23000	250.63	241.26	233.29	226.44	220.53	215.39	210.89	206.94	193.02	185.07	180.32	177.42
24000	261.53	251.75	243.43	236.29	230.12	224.75	220.06	215.94	201.41	193.11	188.16	185.13
25000	272.43	262.24	253.57	246.13	239.71	234.12	229.23	224.94	209.80	201.16	196.00	192.85
26000	283.32	272.73	263.71	255.98	249.29	243.48	238.40	233.93	218.20	209.21	203.84	200.56
27000	294.22	283.22	273.86	265.82	258.88	252.85	247.57	242.93	226.59	217.25	211.68	208.27
28000	305.12	293.71	284.00	275.67	268.47	262.21	256.74	251.93	234.98	225.30	219.52	215.99
29000	316.01	304.20	294.14	285.51	278.06	271.57	265.91	260.93	243.37	233.35	227.36	223.70
30000	326.91	314.69	304.28	295.36	287.65	280.94	275.07	269.92	251.76	241.39	235.20	231.41
31000	337.81	325.18	314.43	305.20	297.23	290.30	284.24	278.92	260.16	249.44	243.04	239.13
32000	348.70	335.67	324.57	315.05	306.82	299.67	293.41	287.92	268.55	257.48	250.88	246.84
33000	359.60	346.15	334.71	324.90	316.41	309.03	302.58	296.91	276.94	265.53	258.72	254.55
34000	370.50	356.64	344.86	334.74	326.00	318.40	311.75	305.91	285.33	273.58	266.56	262.27
35000	381.39	367.13	355.00	344.59	335.59	327.76	320.92	314.91	293.72	281.62	274.40	269.98
36000	392.29	377.62	365.14	354.43	345.17	337.13	330.09	323.91	302.12	289.67	282.24	277.70
37000	403.19	388.11	375.28	364.28	354.76	346.49	339.26	332.90	310.51	297.72	290.08	285.41
38000	414.08	398.60	385.43	374.12	364.35	355.85	348.43	341.90	318.90	305.76	297.92	293.12
39000	424.98	409.09	395.57	383.97	373.94	365.22	357.59	350.90	327.29	313.81	305.76	300.84
40000	435.88	419.58	405.71	393.81	383.53	374.58	366.76	359.90	335.68	321.85	313.60	308.55
41000	446.77	430.07	415.85	403.66	393.11	383.95	375.93	368.89	344.08	329.90	321.44	316.26
42000	457.67	440.56	426.00	413.50	402.70	393.31	385.10	377.89	352.47	337.95	329.28	323.98
43000	468.57	451.05	436.14	423.35	412.29	402.68	394.27	386.89	360.86	345.99	337.12	331.69
44000	479.46	461.54	446.28	433.19	421.88	412.04	403.44	395.88	369.25	354.04	344.96	339.40
45000	490.36	472.03	456.42	443.04	431.47	421.41	412.61	404.88	377.64	362.09	352.80	347.12
46000	501.26	482.52	466.57	452.88	441.05	430.77	421.78	413.88	386.04	370.13	360.64	354.83
47000	512.15	493.01	476.71	462.73	450.64	440.13	430.95	422.88	394.43	378.18	368.48	362.54
48000	523.05	503.50	486.85	472.57	460.23	449.50	440.12	431.87	402.82	386.22	376.32	370.26
49000	533.95	513.98	497.00	482.42	469.82	458.86	449.28	440.87	411.21	394.27	384.16	377.97
50000	544.85	524.47	507.14	492.26	479.41	468.23	458.45	449.87	419.60	402.32	392.00	385.69
55000	599.33	576.92	557.85	541.49	527.35	515.05	504.30	494.85	461.56	442.55	431.20	424.25
60000	653.81	629.37	608.56	590.71	575.29	561.87	550.14	539.84	503.52	482.78	470.40	462.82
65000	708.30	681.81	659.28	639.94	623.23	608.69	595.99	584.83	545.48	523.01	509.60	501.39
70000	762.78	734.26	709.99	689.17	671.17	655.52	641.83	629.81	587.44	563.24	548.80	539.96
75000	817.27	786.71	760.70	738.39	719.11	702.34	687.68	674.80	629.40	603.47	588.00	578.53
80000	871.75	839.16	811.42	787.62	767.05	749.16	733.52	719.79	671.36	643.70	627.20	617.09
85000	926.23	891.60	862.13	836.84	814.99	795.98	779.37	764.77	713.32	683.93	666.40	655.66
90000	980.72	944.05	912.84	886.07	862.93	842.81	825.21	809.76	755.28	724.17	705.60	694.23
95000	1035.20	996.50	963.56	935.30	910.87	889.63	871.06	854.74	797.24	764.40	744.80	732.80
100000	1089.69	1048.94	1014.27	984.52	958.81	936.45	916.90	899.73	839.20	804.63	784.00	771.37

9.50%

MONTHLY

PAYMENT REQUIRED TO AMORTIZE A LOAN

TERM AMOUNT	1 year	2 years	3 years	4 years	5 years	6 years	7 years	8 years	9 years	10 years	11 years	12 years
50	4.39	2.30	1.61	1.26	1.06	.92	.82	.75	.70	.65	.62	.59
100	8.77	4.60	3.21	2.52	2.11	1.83	1.64	1.50	1.39	1.30	1.23	1.17
200	17.54	9.19	6.41	5.03	4.21	3.66	3.27	2.99	2.77	2.59	2.45	2.34
300	26.31	13.78	9.61	7.54	6.31	5.49	4.91	4.48	4.15	3.89	3.68	3.50
400	35.08	18.37	12.82	10.05	8.41	7.31	6.54	5.97	5.53	5.18	4.90	4.67
500	43.85	22.96	16.02	12.57	10.51	9.14	8 18	7.46	6.91	6.47	6.12	5.84
600	52.62	27.55	19.22	15.08	12.61	10.97	9.81	8.95	8.29	7.77	7.35	7.00
700	61.38	32.15	22.43	17.59	14.71	12.80	11.45	10.44	9.67	9.06	8.57	8.17
800	70.15	36.74	25.63	20.10	16.81	14.62	13.08	11.93	11.05	10.36	9.80	9.34
900	78.92	41.33	28.83	22.62	18.91	16.45	14.71	13.42	12.43	11.65	11.02	10.50
1000	87.69	45.92	32.04	25.13	21.01	18.28	16.35	14.92	13.81	12.94	12.24	11.67
2000	175.37	91.83	64.07	50.25	42.01	36.55	32.69	29.83	27.62	25.88	24.48	23.33
3000	263.04	137.75	96.10	75.37	63.01	54.83	49.04	44.74	41.43	38.82	36.72	35.00
4000	350.74	183.66	128.14	100.50	84.01	73.10	65.38	59.65	55 24	51.76	48.96	46.66
5000	438.42	229.58	160.17	125.62	105.01	91.38	81.72	74.56	69.05	64.70	61.20	58.32
6000	526.11	275.49	192.20	150.74	126.02	109.65	98.07	89.47	82.86	77.64	73.44	69.99
7000	613.79	321.41	224.24	175.87	147.02	127.93	114.41	104.38	96.67	90.58	85.68	81.65
8000	701.47	367.32	256.27	200.99	168.02	146.20	130.76	119.29	110.48	103.52	97.91	93.31
9000	789.16	413.24	288.30	226.11	189.02	164.48	147.10	134.20	124.29	116.46	110.15	104.98
10000	876.84	459.15	320.33	251.24	210.02	182.75	163.44	149.11	138.10	129.40	122.39	116.64
11000	964.52	505.06	352.37	276.36	231.03	201.03	179.79	164.02	151.91	142.34	134.63	128.31
12000	1052.21	550.98	384.40	301.48	252.03	219.30	196.13	178.94	165.72	155.28	146.87	139.97
13000	1139.89	596.89	416.43	326.61	273.03	237.58	212.48	193.85	179.53	168.22	159.11	151.63
14000	1227.57	642.81	448.47	351.73	294.03	255.85	228.82	208.76	193.34	181.16	171.35	163.30
15000	1315.26	688.72	480.50	376.85	315.03	274.13	245.16	223.67	207.15	194.10	183.58	174.96
16000	1402.94	734.64	512.53	401.98	336.03	292.40	261.51	238.58	220.95	207.04	195.82	186.62
17000	1490.62	780.55	544.57	427.10	357.04	310.67	277.85	253.49	234.76	219.98	208.06	198.29
18000	1578.31	826.47	576.60	452.22	378.04	328.95	294.20	268.40	248.57	232.92	220.30	209.95
19000	1665.99	872.38	608.63	477.34	399.04	347.22	310.54	283.31	262.38	245.86	232.54	221.62
20000	1753.68	918.29	640.66	502.47	420.04	365.50	326.88	298.22	276.19	258.80	244.78	233.28
21000	1841.36	964.21	672.70	527.59	441.04	383.77	343.23	313.13	290.00	271.74	257.02	244.94
22000	1929.04	1010.12	704.73	552.71	462.05	402.05	359.57	328.04	303.81	284.68	269.26	256.61
23000	2016.73	1056.04	736.76	577.84	483.05	420.32	375.92	342.96	317.62	297.62	281.49	268.27
24000	2104.41	1101.95	768.80	602.96	504.05	438.60	392.26	357.87	331.43	310.56	293.73	279.93
25000	2192.09	1147.87	800.83	628.08	525.05	456.87	408.60	372.78	345.24	323.50	305.97	291.60
26000	2279.78	1193.78	832.86	653.21	546.05	475.15	424.95	387.69	359.05	336.44	318.21	303.26
27000	2367.46	1239.70	864.89	678.33	567.06	493.42	441.29	402.60	372.86	349.38	330.45	314.93
28000	2455.14	1285.61	896.93	703.45	588.06	511.70	457.64	417.51	386.67	362.32	342.69	326.59
29000	2542.83	1331.53	928.96	728.58	609.06	529.97	473.98	432.42	400.48	375.26	354.93	338.25
30000	2630.51	1377.44	960.99	753.70	630.06	548.25	490.32	447.33	414.29	388.20	367.16	349.92
31000	2718.19	1423.35	993.03	778.82	651.06	566.52	506.67	462.24	428.10	401.14	379.40	361.58
32000	2805.88	1469.27	1025.06	803.95	672.06	584.80	523.01	477.15	441.90	414.08	391.64	373.24
33000	2893.56	1515.18	1057.09	829.07	693.07	603.07	539.36	492.06	455.71	427.02	403.88	384.91
34000	2981.24	1561.10	1089.13	854.19	714.07	621.34	555.70	506.98	469.52	439.96	416.12	396.57
35000	3068.93	1607.01	1121.16	879.31	735.07	639.62	572.04	521.89	483.33	452.90	428.36	408.24
36000	3156.61	1652.93	1153.19	904.44	756.07	657.89	588.39	536.80	497.14	465.84	440.60	419.90
37000	3244.29	1698.84	1185.22	929.56	777.07	676.17	604.73	551.71	510.95	478.78	452.83	431.56
38000	3331.98	1744.76	1217.26	954.68	798.08	694.44	621.08	566.62	524.76	491.72	465.07	443.23
39000	3419.66	1790.67	1249.29	979.81	819.08	712.72	637.42	581.53	538.57	504.66	477.31	454.89
40000	3507.35	1836.58	1281.32	1004.93	840.08	730.99	653.76	596.44	552.38	517.60	489.55	466.55
41000	3595.03	1882.50	1313.36	1030.05	861.08	749.27	670.11	611.35	566.19	530.53	501.79	478.22
42000	3682.71	1928.41	1345.39	1055.18	882.08	767.54	686.45	626.26	580.00	543.47	514.03	489.88
43000	3770.40	1974.33	1377.42	1080.30	903.09	785.82	702.80	641.17	593.81	556.41	526.27	501.55
44000	3858.08	2020.24	1409.45	1105.42	924.09	804.09	719.14	656.08	607.62	569.35	538.51	513.21
45000	3945.76	2066.16	1441.49	1130.55	945.09	822.37	735.48	670.99	621.43	582.29	550.74	524.87
46000	4033.45	2112.07	1473.52	1155.67	966.09	840.64	751.83	685.91	635.24	595.23	562.98	536.54
47000	4121.13	2157.99	1505.55	1180.79	987.09	858.92	768.17	700.82	649.04	608.17	575.22	548.20
48000	4208.81	2203.90	1537.59	1205.92	1008.09	877.19	784.52	715.73	662.85	621.11	587.46	559.86
49000	4296.50	2249.82	1569.62	1231.04	1029.10	895.46	800.86	730.64	676.66	634.05	599.70	571.53
50000	4384.18	2295.73	1601.65	1256.16	1050.10	913.74	817.20	745.55	690.47	646.99	611.94	583.19
55000	4822.60	2525.30	1761.82	1381.78	1155.11	1005.11	898.92	820.10	759.52	711.69	673.13	641.51
60000	5261.02	2754.87	1921.98	1507.39	1260.12	1096.49	980.64	894.66	828.57	776.39	734.32	699.83
65000	5699.43	2984.45	2082.15	1633.01	1365.13	1187.86	1062.36	969.21	897.61	841.09	795.52	758.15
70000	6137.85	3214.02	2242.31	1758.62	1470.14	1279.23	1144.08	1043.77	966.66	905.79	856.71	816.47
75000	6576.27	3443.59	2402.48	1884.24	1575.14	1370.61	1225.80	1118.32	1035.71	970.49	917.90	874.78
80000	7014.69	3673.16	2562.64	2009.86	1680.15	1461.98	1307.52	1192.88	1104.75	1035.19	979.10	933.10
85000	7453.10	3902.74	2722.81	2135.47	1785.16	1553.35	1389.24	1267.43	1173.80	1099.88	1040.29	991.42
90000	7891.52	4132.31	2882.97	2261.09	1890.17	1644.73	1470.96	1341.98	1242.85	1164.58	1101.48	1049.74
95000	8329.94	4361.88	3043.14	2386.70	1995.18	1736.10	1552.68	1416.54	1311.89	1229.28	1162.68	1108.06
100000	8768.36	4591.45	3203.30	2512.32	2100.19	1827.47	1634.40	1491.09	1380.94	1293.98	1223.87	1166.38

MONTHLY 9.50%

PAYMENT REQUIRED TO AMORTIZE A LOAN

TERM AMOUNT	13 year	14 years	15 years	16 years	17 years	18 years	19 years	20 years	25 years	30 years	35 years	40 years
50	.56	.54	.53	.51	.50	.49	.48	.47	.44	.43	.42	.41
100	1.12	1.08	1.05	1.02	.99	.97	.95	.94	.88	.85	.83	.82
200	2.24	2.16	2.09	2.03	1.98	1.94	1.90	1.87	1.75	1.69	1.65	1.63
300	3.36	3.24	3.14	3.05	2.97	2.91	2.85	2.80	2.63	2.53	2.47	2.44
400	4.48	4.32	4.18	4.06	3.96	3.88	3.80	3.73	3.50	3.37	3.29	3.25
500	5.60	5.40	5.23	5.08	4.95	4.84	4.75	4.67	4.37	4.21	4.11	4.06
600	6.72	6.48	6.27	6.09	5.94	5.81	5.70	5.60	5.25	5.05	4.93	4.87
700	7.84	7.55	7.31	7.11	6.93	6.78	6.65	6.53	6.12	5.89	5.76	5.68
800	8.95	8.63	8.36	8.12	7.92	7.75	7.60	7.46	6.99	6.73	6.58	6.49
900	10.07	9.71	9.40	9.14	8.91	8.72	8.54	8.39	7.87	7.57	7.40	7.30
1000	11.19	10.79	10.45	10.15	9.90	9.68	9.49	9.33	8.74	8.41	8.22	8.11
2000	22.38	21.57	20.89	20.30	19.80	19.36	18.98	18.65	17.48	16.82	16.44	16.21
3000	33.56	32.36	31.33	30.45	29.70	29.04	28.47	27.97	26.22	25.23	24.65	24.31
4000	44.75	43..*	41.77	40.60	39.60	38.72	37.96	37.29	34.95	33.64	32.87	32.41
5000	55.93	53.92	52.22	50.75	49.49	48.40	47.45	46.61	43.69	42.05	41.09	40.51
6000	67.12	64.71	62.66	60.90	59.39	58.08	56.94	55.93	52.43	50.46	49.30	48.61
7000	78.31	75.49	73.10	71.05	69.29	67.76	66.42	65.25	61.16	58.86	57.52	56.71
8000	89.49	86.27	83.54	81.20	79.19	77.44	75.91	74.58	69.90	67.27	65.73	64.81
9000	100.68	97.06	93.99	91.35	89.09	87.12	85.40	83.90	78.64	75.68	73.95	72.91
10000	111.86	107.84	104.43	101.50	98.98	96.80	94.89	93.22	87.37	84.09	82.17	81.01
11000	123.05	118.63	114.87	111.65	108.88	106.48	104.38	102.54	96.11	92.50	90.38	89.11
12000	134.23	129.41	125.31	121.80	118.78	116.15	113.87	111.86	104.85	100.91	98.60	97.21
13000	145.42	140.19	135.75	131.95	128.68	125.83	123.35	121.18	113.59	109.32	106.81	105.31
14000	156.61	150.98	146.20	142.10	138.57	135.51	132.84	130.50	122.32	117.72	115.03	113.41
15000	167.79	161.76	156.64	152.25	148.47	145.19	142.33	139.82	131.06	126.13	123.25	121.51
16000	178.98	172.54	167.08	162.40	158.37	154.87	151.82	149.15	139.80	134.54	131.46	129.61
17000	190.16	183.33	177.52	172.55	168.27	164.55	161.31	158.47	148.53	142.95	139.68	137.72
18000	201.35	194.11	187.97	182.70	178.17	174.23	170.80	167.79	157.27	151.36	147.90	145.82
19000	212.53	204.89	198.41	192.85	188.06	183.91	180.28	177.11	166.01	159.77	156.11	153.92
20000	223.72	215.68	208.85	203.00	197.96	193.59	189.77	186.43	174.74	168.18	164.33	162.02
21000	234.91	226.46	219.29	213.15	207.86	203.27	199.26	195.75	183.48	176.58	172.54	170.12
22000	246.09	237.25	229.73	223.30	217.76	212.95	208.75	205.07	192.22	184.99	180.76	178.22
23000	257.28	248.03	240.18	233.45	227.65	222.62	218.24	214.40	200.96	193.40	188.98	186.32
24000	268.46	258.81	250.62	243.60	237.55	232.30	227.73	223.72	209.69	201.81	197.19	194.42
25000	279.65	269.60	261.06	253.75	247.45	241.98	237.21	233.04	218.43	210.22	205.41	202.52
26000	290.83	280.38	271.50	263.90	257.35	251.66	246.70	242.36	227.17	218.63	213.62	210.62
27000	302.02	291.16	281.95	274.05	267.25	261.34	256.19	251.68	235.90	227.04	221.84	218.72
28000	313.21	301.95	292.39	284.20	277.14	271.02	265.68	261.00	244.64	235.44	230.06	226.82
29000	324.39	312.73	302.83	294.35	287.04	280.70	275.17	270.32	253.38	243.85	238.27	234.92
30000	335.58	323.52	313.27	304.50	296.94	290.38	284.66	279.64	262.11	252.26	246.49	243.02
31000	346.76	334.30	323.71	314.65	306.84	300.06	294.15	288.97	270.85	260.67	254.70	251.12
32000	357.95	345.08	334.16	324.80	316.73	309.74	303.63	298.29	279.59	269.08	262.92	259.22
33000	369.13	355.87	344.60	334.95	326.63	319.42	313.12	307.61	288.32	277.49	271.14	267.33
34000	380.32	366.65	355.04	345.10	336.53	329.09	322.61	316.93	297.06	285.90	279.35	275.43
35000	391.51	377.43	365.48	355.25	346.43	338.77	332.10	326.25	305.80	294.30	287.57	283.53
36000	402.69	388.22	375.93	365.40	356.33	348.45	341.59	335.57	314.54	302.71	295.79	291.63
37000	413.88	399.00	386.37	375.55	366.22	358.13	351.08	344.89	323.27	311.12	304.00	299.73
38000	425.06	409.78	396.81	385.70	376.12	367.81	360.56	354.21	332.01	319.53	312.22	307.83
39000	436.25	420.57	407.25	395.85	386.02	377.49	370.05	363.54	340.75	327.94	320.43	315.93
40000	447.43	431.35	417.69	406.00	395.92	387.17	379.54	372.86	349.48	336.35	328.65	324.03
41000	458.62	442.14	428.14	416.15	405.82	396.85	389.03	382.18	358.22	344.76	336.87	332.13
42000	469.81	452.92	438.58	426.30	415.71	406.53	398.52	391.50	366.96	353.16	345.08	340.23
43000	480.99	463.70	449.02	436.45	425.61	416.21	408.01	400.82	375.69	361.57	353.30	348.33
44000	492.18	474.49	459.46	446.60	435.51	425.89	417.49	410.14	384.43	369.98	361.51	356.43
45000	503.36	485.27	469.91	456.75	445.41	435.57	426.98	419.46	393.17	378.39	369.73	364.53
46000	514.55	496.05	480.35	466.90	455.30	445.24	436.47	428.79	401.91	386.80	377.95	372.63
47000	525.73	506.84	490.79	477.05	465.20	454.92	445.96	438.11	410.64	395.21	386.16	380.73
48000	536.92	517.62	501.23	487.20	475.10	464.60	455.45	447.43	419.38	403.62	394.38	388.83
49000	548.11	528.41	511.68	497.35	485.00	474.28	464.94	456.75	428.12	412.02	402.59	396.94
50000	559.29	539.19	522.12	507.50	494.90	483.96	474.42	466.07	436.85	420.43	410.81	405.04
55000	615.22	593.11	574.33	558.25	544.38	532.36	521.87	512.68	480.54	462.47	451.89	445.54
60000	671.15	647.03	626.54	609.00	593.87	580.75	569.31	559.28	524.22	504.52	492.97	486.04
65000	727.08	700.94	678.75	659.75	643.36	629.15	616.75	605.89	567.91	546.56	534.05	526.55
70000	783.01	754.86	730.96	710.50	692.85	677.54	664.19	652.50	611.59	588.60	575.13	567.05
75000	838.93	808.78	783.17	761.25	742.34	725.94	711.63	699.10	655.28	630.65	616.21	607.55
80000	894.86	862.70	835.38	812.00	791.83	774.33	759.08	745.71	698.96	672.69	657.29	648.05
85000	950.79	916.62	887.60	862.75	841.32	822.73	806.52	792.32	742.65	714.73	698.37	688.56
90000	1006.72	970.54	939.81	913.50	890.81	871.13	853.96	838.92	786.33	756.77	739.46	729.06
95000	1062.65	1024.45	992.02	964.25	940.30	919.52	901.40	885.53	830.02	798.82	780.54	769.56
100000	1118.58	1078.37	1044.23	1014.99	989.79	967.92	948.84	932.14	873.70	840.86	821.62	810.07

10.00%

MONTHLY

PAYMENT REQUIRED TO AMORTIZE A LOAN

TERM AMOUNT	1 year	2 years	3 years	4 years	5 years	6 years	7 years	8 years	9 years	10 years	11 years	12 years
50	4.40	2.31	1.62	1.27	1.07	.93	.84	.76	.71	.67	63	.60
100	8.80	4.62	3.23	2.54	2.13	1.86	1.67	1.52	1.41	1.33	1.26	1.20
200	17.59	9.23	6.46	5.08	4.25	3.71	3.33	3.04	2.82	2.65	2.51	2.40
300	26.38	13.85	9.69	7.61	6.38	5.56	4.99	4.56	4.23	3.97	3.76	3.59
400	35.17	18.46	12.91	10.15	8.50	7.42	6.65	6.07	5.64	5.29	5.01	4.79
500	43.96	23.08	16.14	12.69	10.63	9.27	8.31	7.59	7.04	6.61	6.26	5.98
600	52.75	27.69	19.37	15.22	12.75	11.12	9.97	9.11	8.45	7.93	7.52	7.18
700	61.55	32.31	22.59	17.76	14.88	12.97	11.63	10.63	9.86	9.26	8.77	8.37
800	70.34	36.92	25.82	20.30	17.00	14.83	13.29	12.14	11.27	10.58	10.02	9.57
900	79.13	41.54	29.05	22.83	19.13	16.68	14.95	13.66	12.68	11.90	11.27	10.76
1000	87.92	46.15	32.27	25.37	21.25	18.53	16.61	15.18	14.08	13.22	12.52	11.96
2000	175.84	92.29	64.54	50.73	42.50	37.06	33.21	30.35	28.16	26.44	25.04	23.91
3000	263.75	138.44	96.81	76.09	63.75	55.58	49.81	45.53	42.24	39.65	37.56	35.86
4000	351.67	184.58	129.07	101.46	84.99	74.11	66.41	60.70	56.32	52.87	50.08	47.81
5000	439.58	230.73	161.34	126.82	106.24	92.63	83.01	75.88	70.40	66.08	62.60	59.76
6000	527.50	276.87	193.61	152.18	127.49	111.16	99.61	91.05	84.48	79.30	75.12	71.71
7000	615.42	323.02	225.88	177.54	148.73	129.69	116.21	106.22	98.56	92.51	87.64	83.66
8000	703.33	369.16	258.14	202.91	169.98	148.21	132.81	121.40	112.63	105.73	100.16	95.61
9000	791.25	415.31	290.41	228.27	191.23	166.74	149.42	136.57	126.71	118.94	112.68	107.56
10000	879.16	461.45	322.68	253.63	212.48	185.26	166.02	151.75	140.79	132.16	125.20	119.51
11000	967.08	507.60	354.94	278.99	233.72	203.79	182.62	166.92	154.87	145.37	137.72	131.46
12000	1055.00	553.74	387.21	304.36	254.97	222.32	199.22	182.09	168.95	158.59	150.24	143.41
13000	1142.91	599.89	419.48	329.72	276.22	240.84	215.82	197.27	183.03	171.80	162.76	155.37
14000	1230.83	646.03	451.75	355.08	297.46	259.37	232.42	212.44	197.11	185.02	175.28	167.32
15000	1318.74	692.18	484.01	380.44	318.71	277.89	249.02	227.62	211.19	198.23	187.80	179.27
16000	1406.66	738.32	516.28	405.81	339.96	296.42	265.62	242.79	225.26	211.45	200.32	191.22
17000	1494.58	784.47	548.55	431.17	361.20	314.94	282.23	257.97	239.34	224.66	212.84	203.17
18000	1582.49	830.61	580.81	456.53	382.45	333.47	298.83	273.14	253.42	237.88	225.36	215.12
19000	1670.41	876.76	613.08	481.89	403.70	352.00	315.43	288.31	267.50	251.09	237.88	227.07
20000	1758.32	922.90	645.35	507.26	424.95	370.52	332.03	303.49	281.58	264.31	250.40	239.02
21000	1846.24	969.05	677.62	532.62	446.19	389.05	348.63	318.66	295.66	277.52	262.92	250.97
22000	1934.15	1015.19	709.88	557.98	467.44	407.57	365.23	333.84	309.74	290.74	275.44	262.92
23000	2022.07	1061.34	742.15	583.34	488.69	426.10	381.83	349.01	323.81	303.95	287.96	274.87
24000	2109.99	1107.48	774.42	608.71	509.93	444.63	398.43	364.18	337.89	317.17	300.48	286.82
25000	2197.90	1153.63	806.68	634.07	531.18	463.15	415.03	379.36	351.97	330.38	313.00	298.77
26000	2285.82	1199.77	838.95	659.43	552.43	481.68	431.64	394.53	366.05	343.60	325.52	310.73
27000	2373.73	1245.92	871.22	684.79	573.68	500.20	448.24	409.71	380.13	356.81	338.04	322.68
28000	2461.65	1292.06	903.49	710.16	594.92	518.73	464.84	424.88	394.21	370.03	350.56	334.63
29000	2549.57	1338.21	935.75	735.52	616.17	537.25	481.44	440.06	408.29	383.24	363.08	346.58
30000	2637.48	1384.35	968.02	760.88	637.42	555.78	498.04	455.23	422.37	396.46	375.60	358.53
31000	2725.40	1430.50	1000.29	786.25	658.66	574.31	514.64	470.40	436.44	409.67	388.12	370.48
32000	2813.31	1476.64	1032.56	811.61	679.91	592.83	531.24	485.58	450.52	422.89	400.64	382.43
33000	2901.23	1522.79	1064.82	836.97	701.16	611.36	547.84	500.75	464.60	436.10	413.16	394.38
34000	2989.15	1568.93	1097.09	862.33	722.40	629.88	564.45	515.93	478.68	449.32	425.68	406.33
35000	3077.06	1615.08	1129.36	887.70	743.65	648.41	581.05	531.10	492.76	462.53	438.20	418.28
36000	3164.98	1661.22	1161.62	913.06	764.90	666.94	597.65	546.27	506.84	475.75	450.72	430.23
37000	3252.89	1707.37	1193.89	938.42	786.15	685.46	614.25	561.45	520.92	488.96	463.24	442.18
38000	3340.81	1753.51	1226.16	963.78	807.39	703.99	630.85	576.62	535.00	502.18	475.76	454.13
39000	3428.72	1799.66	1258.43	989.15	828.64	722.51	647.45	591.80	549.07	515.39	488.28	466.09
40000	3516.64	1845.80	1290.69	1014.51	849.89	741.04	664.05	606.97	563.15	528.61	500.80	478.04
41000	3604.56	1891.95	1322.96	1039.87	871.13	759.56	680.65	622.15	577.23	541.82	513.32	489.99
42000	3692.47	1938.09	1355.23	1065.23	892.38	778.09	697.25	637.32	591.31	555.04	525.84	-501.94
43000	3780.39	1984.24	1387.49	1090.60	913.63	796.62	713.86	652.49	605.39	568.25	538.36	513.89
44000	3868.30	2030.38	1419.76	1115.96	934.87	815.14	730.46	667.67	619.47	581.47	550.88	525.84
45000	3956.22	2076.53	1452.03	1141.32	956.12	833.67	747.06	682.84	633.55	594.68	563.40	537.79
46000	4044.14	2122.67	1484.30	1166.68	977.37	852.19	763.66	698.02	647.62	607.90	575.92	549.74
47000	4132.05	2168.82	1516.56	1192.05	998.62	870.72	780.26	713.19	661.70	621.11	588.44	561.69
48000	4219.97	2214.96	1548.83	1217.41	1019.86	889.25	796.86	728.36	675.78	634.33	600.96	573.64
49000	4307.88	2261.11	1581.10	1242.77	1041.11	907.77	813.46	743.54	689.86	647.54	613.48	585.59
50000	4395.80	2307.25	1613.36	1268.13	1062.36	926.30	830.06	758.71	703.94	660.76	626.00	597.54
55000	4835.38	2537.98	1774.70	1394.95	1168.59	1018.93	913.07	834.58	774.33	726.83	688.60	657.30
60000	5274.96	2768.70	1936.04	1521.76	1274.83	1111.56	996.08	910.45	844.73	792.91	751.20	717.05
65000	5714.54	2999.43	2097.37	1648.57	1381.06	1204.18	1079.08	986.33	915.12	858.98	813.80	776.81
70000	6154.12	3230.15	2258.71	1775.39	1487.30	1296.81	1162.09	1062.20	985.51	925.06	876.40	836.56
75000	6593.70	3460.87	2420.04	1902.20	1593.53	1389.44	1245.09	1138.07	1055.91	991.14	939.00	896.31
80000	7033.28	3691.60	2581.38	2029.01	1699.77	1482.07	1328.10	1213.94	1126.30	1057.21	1001.60	956.07
85000	7472.86	3922.32	2742.72	2155.82	1806.00	1574.70	1411.11	1289.81	1196.69	1123.29	1064.19	1015.82
90000	7912.43	4153.05	2904.05	2282.64	1912.24	1667.33	1494.11	1365.68	1267.09	1189.36	1126.79	1075.58
95000	8352.01	4383.77	3065.39	2409.45	2018.47	1759.96	1577.12	1441.55	1337.48	1255.44	1189.39	1135.33
100000	8791.59	4614.50	3226.72	2536.26	2124.71	1852.59	1660.12	1517.42	1407.87	1321.51	1251.99	1195.08

MONTHLY

10.00%

PAYMENT REQUIRED TO AMORTIZE A LOAN

TERM AMOUNT	13 year	14 years	15 years	16 years	17 years	18 years	19 years	20 years	25 years	30 years	35 years	40 years
50	.58	.56	.54	.53	.52	.50	.50	.49	.46	.44	.43	.43
100	1.15	1.11	1.08	1.05	1.03	1.00	.99	.97	.91	.88	.86	.85
200	2.30	2.22	2.15	2.10	2.05	2.00	1.97	1.94	1.82	1.76	1.72	1.70
300	3.45	3.33	3.23	3.14	3.07	3.00	2.95	2.90	2.73	2.64	2.58	2.55
400	4.60	4.44	4.30	4.19	4.09	4.00	3.93	3.87	3.64	3.52	3.44	3.40
500	5.74	5.55	5.38	5.23	5.11	5.00	4.91	4.83	4.55	4.39	4.30	4.25
600	6.89	6.65	6.45	6.28	6.13	6.00	5.89	5.80	5.46	5.27	5.16	5.10
700	8.04	7.76	7.53	7.33	7.15	7.00	6.87	6.76	6.37	6.15	6.02	5.95
800	9.19	8.87	8.60	8.37	8.17	8.00	7.86	7.73	7.27	7.03	6.88	6.80
900	10.34	9.98	9.68	9.42	9.20	9.00	8.84	8.69	8.18	7.90	7.74	7.65
1000	11.48	11.09	10.75	10.46	10.22	10.00	9.82	9.66	9.09	8.78	8.60	8.50
2000	22.96	22.17	21.50	20.92	20.43	20.00	19.63	19.31	18.18	17.56	17.20	16.99
3000	34.44	33.25	32.24	31.38	30.64	30.00	29.44	28.96	27.27	26.33	25.80	25.48
4000	45.92	44.33	42.99	41.84	40.85	40.00	39.26	38.61	36.35	35.11	34.39	33.97
5000	57.40	55.42	53.74	52.30	51.07	50.00	49.07	48.26	45.44	43.88	42.99	42.46
6000	68.88	66.50	64.48	62.76	61.28	60.00	58.88	57.91	54.53	52.66	51.59	50.95
7000	80.35	77.58	75.23	73.22	71.49	69.99	68.69	67.56	63.61	61.44	60.18	59.45
8000	91.83	88.66	85.97	83.68	81.70	79.99	78.51	77.21	72.70	70.21	68.78	67.94
9000	103.31	99.74	96.72	94.14	91.91	89.99	88.32	86.86	81.79	78.99	77.38	76.43
10000	114.79	110.83	107.47	104.60	102.13	99.99	98.13	96.51	90.88	87.76	85.97	84.92
11000	126.27	121.91	118.21	115.05	112.34	109.99	107.94	106.16	99.96	96.54	94.57	93.41
12000	137.75	132.99	128.96	125.51	122.55	119.99	117.76	115.81	109.05	105.31	103.17	101.90
13000	149.23	144.07	139.70	135.97	132.76	129.98	127.57	125.46	118.14	114.09	111.76	110.39
14000	160.70	155.15	150.45	146.43	142.97	139.98	137.38	135.11	127.22	122.87	120.36	118.89
15000	172.18	166.24	161.20	156.89	153.19	149.98	147.19	144.76	136.31	131.64	128.96	127.38
16000	183.66	177.32	171.94	167.35	163.40	159.98	157.01	154.41	145.40	140.42	137.55	135.87
17000	195.14	188.40	182.69	177.81	173.61	169.98	166.82	164.06	154.48	149.19	146.15	144.36
18000	206.62	199.48	193.43	188.27	183.82	179.98	176.63	173.71	163.57	157.97	154.75	152.85
19000	218.10	210.56	204.18	198.73	194.03	189.98	186.44	183.36	172.66	166.74	163.34	161.34
20000	229.57	221.65	214.93	209.19	204.25	199.97	196.26	193.01	181.75	175.52	171.94	169.83
21000	241.05	232.73	225.67	219.64	214.46	209.97	206.07	202.66	190.83	184.30	180.54	178.33
22000	252.53	243.81	236.42	230.10	224.67	219.97	215.88	212.31	199.92	193.07	189.13	186.82
23000	264.01	254.89	247.16	240.56	234.88	229.97	225.69	221.96	209.01	201.85	197.73	195.31
24000	275.49	265.97	257.91	251.02	245.10	239.97	235.51	231.61	218.09	210.62	206.33	203.80
25000	286.97	277.06	268.66	261.48	255.31	249.97	245.32	241.26	227.18	219.40	214.92	212.29
26000	298.45	288.14	279.40	271.94	265.52	259.96	255.13	250.91	236.27	228.17	223.52	220.78
27000	309.92	299.22	290.15	282.40	275.73	269.96	264.94	260.56	245.35	236.95	232.12	229.27
28000	321.40	310.30	300.89	292.86	285.94	279.96	274.76	270.21	254.44	245.73	240.71	237.77
29000	332.88	321.38	311.64	303.32	296.16	289.96	284.57	279.86	263.53	254.50	249.31	246.26
30000	344.36	332.47	322.39	313.78	306.37	299.96	294.38	289.51	272.62	263.28	257.91	254.75
31000	355.84	343.55	333.13	324.23	316.58	309.96	304.20	299.16	281.70	272.05	266.50	263.24
32000	367.32	354.63	343.88	334.69	326.79	319.95	314.01	308.81	290.79	280.83	275.10	271.73
33000	378.79	365.71	354.62	345.15	337.00	329.95	323.82	318.46	299.88	289.60	283.70	280.22
34000	390.27	376.79	365.37	355.61	347.22	339.95	333.63	328.11	308.96	298.38	292.29	288.71
35000	401.75	387.88	376.12	366.07	357.43	349.95	343.45	337.76	318.05	307.16	300.89	297.21
36000	413.23	398.96	386.86	376.53	367.64	359.95	353.26	347.41	327.14	315.93	309.49	305.70
37000	424.71	410.04	397.61	386.99	377.85	369.95	363.07	357.06	336.22	324.71	318.08	314.19
38000	436.19	421.12	408.35	397.45	388.06	379.95	372.88	366.71	345.31	333.48	326.68	322.68
39000	447.67	432.20	419.10	407.91	398.28	389.94	382.70	376.36	354.40	342.26	335.28	331.17
40000	459.14	443.29	429.85	418.37	408.49	399.94	392.51	386.01	363.49	351.03	343.87	339.66
41000	470.62	454.37	440.59	428.82	418.70	409.94	402.32	395.66	372.57	359.81	352.47	348.15
42000	482.10	465.45	451.34	439.28	428.91	419.94	412.13	405.31	381.66	368.59	361.07	356.65
43000	493.58	476.53	462.09	449.74	439.13	429.94	421.95	414.96	390.75	377.36	369.66	365.14
44000	505.06	487.61	472.83	460.20	449.34	439.94	431.76	424.61	399.83	386.14	378.26	373.63
45000	516.54	498.70	483.58	470.66	459.55	449.93	441.57	434.26	408.92	394.91	386.86	382.12
46000	528.02	509.78	494.32	481.12	469.76	459.93	451.38	443.91	418.01	403.69	395.45	390.61
47000	539.49	520.86	505.07	491.58	479.97	469.93	461.20	453.57	427.09	412.46	404.05	399.10
48000	550.97	531.94	515.82	502.04	490.19	479.93	471.01	463.22	436.18	421.24	412.65	407.60
49000	562.45	543.02	526.56	512.50	500.40	489.93	480.82	472.87	445.27	430.02	421.24	416.09
50000	573.93	554.11	537.31	522.96	510.61	499.93	490.63	482.52	454.36	438.79	429.84	424.58
55000	631.32	609.52	591.04	575.25	561.67	549.92	539.70	530.77	499.79	482.67	472.82	467.04
60000	688.71	664.93	644.77	627.55	612.73	599.91	588.76	579.02	545.23	526.55	515.81	509.49
65000	746.11	720.34	698.50	679.84	663.79	649.90	637.82	627.27	590.66	570.43	558.79	551.95
70000	803.50	775.75	752.23	732.14	714.85	699.90	686.89	675.52	636.10	614.31	601.78	594.41
75000	860.89	831.16	805.96	784.43	765.91	749.89	735.95	723.77	681.53	658.18	644.76	636.86
80000	918.28	886.57	859.69	836.73	816.97	799.88	785.01	772.02	726.97	702.06	687.74	679.32
85000	975.68	941.98	913.42	889.02	868.03	849.87	834.08	820.27	772.40	745.94	730.73	721.78
90000	1033.07	997.39	967.15	941.32	919.09	899.86	883.14	868.52	817.84	789.82	773.71	764.24
95000	1090.46	1052.80	1020.88	993.61	970.15	949.86	932.20	916.78	863.27	833.70	816.69	806.69
100000	1147.85	1108.21	1074.61	1045.91	1021.22	999.85	981.26	965.03	908.71	877.58	859.68	849.15

MONTHLY

10.50%

PAYMENT REQUIRED TO AMORTIZE A LOAN

TERM AMOUNT	1 year	2 years	3 years	4 years	5 years	6 years	7 years	8 years	9 years	10 years	11 years	12 years
50	4.41	2.32	1.63	1.29	1.08	.94	.85	.78	.72	.68	.65	.62
100	8.82	4.64	3.26	2.57	2.15	1.88	1.69	1.55	1.44	1.35	1.29	1.23
200	17.63	9.28	6.51	5.13	4.30	3.76	3.38	3.09	2.88	2.70	2.57	2.45
300	26.45	13.92	9.76	7.69	6.45	5.64	5.06	4.64	4.31	4.05	3.85	3.68
400	35.26	18.56	13.01	10.25	8.60	7.52	6.75	6.18	5.75	5.40	5.13	4.90
500	44.08	23.19	16.26	12.81	10.75	9.39	8.44	7.73	7.18	6.75	6.41	6.13
600	52.89	27.83	19.51	15.37	12.90	11.27	10.12	9.27	8.62	8.10	7.69	7.35
700	61.71	32.47	22.76	17.93	15.05	13.15	11.81	10.81	10.05	9.45	8.97	8.57
800	70.52	37.11	26.01	20.49	17.20	15.03	13.49	12.36	11.49	10.80	10.25	9.80
900	79.34	41.74	29.26	23.05	19.35	16.91	15.18	13.90	12.92	12.15	11.53	11.02
1000	88.15	46.38	32.51	25.61	21.50	18.78	16.87	15.45	14.36	13.50	12.81	12.25
2000	176.30	92.76	65.01	51.21	42.99	37.56	33.73	30.89	28.71	26.99	25.61	24.49
3000	264.45	139.13	97.51	76.82	64.49	56.34	50.59	46.33	43.06	40.49	38.42	36.73
4000	352.60	185.51	130.01	102.42	85.98	75.12	67.45	61.77	57.41	53.98	51.22	48.97
5000	440.75	231.89	162.52	128.02	107.47	93.90	84.31	77.21	71.76	67.47	64.03	61.21
6000	528.90	278.26	195.02	153.63	128.97	112.68	101.17	92.65	86.11	80.97	76.83	73.45
7000	617.05	324.64	227.52	179.23	150.46	131.46	118.03	108.09	100.46	94.46	89.64	85.69
8000	705.19	371.01	260.02	204.83	171.96	150.24	134.89	123.53	114.81	107.95	102.44	97.94
9000	793.34	417.39	292.53	230.44	193.45	169.02	151.75	138.97	129.16	121.45	115.25	110.18
10000	881.49	463.77	325.03	256.04	214.94	187.79	168.61	154.41	143.51	134.94	128.05	122.42
11000	969.64	510.14	357.53	281.64	236.44	206.57	185.47	169.85	157.86	148.43	140.85	134.66
12000	1057.79	556.52	390.03	307.25	257.93	225.35	202.33	185.29	172.22	161.93	153.66	146.90
13000	1145.94	602.89	422.54	332.85	279.43	244.13	219.19	200.73	186.57	175.42	166.46	159.14
14000	1234.09	649.27	455.04	358.45	300.92	262.91	236.05	216.17	200.92	188.91	179.27	171.38
15000	1322.23	695.65	487.54	384.06	322.41	281.69	252.92	231.61	215.27	202.41	192.07	183.63
16000	1410.38	742.02	520.04	409.66	343.91	300.47	269.78	247.05	229.62	215.90	204.88	195.87
17000	1498.53	788.40	552.55	435.26	365.40	319.25	286.64	262.49	243.97	229.39	217.68	208.11
18000	1586.68	834.77	585.05	460.87	386.90	338.03	303.50	277.93	258.32	242.89	230.49	220.35
19000	1674.83	881.15	617.55	486.47	408.39	356.81	320.34	293.37	272.67	256.38	243.29	232.59
20000	1762.98	927.53	650.05	512.07	429.88	375.58	337.22	308.81	287.02	269.87	256.09	244.83
21000	1851.13	973.90	682.56	537.68	451.38	394.36	354.08	324.25	301.37	283.37	268.90	257.07
22000	1939.27	1020.28	715.06	563.28	472.87	413.14	370.94	339.69	315.72	296.86	281.70	269.32
23000	2027.42	1066.65	747.56	588.88	494.36	431.92	387.80	355.13	330.07	310.36	294.51	281.56
24000	2115.57	1113.03	780.06	614.49	515.86	450.70	404.66	370.57	344.43	323.85	307.31	293.80
25000	2203.72	1159.41	812.57	640.09	537.35	469.48	421.52	386.01	358.78	337.34	320.12	306.04
26000	2291.87	1205.78	845.07	665.69	558.85	488.26	438.38	401.45	373.13	350.84	332.92	318.28
27000	2380.02	1252.16	877.57	691.30	580.34	507.04	455.24	416.89	387.48	364.33	345.73	330.52
28000	2468.17	1298.53	910.07	716.90	601.83	525.82	472.10	432.33	401.83	377.82	358.53	342.76
29000	2556.31	1344.91	942.58	742.50	623.33	544.60	488.96	447.77	416.18	391.32	371.33	355.01
30000	2644.46	1391.29	975.08	768.11	644.82	563.37	505.83	463.21	430.53	404.81	384.14	367.25
31000	2732.41	1437.66	1007.58	793.71	666.32	582.15	522.69	478.65	444.88	418.30	396.94	379.49
32000	2820.76	1484.04	1040.08	819.31	687.81	600.93	539.55	494.09	459.23	431.80	409.75	391.73
33000	2908.91	1530.41	1072.59	844.92	709.30	619.71	556.41	509.53	473.58	445.29	422.55	403.97
34000	2997.06	1576.79	1105.09	870.52	730.80	638.49	573.27	524.97	487.93	458.78	435.36	416.21
35000	3085.21	1623.17	1137.59	896.12	752.29	657.27	590.13	540.41	502.29	472.28	448.16	428.45
36000	3173.35	1669.54	1170.09	921.73	773.79	676.05	606.99	555.85	516.64	485.77	460.97	440.70
37000	3261.50	1715.92	1202.60	947.33	795.28	694.83	623.85	571.29	530.99	499.26	473.77	452.94
38000	3349.65	1762.29	1235.10	972.93	816.77	713.61	640.71	586.73	545.34	512.76	486.57	465.18
39000	3437.80	1808.67	1267.60	998.54	838.27	732.38	657.57	602.17	559.69	526.25	499.38	477.42
40000	3525.95	1855.05	1300.10	1024.14	859.76	751.16	674.43	617.61	574.04	539.74	512.18	489.66
41000	3614.10	1901.42	1332.61	1049.74	881.25	769.94	691.29	633.05	588.39	553.24	524.99	501.90
42000	3702.25	1947.80	1365.11	1075.35	902.75	788.72	708.15	648.49	602.74	566.73	537.79	514.14
43000	3790.39	1994.17	1397.61	1100.95	924.24	807.50	725.01	663.93	617.09	580.23	550.60	526.39
44000	3878.54	2040.55	1430.11	1126.55	945.74	826.28	741.87	679.37	631.44	593.72	563.40	538.63
45000	3966.69	2086.93	1462.61	1152.16	967.23	845.06	758.74	694.81	645.79	607.21	576.21	550.87
46000	4054.84	2133.30	1495.12	1177.76	988.72	863.84	775.60	710.25	660.14	620.71	589.01	563.11
47000	4142.99	2179.68	1527.62	1203.36	1010.22	882.62	792.46	725.69	674.50	634.20	601.81	575.35
48000	4231.14	2226.06	1560.12	1228.97	1031.71	901.40	809.32	741.13	688.85	647.69	614.62	587.59
49000	4319.29	2272.43	1592.62	1254.57	1053.21	920.17	826.18	756.57	703.20	661.19	627.42	599.83
50000	4407.44	2318.81	1625.13	1280.17	1074.70	938.95	843.04	772.01	717.55	674.68	640.23	612.08
55000	4848.18	2550.69	1787.64	1408.19	1182.17	1032.85	927.34	849.21	789.30	742.15	704.25	673.28
60000	5288.92	2782.57	1950.15	1536.21	1289.64	1126.74	1011.65	926.41	861.06	809.61	768.27	734.49
65000	5729.66	3014.45	2112.66	1664.22	1397.11	1220.64	1095.95	1003.61	932.81	877.08	832.29	795.70
70000	6170.41	3246.33	2275.18	1792.24	1504.58	1314.53	1180.25	1080.81	1004.57	944.55	896.32	856.90
75000	6611.15	3478.21	2437.69	1920.26	1612.05	1408.43	1264.56	1158.01	1076.32	1012.02	960.34	918.11
80000	7051.89	3710.09	2600.20	2048.28	1719.52	1502.32	1348.86	1235.21	1148.07	1079.49	1024.36	979.32
85000	7492.64	3941.97	2762.71	2176.29	1826.99	1596.22	1433.16	1312.41	1219.83	1146.95	1088.38	1040.52
90000	7933.38	4173.85	2925.22	2304.31	1934.46	1690.11	1517.47	1389.61	1291.58	1214.42	1152.41	1101.73
95000	8374.12	4405.73	3087.74	2432.33	2041.93	1784.01	1601.77	1466.81	1363.34	1281.89	1216.43	1162.94
100000	8814.87	4637.61	3250.25	2560.34	2149.40	1877.90	1686.07	1544.01	1435.09	1349.36	1280.45	1224.15

MONTHLY   10.50%

PAYMENT REQUIRED TO AMORTIZE A LOAN

TERM AMOUNT	13 year	14 years	15 years	16 years	17 years	18 years	19 years	20 years	25 years	30 years	35 years	40 years
50	.59	.57	.56	.54	.53	.52	.51	.50	.48	.46	.45	.45
100	1.18	1.14	1.11	1.08	1.06	1.04	1.02	1.00	.95	.92	.90	.89
200	2.36	2.28	2.22	2.16	2.11	2.07	2.03	2.00	1.89	1.83	1.80	1.78
300	3.54	3.42	3.32	3.24	3.16	3.10	3.05	3.00	2.84	2.75	2.70	2.67
400	4.72	4.56	4.43	4.31	4.22	4.13	4.06	4.00	3.78	3.66	3.60	3.56
500	5.89	5.70	5.53	5.39	5.27	5.17	5.08	5.00	4.73	4.58	4.50	4.45
600	7.07	6.84	6.64	6.47	6.32	6.20	6.09	6.00	5.67	5.49	5.39	5.34
700	8.25	7.97	7.74	7.55	7.38	7.23	7.10	6.99	6.61	6.41	6.29	6.22
800	9.43	9.11	8.85	8.62	8.43	8.26	8.12	7.99	7.56	7.32	7.19	7.11
900	10.60	10.25	9.95	9.70	9.48	9.30	9.13	8.99	8.50	8.24	8.09	8.00
1000	11.78	11.39	11.06	10.78	10.54	10.33	10.15	9.99	9.45	9.15	8.99	8.89
2000	23.56	22.77	22.11	21.55	21.07	20.65	20.29	19.97	18.89	18.30	17.97	17.78
3000	35.33	34.16	33.17	32.32	31.60	30.97	30.43	29.96	28.33	27.45	26.95	26.66
4000	47.11	45.54	44.22	43.09	42.13	41.29	40.57	39.94	37.77	36.59	35.93	35.55
5000	58.88	56.93	55.27	53.87	52.66	51.62	50.71	49.92	47.21	45.74	44.91	44.43
6000	70.66	68.31	66.33	64.64	63.19	61.94	60.85	59.91	56.66	54.89	53.89	53.32
7000	82.43	79.70	77.38	75.41	73.72	72.26	70.99	69.89	66.10	64.04	62.87	62.20
8000	94.21	91.08	88.44	86.18	84.25	82.58	81.14	79.88	75.54	73.18	71.86	71.09
9000	105.98	102.46	99.49	96.96	94.78	92.91	91.28	89.86	84.98	82.33	80.84	79.98
10000	117.76	113.85	110.54	107.73	105.31	103.23	101.42	99.84	94.42	91.48	89.82	88.86
11000	129.53	125.23	121.60	118.50	115.84	113.55	111.56	109.83	103.86	100.63	98.80	97.75
12000	141.31	136.62	132.65	129.27	126.37	123.87	121.70	119.81	113.31	109.77	107.78	106.63
13000	153.08	148.00	143.71	140.05	136.91	134.19	131.84	129.79	122.75	118.92	116.76	115.52
14000	164.86	159.39	154.76	150.82	147.44	144.52	141.98	139.78	132.19	128.07	125.74	124.40
15000	176.63	170.77	165.81	161.59	157.97	154.84	152.13	149.76	141.63	137.22	134.73	133.29
16000	188.41	182.15	176.87	172.36	168.50	165.16	162.27	159.75	151.07	146.36	143.71	142.18
17000	200.18	193.54	187.92	183.14	179.03	175.48	172.41	169.73	160.52	155.51	152.69	151.06
18000	211.96	204.92	198.98	193.91	189.56	185.81	182.55	179.71	169.96	164.66	161.67	159.95
19000	223.73	216.31	210.03	204.68	200.09	196.13	192.69	189.70	179.40	173.81	170.65	168.83
20000	235.51	227.69	221.08	215.45	210.62	206.45	202.83	199.68	188.84	182.95	179.63	177.72
21000	247.28	239.08	232.14	226.23	221.15	216.77	212.97	209.66	198.28	192.10	188.61	186.60
22000	259.06	250.46	243.19	237.00	231.68	227.10	223.12	219.65	207.72	201.25	197.59	195.49
23000	270.83	261.84	254.25	247.77	242.21	237.42	233.26	229.63	217.17	210.40	206.58	204.38
24000	282.61	273.23	265.30	258.54	252.74	247.74	243.40	239.62	226.61	219.54	215.56	213.26
25000	294.38	284.61	276.35	269.32	263.28	258.06	253.54	249.60	236.05	228.69	224.54	222.15
26000	306.16	296.00	287.41	280.09	273.81	268.38	263.68	259.58	245.49	237.84	233.52	231.03
27000	317.93	307.38	298.46	290.86	284.34	278.71	273.82	269.57	254.93	246.98	242.50	239.92
28000	329.71	318.77	309.52	301.63	294.87	289.03	283.96	279.55	264.38	256.13	251.48	248.80
29000	341.48	330.15	320.57	312.41	305.40	299.35	294.11	289.54	273.82	265.28	260.46	257.69
30000	353.26	341.54	331.62	323.18	315.93	309.67	304.25	299.52	283.26	274.43	269.45	266.58
31000	365.03	352.92	342.68	333.95	326.46	320.00	314.39	309.50	292.70	283.57	278.43	275.46
32000	376.81	364.30	353.73	344.72	336.99	330.32	324.53	319.49	302.14	292.72	287.41	284.35
33000	388.58	375.69	364.79	355.50	347.52	340.64	334.67	329.47	311.58	301.87	296.39	293.23
34000	400.36	387.07	375.84	366.27	358.05	350.96	344.81	339.45	321.03	311.02	305.37	302.12
35000	412.13	398.46	386.89	377.04	368.58	361.28	354.95	349.44	330.47	320.16	314.35	311.00
36000	423.91	409.84	397.95	387.81	379.11	371.61	365.10	359.42	339.91	329.31	323.33	319.89
37000	435.68	421.23	409.00	398.58	389.65	381.93	375.24	369.41	349.35	338.46	332.31	328.78
38000	447.46	432.61	420.06	409.36	400.18	392.25	385.38	379.39	358.79	347.61	341.30	337.66
39000	459.23	443.99	431.11	420.13	410.71	402.57	395.52	389.37	368.24	356.75	350.28	346.55
40000	471.01	455.38	442.16	430.90	421.24	412.90	405.66	399.36	377.68	365.90	359.26	355.43
41000	482.78	466.76	453.22	441.67	431.77	423.22	415.80	409.34	387.12	375.05	368.24	364.32
42000	494.56	478.15	464.27	452.45	442.30	433.54	425.94	419.32	396.56	384.20	377.22	373.20
43000	506.33	489.53	475.33	463.22	452.83	443.86	436.08	429.31	406.00	393.34	386.20	382.09
44000	518.11	500.92	486.38	473.99	463.36	454.19	446.23	439.29	415.44	402.49	395.18	390.98
45000	529.88	512.30	497.43	484.76	473.89	464.51	456.37	449.28	424.89	411.64	404.17	399.86
46000	541.66	523.68	508.49	495.54	484.42	474.83	466.51	459.26	434.33	420.79	413.15	408.75
47000	553.43	535.07	519.54	506.31	494.95	485.15	476.65	469.24	443.77	429.93	422.13	417.63
48000	565.21	546.45	530.60	517.08	505.48	495.47	486.79	479.23	453.21	439.08	431.11	426.52
49000	576.98	557.84	541.65	527.85	516.01	505.80	496.93	489.21	462.65	448.23	440.09	435.40
50000	588.76	569.22	552.70	538.63	526.55	516.12	507.07	499.19	472.10	457.37	449.07	444.29
55000	647.63	626.14	607.97	592.49	579.20	567.73	557.78	549.11	519.30	503.11	493.98	488.72
60000	706.51	683.07	663.24	646.35	631.85	619.34	608.49	599.03	566.51	548.85	538.89	533.15
65000	765.38	739.99	718.51	700.21	684.51	670.95	659.20	648.95	613.72	594.59	583.79	577.58
70000	824.26	796.91	773.78	754.07	737.16	722.56	709.90	698.87	660.93	640.32	628.70	622.00
75000	883.13	853.83	829.05	807.94	789.82	774.18	760.61	748.79	708.14	686.06	673.61	666.43
80000	942.01	910.75	884.32	861.80	842.47	825.79	811.32	798.71	755.35	731.80	718.51	710.86
85000	1000.88	967.67	939.59	915.66	895.12	877.40	862.02	848.63	802.56	777.53	763.42	755.29
90000	1059.76	1024.60	994.86	969.52	947.78	929.01	912.73	898.55	849.77	823.27	808.33	799.72
95000	1118.63	1081.52	1050.13	1023.39	1000.43	980.62	963.44	948.47	896.98	869.01	853.23	844.15
100000	1177.51	1138.44	1105.40	1077.25	1053.09	1032.23	1014.14	998.38	944.19	914.74	898.14	888.58

11.00%
MONTHLY
PAYMENT REQUIRED TO AMORTIZE A LOAN

TERM AMOUNT	1 year	2 years	3 years	4 years	5 years	6 years	7 years	8 years	9 years	10 years	11 years	12 years
50	4.42	2.34	1.64	1.30	1.09	.96	.86	.79	.74	.69	.66	.63
100	8.84	4.67	3.28	2.59	2.18	1.91	1.72	1.58	1.47	1.38	1.31	1.26
200	17.68	9.33	6.55	5.17	4.35	3.81	3.43	3.15	2.93	2.76	2.62	2.51
300	26.52	13.99	9.83	7.76	6.53	5.72	5.14	4.72	4.39	4.14	3.93	3.77
400	35.36	18.65	13.10	10.34	8.70	7.62	6.85	6.29	5.86	5.52	5.24	5.02
500	44.20	23.31	16.37	12.93	10.88	9.52	8.57	7.86	7.32	6.89	6.55	6.27
600	53.03	27.97	19.65	15.51	13.05	11.43	10.28	9.43	8.78	8.27	7.86	7.53
700	61.87	32.63	22.92	18.10	15.22	13.33	11.99	11.00	10.24	9.65	9.17	8.78
800	70.71	37.29	26.20	20.68	17.40	15.23	13.70	12.57	11.71	11.03	10.48	10.03
900	79.55	41.95	29.47	23.27	19.57	17.14	15.42	14.14	13.17	12.40	11.79	11.29
1000	88.39	46.61	32.74	25.85	21.75	19.04	17.13	15.71	14.63	13.78	13.10	12.54
2000	176.77	93.22	65.48	51.70	43.49	38.07	34.25	31.42	29.26	27.56	26.19	25.08
3000	265.15	139.83	98.22	77.54	65.23	57.11	51.37	47.13	43.88	41.33	39.28	37.61
4000	353.53	186.44	130.96	103.39	86.97	76.14	68.49	62.84	58.51	55.11	52.37	50.15
5000	441.91	233.04	163.70	129.23	108.72	95.18	85.62	78.55	73.13	68.88	65.47	62.68
6000	530.29	279.65	196.44	155.08	130.46	114.21	102.74	94.26	87.76	82.66	78.56	75.22
7000	618.68	326.26	229.18	180.92	152.20	133.24	119.86	109.96	102.39	96.43	91.65	87.75
8000	707.06	372.87	261.91	206.77	173.94	152.28	136.98	125.67	117.01	110.21	104.74	100.29
9000	795.44	419.48	294.65	232.61	195.69	171.31	154.11	141.38	131.64	123.98	117.84	112.82
10000	883.82	466.08	327.39	258.46	217.43	190.35	171.23	157.09	146.26	137.76	130.93	125.36
11000	972.20	512.69	360.13	284.31	239.17	209.38	188.35	172.80	160.89	151.53	144.02	137.90
12000	1060.58	559.30	392.87	310.15	260.91	228.41	205.47	188.51	175.52	165.31	157.11	150.43
13000	1148.97	605.91	425.61	336.00	282.66	247.45	222.60	204.21	190.14	179.08	170.21	162.97
14000	1237.35	652.51	458.35	361.84	304.40	266.48	239.72	219.92	204.77	192.86	183.30	175.50
15000	1325.73	699.12	491.09	387.69	326.14	285.52	256.84	235.63	219.39	206.63	196.39	188.04
16000	1414.11	745.73	523.82	413.53	347.88	304.55	273.96	251.34	234.02	220.41	209.48	200.57
17000	1502.49	792.34	556.56	439.38	369.63	323.58	291.09	267.05	248.64	234.18	222.57	213.11
18000	1590.87	838.95	589.30	465.22	391.37	342.62	308.21	282.76	263.27	247.96	235.67	225.64
19000	1679.26	885.55	622.04	491.07	413.11	361.65	325.33	298.47	277.90	261.73	248.76	238.18
20000	1767.64	932.16	654.78	516.92	434.85	380.69	342.45	314.17	292.52	275.51	261.85	250.72
21000	1856.02	978.77	687.52	542.76	456.60	399.72	359.58	329.88	307.15	289.28	274.94	263.25
22000	1944.40	1025.38	720.26	568.61	478.34	418.75	376.70	345.59	321.77	303.06	288.04	275.79
23000	2032.78	1071.99	753.00	594.45	500.08	437.79	393.82	361.30	336.40	316.83	301.13	288.32
24000	2121.16	1118.59	785.73	620.30	521.82	456.82	410.94	377.01	351.03	330.61	314.22	300.86
25000	2209.55	1165.20	818.47	646.14	543.57	475.86	428.07	392.72	365.65	344.38	327.31	313.39
26000	2297.93	1211.81	851.21	671.99	565.31	494.89	445.19	408.42	380.28	358.16	340.41	325.93
27000	2386.31	1258.42	883.95	697.83	587.05	513.93	462.31	424.13	394.90	371.93	353.50	338.46
28000	2474.69	1305.02	916.69	723.68	608.79	532.96	479.43	439.84	409.53	385.71	366.59	351.00
29000	2563.07	1351.63	949.43	749.53	630.54	551.99	496.56	455.55	424.15	399.48	379.68	363.54
30000	2651.45	1398.24	982.17	775.37	652.28	571.03	513.68	471.26	438.78	413.26	392.78	376.07
31000	2739.84	1444.85	1014.91	801.22	674.02	590.06	530.80	486.97	453.41	427.03	405.87	388.61
32000	2828.22	1491.46	1047.64	827.06	695.76	609.10	547.92	502.67	468.03	440.81	418.96	401.14
33000	2916.60	1538.06	1080.38	852.91	717.50	628.13	565.05	518.38	482.66	454.58	432.05	413.68
34000	3004.98	1584.67	1113.12	878.75	739.25	647.16	582.17	534.09	497.28	468.36	445.14	426.21
35000	3093.36	1631.28	1145.86	904.60	760.99	666.20	599.29	549.80	511.91	482.13	458.24	438.75
36000	3181.74	1677.89	1178.60	930.44	782.73	685.23	616.41	565.51	526.54	495.91	471.33	451.28
37000	3270.13	1724.50	1211.34	956.29	804.47	704.27	633.54	581.22	541.16	509.68	484.42	463.82
38000	3358.51	1771.10	1244.08	982.13	826.22	723.30	650.66	596.93	555.79	523.46	497.51	476.36
39000	3446.89	1817.71	1276.82	1007.98	847.96	742.33	667.78	612.63	570.41	537.23	510.61	488.89
40000	3535.27	1864.32	1309.55	1033.83	869.70	761.37	684.90	628.34	585.04	551.01	523.70	501.43
41000	3623.65	1910.93	1342.29	1059.67	891.44	780.40	702.02	644.05	599.67	564.78	536.79	513.96
42000	3712.03	1957.53	1375.03	1085.52	913.19	799.44	719.15	659.76	614.29	578.56	549.88	526.50
43000	3800.42	2004.14	1407.77	1111.36	934.93	818.47	736.27	675.47	628.92	592.33	562.98	539.03
44000	3888.80	2050.75	1440.51	1137.21	956.67	837.50	753.39	691.18	643.54	606.11	576.07	551.57
45000	3977.18	2097.36	1473.25	1163.05	978.41	856.54	770.51	706.88	658.17	619.88	589.16	564.10
46000	4065.56	2143.97	1505.99	1188.90	1000.16	875.57	787.64	722.59	672.79	633.66	602.25	576.64
47000	4153.94	2190.57	1538.72	1214.74	1021.90	894.61	804.76	738.30	687.42	647.43	615.35	589.18
48000	4242.32	2237.18	1571.46	1240.59	1043.64	913.64	821.88	754.01	702.05	661.21	628.44	601.71
49000	4330.71	2283.79	1604.20	1266.44	1065.38	932.67	839.00	769.72	716.67	674.98	641.53	614.25
50000	4419.09	2330.40	1636.94	1292.28	1087.13	951.71	856.13	785.43	731.30	688.76	654.62	626.78
55000	4861.00	2563.44	1800.63	1421.51	1195.84	1046.88	941.74	863.97	804.43	757.63	720.08	689.46
60000	5302.90	2796.48	1964.33	1550.74	1304.55	1142.05	1027.35	942.51	877.56	826.51	785.55	752.14
65000	5744.81	3029.51	2128.02	1679.96	1413.26	1237.22	1112.96	1021.05	950.69	895.38	851.01	814.82
70000	6186.72	3262.55	2291.72	1809.19	1521.97	1332.39	1198.58	1099.59	1023.82	964.26	916.47	877.49
75000	6628.63	3495.59	2455.41	1938.42	1630.69	1427.56	1284.19	1178.14	1096.94	1033.13	981.93	940.17
80000	7070.54	3728.63	2619.10	2067.65	1739.40	1522.73	1369.80	1256.68	1170.07	1102.01	1047.39	1002.85
85000	7512.45	3961.67	2782.80	2196.87	1848.11	1617.90	1455.41	1335.22	1243.20	1170.88	1112.85	1065.53
90000	7954.35	4194.71	2946.49	2326.10	1956.82	1713.07	1541.02	1413.76	1316.33	1239.76	1178.32	1128.20
95000	8396.26	4427.75	3110.18	2455.33	2065.54	1808.24	1626.64	1492.31	1389.46	1308.63	1243.78	1190.88
100000	8838.17	4660.79	3273.88	2584.56	2174.25	1903.41	1712.25	1570.85	1462.59	1377.51	1309.24	1253.56

MONTHLY 11.00%

PAYMENT REQUIRED TO AMORTIZE A LOAN

TERM AMOUNT	13 year	14 years	15 years	16 years	17 years	18 years	19 years	20 years	25 years	30 years	35 years	40 years
50	.61	.59	.57	.56	.55	.54	.53	.52	.50	.48	.47	.47
100	1.21	1.17	1.14	1.11	1.09	1.07	1.05	1.04	.99	.96	.94	.93
200	2.42	2.34	2.28	2.22	2.18	2.14	2.10	2.07	1.97	1.91	1.88	1.86
300	3.63	3.51	3.41	3.33	3.26	3.20	3.15	3.10	2.86	2.86	2.82	2.79
400	4.84	4.68	4.55	4.44	4.35	4.27	4.19	4.13	3.93	3.81	3.75	3.72
500	6.04	5.85	5.69	5.55	5.43	5.33	5.24	5.17	4.91	4.77	4.69	4.65
600	7.25	7.02	6.82	6.66	6.52	6.40	6.29	6.20	5.89	5.72	5.63	5.57
700	8.46	8.19	7.96	7.77	7.60	7.46	7.34	7.23	6.87	6.67	6.56	6.50
800	9.67	9.36	9.10	8.88	8.69	8.53	8.38	8.26	7.85	7.62	7.50	7.43
900	10.87	10.53	10.23	9.99	9.77	9.59	9.43	9.29	8.83	8.58	8.44	8.36
1000	12.08	11.70	11.37	11.10	10.86	10.66	10.48	10.33	9.81	9.53	9.37	9.29
2000	24.16	23.39	22.74	22.19	21.71	21.31	20.95	20.65	19.61	19.05	18.74	18.57
3000	36.23	35.08	34.10	33.28	32.57	31.96	31.43	30.97	29.41	28.57	28.11	27.85
4000	48.31	46.77	45.47	44.37	43.42	42.61	41.90	41.29	39.21	38.10	37.48	37.14
5000	60.38	58.46	56.83	55.46	54.27	53.26	52.38	51.61	49.01	47.62	46.85	46.42
6000	72.46	70.15	68.20	66.55	65.13	63.91	62.85	61.94	58.81	57.14	56.22	55.70
7000	84.53	81.84	79.57	77.64	75.98	74.56	73.33	72.26	68.61	66.67	65.59	64.99
8000	96.61	93.53	90.93	88.73	86.84	85.21	83.80	82.58	78.41	76.19	74.96	74.27
9000	108.68	105.22	102.30	99.82	97.69	95.86	94.28	92.90	88.22	85.71	84.33	83.55
10000	120.76	116.91	113.66	110.91	108.54	106.51	104.75	103.22	98.02	95.24	93.70	92.83
11000	132.83	128.60	125.03	122.00	119.40	117.16	115.23	113.55	107.82	104.76	103.07	102.12
12000	144.91	140.29	136.40	133.09	130.25	127.81	125.70	123.87	117.62	114.28	112.44	111.40
13000	156.98	151.98	147.76	144.18	141.10	138.46	136.18	134.19	127.42	123.81	121.81	120.68
14000	169.06	163.67	159.13	155.27	151.96	149.11	146.65	144.51	137.22	133.33	131.18	129.97
15000	181.13	175.36	170.49	166.36	162.81	159.76	157.12	154.83	147.02	142.85	140.55	139.25
16000	193.21	187.05	181.86	177.45	173.67	170.41	167.60	165.16	156.82	152.38	149.92	148.53
17000	205.28	198.74	193.23	188.54	184.52	181.06	178.07	175.48	166.62	161.90	159.29	157.82
18000	217.36	210.43	204.59	199.63	195.37	191.71	188.55	185.80	176.43	171.42	168.66	167.10
19000	229.44	222.13	215.96	210.72	206.23	202.36	199.02	196.12	186.23	180.95	178.03	176.38
20000	241.51	233.82	227.32	221.81	217.08	213.01	209.50	206.44	196.03	190.47	187.40	185.66
21000	253.59	245.51	238.69	232.90	227.93	223.67	219.97	216.76	205.83	199.99	196.77	194.95
22000	265.66	257.20	250.06	243.99	238.79	234.32	230.45	227.09	215.63	209.52	206.14	204.23
23000	277.74	268.89	261.42	255.08	249.64	244.97	240.92	237.41	225.43	219.04	215.51	213.51
24000	289.81	280.58	272.79	266.17	260.50	255.62	251.40	247.73	235.23	228.56	224.87	222.80
25000	301.89	292.27	284.15	277.26	271.35	266.27	261.87	258.05	245.03	238.09	234.24	232.08
26000	313.96	303.96	295.52	288.35	282.20	276.92	272.35	268.37	254.83	247.61	243.61	241.36
27000	326.04	315.65	306.89	299.44	293.06	287.57	282.82	278.70	264.64	257.13	252.98	250.64
28000	338.11	327.34	318.25	310.53	303.91	298.22	293.29	289.02	274.44	266.66	262.35	259.93
29000	350.19	339.03	329.62	321.62	314.77	308.87	303.77	299.34	284.24	276.18	271.72	269.21
30000	362.26	350.72	340.98	332.71	325.62	319.52	314.24	309.66	294.04	285.70	281.09	278.49
31000	374.34	362.41	352.35	343.80	336.47	330.17	324.72	319.98	303.84	295.23	290.46	287.78
32000	386.41	374.10	363.72	354.89	347.33	340.82	335.19	330.31	313.64	304.75	299.83	297.06
33000	398.49	385.79	375.08	365.98	358.18	351.47	345.67	340.63	323.44	314.27	309.20	306.34
34000	410.56	397.48	386.45	377.07	369.03	362.12	356.14	350.95	333.24	323.79	318.57	315.63
35000	422.64	409.17	397.81	388.16	379.89	372.77	366.62	361.27	343.04	333.32	327.94	324.91
36000	434.71	420.86	409.18	399.25	390.74	383.42	377.09	371.59	352.85	342.84	337.31	334.19
37000	446.79	432.56	420.55	410.34	401.60	394.07	387.57	381.91	362.65	352.36	346.68	343.47
38000	458.87	444.25	431.91	421.43	412.45	404.72	398.04	392.24	372.45	361.89	356.05	352.76
39000	470.94	455.94	443.28	432.52	423.30	415.37	408.52	402.56	382.25	371.41	365.42	362.04
40000	483.02	467.63	454.64	443.61	434.16	426.02	418.99	412.88	392.05	380.93	374.79	371.32
41000	495.09	479.32	466.01	454.70	445.01	436.68	429.47	423.20	401.85	390.46	384.16	380.61
42000	507.17	491.01	477.38	465.79	455.86	447.33	439.94	433.52	411.65	399.98	393.53	389.89
43000	519.24	502.70	488.74	476.88	466.72	457.98	450.41	443.85	421.45	409.50	402.90	399.17
44000	531.32	514.39	500.11	487.97	477.57	468.63	460.89	454.17	431.25	419.03	412.27	408.45
45000	543.39	526.08	511.47	499.06	488.43	479.28	471.36	464.49	441.06	428.55	421.64	417.74
46000	555.47	537.77	522.84	510.15	499.28	489.93	481.84	474.81	450.86	438.07	431.01	427.02
47000	567.54	549.46	534.21	521.24	510.13	500.58	492.31	485.13	460.66	447.60	440.38	436.30
48000	579.62	561.15	545.57	532.33	520.99	511.23	502.79	495.46	470.46	457.12	449.74	445.59
49000	591.69	572.84	556.94	543.42	531.84	521.88	513.26	505.78	480.26	466.64	459.11	454.87
50000	603.77	584.53	568.30	554.51	542.70	532.53	523.74	516.10	490.06	476.17	468.48	464.15
55000	664.15	642.98	625.13	609.96	596.96	585.78	576.11	567.71	539.07	523.78	515.33	510.57
60000	724.52	701.44	681.96	665.41	651.23	639.03	628.48	619.32	588.07	571.40	562.18	556.98
65000	784.90	759.89	738.79	720.86	705.50	692.29	680.86	670.93	637.08	619.02	609.03	603.40
70000	845.27	818.34	795.62	776.31	759.77	745.54	733.23	722.54	686.08	666.63	655.88	649.81
75000	905.65	876.80	852.45	831.76	814.04	798.79	785.60	774.15	735.09	714.25	702.72	696.23
80000	966.03	935.25	909.28	887.21	868.31	852.04	837.98	825.76	784.10	761.86	749.57	742.64
85000	1026.40	993.70	966.11	942.66	922.58	905.30	890.35	877.37	833.10	809.48	796.42	789.06
90000	1086.78	1052.15	1022.94	998.11	976.85	958.55	942.72	928.97	882.11	857.10	843.27	835.47
95000	1147.16	1110.61	1079.77	1053.56	1031.12	1011.80	995.10	980.58	931.11	904.71	890.11	881.88
100000	1207.53	1169.06	1136.60	1109.01	1085.39	1065.05	1047.47	1032.19	980.12	952.33	936.96	928.30

MONTHLY

11.50%

PAYMENT REQUIRED TO AMORTIZE A LOAN

TERM AMOUNT	1 year	2 years	3 years	4 years	5 years	6 years	7 years	8 years	9 years	10 years	11 years	12 years
50	4.44	2.35	1.65	1.31	1.10	.97	.87	.80	.75	.71	.67	.65
100	8.87	4.69	3.30	2.61	2.20	1.93	1.74	1.60	1.50	1.41	1.34	1.29
200	17.73	9.37	6.60	5.22	4.40	3.86	3.48	3.20	2.99	2.82	2.68	2.57
300	26.59	14.06	9.90	7.83	6.60	5.79	5.22	4.80	4.48	4.22	4.02	3.85
400	35.45	18.74	13.20	10.44	8.80	7.72	6.96	6.40	5.97	5.63	5.36	5.14
500	44.31	23.43	16.49	13.05	11.00	9.65	8.70	7.99	7.46	7.03	6.70	6.42
600	53.17	28.11	19.79	15.66	13.20	11.58	10.44	9.59	8.95	8.44	8.04	7.70
700	62.04	32.79	23.09	18.27	15.40	13.51	12.18	11.19	10.44	9.85	9.37	8.99
800	70.90	37.48	26.39	20.88	17.60	15.44	13.91	12.79	11.93	11.25	10.71	10.27
900	79.76	42.16	29.68	23.49	19.80	17.37	15.65	14.39	13.42	12.66	12.05	11.55
1000	88.62	46.85	32.98	26.09	22.00	19.30	17.39	15.98	14.91	14.06	13.39	12.84
2000	177.24	93.69	65.96	52.18	43.99	38.59	34.78	31.96	29.81	28.12	26.77	25.67
3000	265.85	140.53	98.93	78.27	65.98	57.88	52.16	47.94	44.72	42.18	40.16	38.50
4000	354.47	187.37	131.91	104.36	87.98	77.17	69.55	63.92	59.62	56.24	53.54	51.34
5000	443.08	234.21	164.89	130.45	109.97	96.46	86.94	79.90	74.52	70.30	66.92	64.17
6000	531.70	281.05	197.86	156.54	131.96	115.75	104.32	95.88	89.43	84.36	80.31	77.00
7000	620.31	327.89	230.84	182.63	153.95	135.04	121.71	111.86	104.33	98.42	93.69	89.84
8000	708.93	374.73	263.81	208.72	175.95	154.33	139.10	127.84	119.23	112.48	107.07	102.67
9000	797.54	421.57	296.79	234.81	197.94	173.63	156.48	143.82	134.14	126.54	120.46	115.50
10000	886.16	468.41	329.77	260.90	219.93	192.92	173.87	159.80	149.04	140.60	133.84	128.34
11000	974.77	515.25	362.74	286.98	241.92	212.21	191.26	175.78	163.95	154.66	147.22	141.17
12000	1063.39	562.09	395.72	313.07	263.92	231.50	208.64	191.76	178.85	168.72	160.61	154.00
13000	1152.00	608.93	428.69	339.16	285.91	250.79	226.03	207.74	193.75	182.78	173.99	166.84
14000	1240.62	655.77	461.67	365.25	307.90	270.08	243.42	223.72	208.66	196.84	187.37	179.67
15000	1329.23	702.61	494.65	391.34	329.89	289.37	260.80	239.70	223.56	210.90	200.76	192.50
16000	1417.85	749.45	527.62	417.43	351.89	308.66	278.19	255.67	238.46	224.96	214.14	205.34
17000	1506.46	796.29	560.60	443.52	373.88	327.95	295.57	271.65	253.37	239.02	227.52	218.17
18000	1595.08	843.13	593.57	469.61	395.87	347.25	312.96	287.63	268.27	253.08	240.91	231.00
19000	1683.69	889.97	626.55	495.70	417.86	366.54	330.35	303.61	283.17	267.14	254.29	243.84
20000	1772.31	936.81	659.53	521.79	439.86	385.83	347.73	319.59	298.08	281.20	267.68	256.67
21000	1860.92	983.65	692.50	547.87	461.85	405.12	365.12	335.57	312.98	295.26	281.06	269.50
22000	1949.54	1030.49	725.48	573.96	483.84	424.41	382.51	351.55	327.89	309.31	294.44	282.33
23000	2038.15	1077.33	758.45	600.05	505.83	443.70	399.89	367.53	342.79	323.37	307.83	295.17
24000	2126.77	1124.17	791.43	626.14	527.83	462.99	417.28	383.51	357.69	337.43	321.21	308.00
25000	2215.38	1171.01	824.41	652.23	549.82	482.28	434.67	399.49	372.60	351.49	334.59	320.83
26000	2304.00	1217.85	857.38	678.32	571.81	501.58	452.05	415.47	387.50	365.55	347.98	333.67
27000	2392.61	1264.69	890.36	704.41	593.81	520.87	469.44	431.45	402.40	379.61	361.36	346.50
28000	2481.23	1311.53	923.33	730.50	615.80	540.16	486.83	447.43	417.31	393.67	374.74	359.33
29000	2569.84	1358.37	956.31	756.59	637.79	559.45	504.21	463.41	432.21	407.73	388.13	372.17
30000	2658.46	1405.21	989.29	782.68	659.78	578.74	521.60	479.39	447.11	421.79	401.51	385.00
31000	2747.07	1452.05	1022.26	808.76	681.78	598.03	538.99	495.37	462.02	435.85	414.89	397.83
32000	2835.69	1498.90	1055.24	834.85	703.77	617.32	556.37	511.34	476.92	449.91	428.28	410.67
33000	2924.30	1545.74	1088.21	860.94	725.76	636.61	573.76	527.32	491.83	463.97	441.66	423.50
34000	3012.92	1592.58	1121.19	887.03	747.75	655.90	591.14	543.30	506.73	478.03	455.04	436.33
35000	3101.53	1639.42	1154.17	913.12	769.75	675.20	608.53	559.28	521.63	492.09	468.43	449.17
36000	3190.15	1686.26	1187.14	939.21	791.74	694.49	625.92	575.26	536.54	506.15	481.81	462.00
37000	3278.76	1733.10	1220.12	965.30	813.73	713.78	643.30	591.24	551.44	520.21	495.19	474.83
38000	3367.38	1779.94	1253.09	991.39	835.72	733.07	660.69	607.22	566.34	534.27	508.58	487.67
39000	3455.99	1826.78	1286.07	1017.48	857.72	752.36	678.08	623.20	581.25	548.33	521.96	500.50
40000	3544.61	1873.62	1319.05	1043.57	879.71	771.65	695.46	639.18	596.15	562.39	535.35	513.33
41000	3633.22	1920.46	1352.02	1069.65	901.70	790.94	712.85	655.16	611.06	576.45	548.73	526.16
42000	3721.84	1967.30	1385.00	1095.74	923.69	810.23	730.24	671.14	625.96	590.51	562.11	539.00
43000	3810.45	2014.14	1417.97	1121.83	945.69	829.52	747.62	687.12	640.86	604.57	575.50	551.83
44000	3899.07	2060.98	1450.95	1147.92	967.68	848.82	765.01	703.10	655.77	618.62	588.88	564.66
45000	3987.68	2107.82	1483.93	1174.01	989.67	868.11	782.40	719.08	670.67	632.68	602.26	577.50
46000	4076.30	2154.66	1516.90	1200.10	1011.66	887.40	799.78	735.06	685.57	646.74	615.65	590.33
47000	4164.91	2201.50	1549.88	1226.19	1033.66	906.69	817.17	751.04	700.48	660.80	629.03	603.16
48000	4253.53	2248.34	1582.85	1252.28	1055.65	925.98	834.56	767.01	715.38	674.86	642.41	616.00
49000	4342.14	2295.18	1615.83	1278.37	1077.64	945.27	851.94	782.99	730.28	688.92	655.80	628.83
50000	4430.76	2342.02	1648.81	1304.46	1099.64	964.56	869.33	798.97	745.19	702.98	669.18	641.66
55000	4873.83	2576.22	1813.69	1434.90	1209.60	1061.02	956.26	878.87	819.71	773.28	736.10	705.83
60000	5316.91	2810.42	1978.57	1565.35	1319.56	1157.47	1043.19	958.77	894.22	843.58	803.02	769.99
65000	5759.98	3044.63	2143.45	1695.79	1429.52	1253.93	1130.12	1038.66	968.74	913.88	869.93	834.16
70000	6203.06	3278.83	2308.33	1826.24	1539.49	1350.39	1217.06	1118.56	1043.26	984.17	936.85	898.33
75000	6646.13	3513.03	2473.21	1956.68	1649.45	1446.84	1303.99	1198.46	1117.78	1054.47	1003.77	962.49
80000	7089.21	3747.23	2638.09	2087.13	1759.41	1543.30	1390.92	1278.35	1192.30	1124.77	1070.69	1026.66
85000	7532.28	3981.43	2802.97	2217.57	1869.38	1639.75	1477.85	1358.25	1266.82	1195.07	1137.60	1090.82
90000	7975.36	4215.63	2967.85	2348.02	1979.34	1736.21	1564.79	1438.15	1341.33	1265.36	1204.52	1154.99
95000	8418.44	4449.83	3132.73	2478.46	2089.30	1832.66	1651.72	1518.05	1415.85	1335.66	1271.44	1219.16
100000	8861.51	4684.04	3297.61	2608.91	2199.27	1929.12	1738.65	1597.94	1490.37	1405.96	1338.36	1283.32

MONTHLY 11.50%

PAYMENT REQUIRED TO AMORTIZE A LOAN

TERM AMOUNT	13 year	14 years	15 years	16 years	17 years	18 years	19 years	20 years	25 years	30 years	35 years	40 years
50	.62	.61	.59	.58	.56	.55	.55	.54	.51	.50	49	.49
100	1.24	1.21	1.17	1.15	1.12	1.10	1.09	1.07	1.02	1.00	98	.97
200	2.48	2.41	2.34	2.29	2.24	2.20	2.17	2.14	2.04	1.99	1.96	1.94
300	3.72	3.61	3.51	3.43	3.36	3.30	3.25	3.20	3.05	2.98	2.93	2.91
400	4.96	4.81	4.68	4.57	4.48	4.40	4.33	4.27	4.07	3.97	3.91	3.88
500	6.19	6.01	5.85	5.71	5.60	5.50	5.41	5.34	5.09	4.96	4.89	4.85
600	7.43	7.21	7.01	6.85	6.71	6.59	6.49	6.40	6.10	5.95	5.86	5.81
700	8.67	8.41	8.18	7.99	7.83	7.69	7.57	7.47	7.12	6.94	6.84	6.78
800	9.91	9.61	9.35	9.13	8.95	8.79	8.65	8.54	8.14	7.93	7.81	7.75
900	11.15	10.81	10.52	10.28	10.07	9.69	9.74	9.60	9.15	8.92	8.79	8.72
1000	12.38	12.01	11.69	11.42	11.19	10.99	10.82	10.67	10.17	9.91	9.77	9.69
2000	24.76	24.01	23.37	22.83	22.37	21.97	21.63	21.33	20.33	19.81	19.53	19.37
3000	37.14	36.01	35.05	34.24	33.55	32.95	32.44	32.00	30.50	29.71	29.29	29.05
4000	49.52	48.01	46.73	45.65	44.73	43.94	43.25	42.66	40.66	39.62	39.05	38.74
5000	61.90	60.01	58.41	57.06	55.91	54.92	54.07	53.33	50.83	49.52	48.81	48.42
6000	74.28	72.01	70.10	68.47	67.09	65.90	64.88	63.99	60.99	59.42	58.57	58.10
7000	86.66	84.01	81.78	79.89	78.27	76.89	75.69	74.66	71.16	69.33	68.33	67.78
8000	99.04	96.01	93.46	91.30	89.45	87.87	86.50	85.32	81.32	79.23	78.09	77.47
9000	111.42	108.01	105.14	102.71	100.63	98.85	97.31	95.98	91.49	89.13	87.85	87.15
10000	123.80	120.01	116.82	114.12	111.81	109.83	108.13	106.65	101.65	99.03	97.62	96.83
11000	136.18	132.01	128.51	125.53	123.00	120.82	118.94	117.31	111.82	108.94	107.38	106.52
12000	148.56	144.01	140.19	136.94	134.18	131.80	129.75	127.98	121.98	118.84	117.14	116.20
13000	160.93	156.01	151.87	148.36	145.36	142.78	140.56	138.64	132.15	128.74	126.90	125.88
14000	173.31	168.01	163.55	159.77	156.54	153.77	151.38	149.31	142.31	138.65	136.66	135.56
15000	185.69	180.01	175.23	171.18	167.72	164.75	162.19	159.97	152.48	148.55	146.42	145.25
16000	198.07	192.01	186.92	182.59	178.90	175.73	173.00	170.63	162.64	158.45	156.18	154.93
17000	210.45	204.01	198.60	194.00	190.08	186.72	183.81	181.30	172.80	168.35	165.94	164.61
18000	222.83	216.01	210.28	205.41	201.26	197.70	194.62	191.96	182.97	178.26	175.70	174.30
19000	235.21	228.02	221.96	216.83	212.44	208.68	205.44	202.63	193.13	188.16	185.47	183.98
20000	247.59	240.02	233.64	228.24	223.62	219.66	216.25	213.29	203.30	198.06	195.23	193.66
21000	259.97	252.02	245.32	239.65	234.81	230.65	227.06	223.96	213.46	207.97	204.99	203.34
22000	272.35	264.02	257.01	251.06	245.99	241.63	237.87	234.62	223.63	217.87	214.75	213.03
23000	284.73	276.02	268.69	262.47	257.17	252.61	248.69	245.28	233.79	227.77	224.51	222.71
24000	297.11	288.02	280.37	273.88	268.35	263.60	259.50	255.95	243.96	237.67	234.27	232.39
25000	309.48	300.02	292.05	285.30	279.53	274.58	270.31	266.61	254.12	247.58	244.03	242.08
26000	321.86	312.02	303.73	296.71	290.71	285.56	281.12	277.28	264.29	257.48	253.79	251.76
27000	334.24	324.02	315.42	308.12	301.89	296.54	291.93	287.94	274.45	267.38	263.55	261.44
28000	346.62	336.02	327.10	319.53	313.07	307.53	302.75	298.61	284.62	277.29	273.32	271.12
29000	359.00	348.02	338.78	330.94	324.25	318.51	313.56	309.27	294.78	287.19	283.08	280.81
30000	371.38	360.02	350.46	342.35	335.43	329.49	324.37	319.93	304.95	297.09	292.84	290.49
31000	383.76	372.02	362.14	353.77	346.61	340.48	335.18	330.60	315.11	307.00	302.60	300.17
32000	396.14	384.02	373.83	365.18	357.80	351.46	345.99	341.26	325.28	316.90	312.36	309.86
33000	408.52	396.02	385.51	376.59	368.98	362.44	356.81	351.93	335.44	326.80	322.12	319.54
34000	420.90	408.02	397.19	388.00	380.16	373.43	367.62	362.59	345.60	336.70	331.88	329.22
35000	433.28	420.02	408.87	399.41	391.34	384.41	378.43	373.26	355.77	346.61	341.64	338.90
36000	445.66	432.02	420.55	410.82	402.52	395.39	389.24	383.92	365.93	356.51	351.40	348.59
37000	458.03	444.03	432.24	422.24	413.70	406.37	400.06	394.58	376.10	366.41	361.16	358.27
38000	470.41	456.03	443.92	433.65	424.88	417.36	410.87	405.25	386.26	376.32	370.93	367.95
39000	482.79	468.03	455.60	445.06	436.06	428.34	421.68	415.91	396.43	386.22	380.69	377.63
40000	495.17	480.03	467.28	456.47	447.24	439.32	432.49	426.58	406.59	396.12	390.45	387.32
41000	507.55	492.03	478.96	467.88	458.42	450.31	443.30	437.24	416.76	406.02	400.21	397.00
42000	519.93	504.03	490.64	479.29	469.61	461.29	454.12	447.91	426.92	415.93	409.97	406.68
43000	532.31	516.03	502.33	490.71	480.79	472.27	464.93	458.57	437.09	425.83	419.73	416.37
44000	544.69	528.03	514.01	502.12	491.97	483.25	475.74	469.23	447.25	435.73	429.49	426.05
45000	557.07	540.03	525.69	513.53	503.15	494.24	486.55	479.90	457.42	445.64	439.25	435.73
46000	569.45	552.03	537.37	524.94	514.33	505.22	497.37	490.56	467.58	455.54	449.01	445.41
47000	581.83	564.03	549.05	536.35	525.51	516.20	508.18	501.23	477.75	465.44	458.78	455.10
48000	594.21	576.03	560.74	547.76	536.69	527.19	518.99	511.89	487.91	475.34	468.54	464.78
49000	606.58	588.03	572.42	559.18	547.87	538.17	529.80	522.56	498.07	485.25	478.30	474.46
50000	618.96	600.03	584.10	570.59	559.05	549.15	540.61	533.22	508.24	495.15	488.06	484.15
55000	680.86	660.04	642.51	627.65	614.96	604.07	594.67	586.54	559.06	544.67	536.86	532.56
60000	742.76	720.04	700.92	684.70	670.86	658.98	648.74	639.86	609.89	594.18	585.67	580.97
65000	804.65	780.04	759.33	741.76	726.77	713.90	702.80	693.18	660.71	643.69	634.47	629.39
70000	866.55	840.04	817.74	798.82	782.67	768.81	756.86	746.51	711.53	693.21	683.28	677.80
75000	928.44	900.05	876.15	855.88	838.58	823.73	810.92	799.83	762.36	742.72	732.09	726.22
80000	990.34	960.05	934.56	912.94	894.48	878.64	864.98	853.15	813.18	792.24	780.89	774.63
85000	1052.24	1020.05	992.97	970.00	950.39	933.56	919.04	906.47	864.00	841.75	829.70	823.04
90000	1114.13	1080.05	1051.28	1027.05	1006.29	988.47	973.10	959.79	914.83	891.27	878.50	871.46
95000	1176.03	1140.06	1109.79	1084.11	1062.20	1043.39	1027.16	1013.11	965.65	940.78	927.31	919.87
100000	1237.92	1200.06	1168.19	1141.17	1118.10	1098.30	1081.22	1066.43	1016.47	990.30	976.11	968.29

12.00% MONTHLY

PAYMENT REQUIRED TO AMORTIZE A LOAN

TERM AMOUNT	1 year	2 years	3 years	4 years	5 years	6 years	7 years	8 years	9 years	10 years	11 years	12 years
50	4.45	2.36	1.67	1.32	1.12	.98	.89	.82	.76	.72	.69	.66
100	8.89	4.71	3.33	2.64	2.23	1.96	1.77	1.63	1.52	1.44	1.37	1.32
200	17.77	9.42	6.65	5.27	4.45	3.92	3.54	3.26	3.04	2.87	2.74	2.63
300	26.66	14.13	9.97	7.91	6.68	5.87	5.30	4.88	4.56	4.31	4.11	3.95
400	35.54	18.83	13.29	10.54	8.90	7.83	7.07	6.51	6.08	5.74	5.48	5.26
500	44.43	23.54	16.61	13.17	11.13	9.78	8.83	8.13	7.60	7.18	6.84	6.57
600	53.31	28.25	19.93	15.81	13.35	11.74	10.60	9.76	9.12	8.61	8.21	7.89
700	62.20	32.96	23.26	18.44	15.58	13.69	12.36	11.38	10.63	10.05	9.58	9.20
800	71.08	37.66	26.58	21.07	17.80	15.65	14.13	13.01	12.15	11.48	10.95	10.51
900	79.97	42.37	29.90	23.71	20.03	17.60	15.89	14.63	13.67	12.92	12.32	11.83
1000	88.85	47.08	33.22	26.34	22.25	19.56	17.66	16.26	15.19	14.35	13.68	13.14
2000	177.70	94.15	66.43	52.67	44.49	39.11	35.31	32.51	30.37	28.70	27.36	26.27
3000	266.55	141.23	99.65	79.01	66.74	58.66	52.96	48.76	45.56	43.05	41.04	39.41
4000	355.40	188.30	132.86	105.34	88.98	78.21	70.62	65.02	60.74	57.39	54.72	52.54
5000	444.25	235.37	166.08	131.67	111.23	97.76	88.27	81.27	75.93	71.74	68.39	65.68
6000	533.10	282.45	199.29	158.01	133.47	117.31	105.92	97.52	91.11	86.09	82.07	78.81
7000	621.95	329.52	232.51	184.34	155.72	136.86	123.57	113.77	106.29	100.43	95.75	91.94
8000	710.80	376.59	265.72	210.68	177.96	156.41	141.23	130.03	121.48	114.78	109.43	105.08
9000	799.64	423.67	298.93	237.01	200.21	175.96	158.88	146.28	136.66	129.13	123.11	118.21
10000	888.49	470.74	332.15	263.34	222.45	195.51	176.53	162.53	151.85	143.48	136.78	131.35
11000	977.34	517.81	365.36	289.68	244.69	215.06	194.19	178.79	167.03	157.82	150.46	144.48
12000	1066.19	564.89	398.58	316.01	266.94	234.61	211.84	195.04	182.22	172.17	164.14	157.62
13000	1155.04	611.96	431.79	342.34	289.18	254.16	229.49	211.29	197.40	186.52	177.82	170.75
14000	1243.89	659.03	465.01	368.68	311.43	273.71	247.14	227.54	212.58	200.86	191.50	183.88
15000	1332.74	706.11	498.22	395.01	333.67	293.26	264.80	243.80	227.77	215.21	205.17	197.02
16000	1421.59	753.18	531.43	421.35	355.92	312.81	282.45	260.05	242.95	229.56	218.85	210.15
17000	1510.43	800.25	564.65	447.68	378.16	332.36	300.10	276.30	258.14	243.91	232.53	223.29
18000	1599.28	847.33	597.86	474.01	400.41	351.91	317.75	292.56	273.32	258.25	246.21	236.42
19000	1688.13	894.40	631.08	500.35	422.65	371.46	335.41	308.81	288.51	272.60	259.88	249.55
20000	1776.98	941.47	664.29	526.68	444.89	391.01	353.06	325.06	303.69	286.95	273.56	262.69
21000	1865.83	988.55	697.51	553.02	467.14	410.56	370.71	341.31	318.87	301.29	287.24	275.82
22000	1954.68	1035.62	730.72	579.35	489.38	430.11	388.37	357.57	334.06	315.64	300.92	288.96
23000	2043.53	1082.69	763.93	605.68	511.63	449.66	406.02	373.82	349.24	329.99	314.60	302.09
24000	2132.38	1129.77	797.15	632.02	533.87	469.21	423.67	390.07	364.43	344.34	328.27	315.23
25000	2221.22	1176.84	830.36	658.35	556.12	488.76	441.32	406.33	379.61	358.68	341.95	328.36
26000	2310.07	1223.92	863.58	684.68	578.36	508.31	458.98	422.58	394.80	373.03	355.63	341.49
27000	2398.92	1270.99	896.79	711.02	600.61	527.86	476.63	438.83	409.98	387.38	369.31	354.63
28000	2487.77	1318.06	930.01	737.35	622.85	547.41	494.28	455.08	425.16	401.72	382.99	367.76
29000	2576.62	1365.14	963.22	763.69	645.09	566.96	511.93	471.34	440.35	416.07	396.66	380.90
30000	2665.47	1412.21	996.43	790.02	667.34	586.51	529.59	487.59	455.53	430.42	410.34	394.03
31000	2754.32	1459.28	1029.65	816.35	689.58	606.06	547.24	503.84	470.72	444.76	424.02	407.16
32000	2843.17	1506.36	1062.86	842.69	711.83	625.61	564.89	520.10	485.90	459.11	437.70	420.30
33000	2932.02	1553.43	1096.08	869.02	734.07	645.16	582.55	536.35	501.08	473.46	451.38	433.43
34000	3020.86	1600.50	1129.29	895.36	756.32	664.71	600.20	552.60	516.27	487.81	465.05	446.57
35000	3109.71	1647.58	1162.51	921.69	778.56	684.26	617.85	568.85	531.45	502.15	478.73	459.70
36000	3198.56	1694.65	1195.72	948.02	800.81	703.81	635.50	585.11	546.64	516.50	492.41	472.84
37000	3287.41	1741.72	1228.93	974.36	823.05	723.36	653.16	601.36	561.82	530.85	506.09	485.97
38000	3376.26	1788.80	1262.15	1000.69	845.29	742.91	670.81	617.61	577.01	545.19	519.76	499.10
39000	3465.11	1835.87	1295.36	1027.02	867.54	762.46	688.46	633.87	592.19	559.54	533.44	512.24
40000	3553.96	1882.94	1328.58	1053.36	889.78	782.01	706.11	650.12	607.37	573.89	547.12	525.37
41000	3642.81	1930.02	1361.79	1079.69	912.03	801.56	723.77	666.37	622.56	588.24	560.80	538.51
42000	3731.65	1977.09	1395.01	1106.03	934.27	821.11	741.42	682.62	637.74	602.58	574.48	551.64
43000	3820.50	2024.16	1428.22	1132.36	956.52	840.66	759.07	698.88	652.93	616.93	588.15	564.78
44000	3909.35	2071.24	1461.43	1158.69	978.76	860.21	776.73	715.13	668.11	631.28	601.83	577.91
45000	3998.20	2118.31	1494.65	1185.03	1001.01	879.76	794.38	731.38	683.30	645.62	615.51	591.04
46000	4087.05	2165.38	1527.86	1211.36	1023.25	899.31	812.03	747.64	698.48	659.97	629.19	604.18
47000	4175.90	2212.46	1561.08	1237.70	1045.49	918.86	829.68	763.89	713.66	674.32	642.87	617.31
48000	4264.75	2259.53	1594.29	1264.03	1067.74	938.41	847.34	780.14	728.85	688.67	656.54	630.45
49000	4353.60	2306.61	1627.51	1290.36	1089.98	957.96	864.99	796.39	744.03	703.01	670.22	643.58
50000	4442.44	2353.68	1660.72	1316.70	1112.23	977.51	882.64	812.65	759.22	717.36	683.90	656.71
55000	4886.69	2589.05	1826.79	1448.37	1223.45	1075.27	970.91	893.91	835.14	789.10	752.29	722.39
60000	5330.93	2824.41	1992.86	1580.04	1334.67	1173.02	1059.17	975.18	911.06	860.83	820.68	788.06
65000	5775.18	3059.78	2158.94	1711.70	1445.89	1270.77	1147.43	1056.44	986.98	932.57	889.07	853.73
70000	6219.42	3295.15	2325.01	1843.37	1557.12	1368.52	1235.70	1137.70	1062.90	1004.30	957.46	919.40
75000	6663.66	3530.52	2491.08	1975.04	1668.34	1466.27	1323.96	1218.97	1138.82	1076.04	1025.85	985.07
80000	7107.91	3765.88	2657.15	2106.71	1779.56	1564.02	1412.22	1300.23	1214.74	1147.77	1094.24	1050.74
85000	7552.15	4001.25	2823.22	2238.38	1890.78	1661.77	1500.49	1381.50	1290.66	1219.51	1162.62	1116.41
90000	7996.40	4236.62	2989.29	2370.05	2002.01	1759.52	1588.75	1462.76	1366.59	1291.24	1231.01	1182.08
95000	8440.64	4471.98	3155.36	2501.72	2113.23	1857.27	1677.01	1544.02	1442.51	1362.98	1299.40	1247.75
100000	8884.88	4707.35	3321.44	2633.39	2224.45	1955.02	1765.28	1625.29	1518.43	1434.71	1367.79	1313.42

MONTHLY

12.00%

PAYMENT REQUIRED TO AMORTIZE A LOAN

TERM AMOUNT	13 year	14 years	15 years	16 years	17 years	18 years	19 years	20 years	25 years	30 years	35 years	40 years
50	.64	.62	.6i	.59	.58	.57	.56	.56	.53	.52	.51	.51
100	1.27	1.24	1.21	1.18	1.16	1.14	1.12	1.11	1.06	1.03	1.02	1.01
200	2.54	2.47	2.41	2.35	2.31	2.27	2.24	2.21	2.11	2.06	2.04	2.02
300	3.81	3.70	3.61	3.53	3.46	3.40	3.35	3.31	3.16	3.09	3.05	3.03
400	5.08	4.93	4.81	4.70	4.61	4.53	4.47	4.41	4.22	4.12	4.07	4.04
500	6.35	6.16	6.01	5.87	5.76	5.66	5.58	5.51	5.27	5.15	5.08	5.05
600	7.62	7.39	7.21	7.05	6.91	6.80	6.70	6.61	6.32	6.18	6.10	6.06
700	8.89	8.63	8.41	8.22	8.06	7.93	7.81	7.71	7.38	7.21	7.11	7.06
800	10.15	9.86	9.61	9.39	9.21	9.06	8.93	8.81	8.43	8.23	8.13	8.07
900	11.42	11.09	10.81	10.57	10.37	10.19	10.04	9.91	9.48	9.26	9.14	9.08
1000	12.69	12.32	12.01	11.74	11.52	11.32	11.16	11.02	10.54	10.29	10.16	10.09
2000	25.38	24.63	24.01	23.48	23.03	22.64	22.31	22.03	21.07	20.58	20.32	20.17
3000	38.06	36.95	36.01	35.22	34.54	33.96	33.47	33.04	31.60	30.86	30.47	30.26
4000	50.75	49.26	48.01	46.95	46.05	45.28	44.62	44.05	42.13	41.15	40.63	40.34
5000	63.44	61.58	60.01	58.69	57.57	56.60	55.77	55.06	52.67	51.44	50.78	50.43
6000	76.12	73.89	72.02	70.43	69.08	67.92	66.93	66.07	63.20	61.72	60.94	60.51
7000	88.81	86.21	84.02	82.17	80.59	79.24	78.08	77.08	73.73	72.01	71.09	70.60
8000	101.50	98.52	96.02	93.90	92.10	90.56	89.24	88.09	84.26	82.29	81.25	80.68
9000	114.18	110.83	108.02	105.64	103.61	101.88	100.39	99.10	94.80	92.58	91.40	90.77
10000	126.87	123.15	120.02	117.38	115.13	113.20	111.54	110.11	105.33	102.87	101.56	100.85
11000	139.56	135.46	132.02	129.11	126.64	124.52	122.70	121.12	115.86	113.15	111.72	110.94
12000	152.24	147.78	144.03	140.85	138.15	135.84	133.85	132.14	126.39	123.44	121.87	121.02
13000	164.93	160.09	156.03	152.59	149.66	147.16	145.01	143.15	136.92	133.72	132.03	131.11
14000	177.62	172.41	168.03	164.33	161.18	158.48	156.16	154.16	147.46	144.01	142.18	141.19
15000	190.30	184.72	180.03	176.06	172.69	169.80	167.31	165.17	157.99	154.30	152.34	151.28
16000	202.99	197.03	192.03	187.80	184.20	181.12	178.47	176.18	168.52	164.58	162.49	161.36
17000	215.68	209.35	204.03	199.54	195.71	192.44	189.62	187.19	179.05	174.87	172.65	171.45
18000	228.36	221.66	216.04	211.28	207.22	203.76	200.77	198.20	189.59	185.16	182.80	181.53
19000	241.05	233.98	228.04	223.01	218.74	215.08	211.93	209.21	200.12	195.44	192.96	191.62
20000	253.74	246.29	240.04	234.75	230.25	226.40	223.08	220.22	210.65	205.73	203.11	201.70
21000	266.42	258.61	252.04	246.49	241.76	237.71	234.24	231.23	221.18	216.01	213.27	211.79
22000	279.11	270.92	264.04	258.22	253.27	249.03	245.39	242.24	231.71	226.30	223.43	221.87
23000	291.80	283.23	276.04	269.96	264.78	260.35	256.54	253.25	242.25	236.59	233.58	231.96
24000	304.48	295.55	288.05	281.70	276.30	271.67	267.70	264.27	252.78	246.87	243.74	242.04
25000	317.17	307.86	300.05	293.44	287.81	282.99	278.85	275.28	263.31	257.16	253.89	252.13
26000	329.86	320.18	312.05	305.17	299.32	294.31	290.01	286.29	273.84	267.44	264.05	262.21
27000	342.54	332.49	324.05	316.91	310.83	305.63	301.16	297.30	284.38	277.73	274.20	272.30
28000	355.23	344.81	336.05	328.65	322.35	316.95	312.31	308.31	294.91	288.02	284.36	282.38
29000	367.92	357.12	348.05	340.39	333.86	328.27	323.47	319.32	305.44	298.30	294.51	292.47
30000	380.60	369.43	360.06	352.12	345.37	339.59	334.62	330.33	315.97	308.59	304.67	302.55
31000	393.29	381.75	372.06	363.86	356.88	350.91	345.77	341.34	326.50	318.87	314.83	312.64
32000	405.98	394.06	384.06	375.60	368.39	362.23	356.93	352.35	337.04	329.16	324.98	322.72
33000	418.66	406.38	396.06	387.33	379.91	373.55	368.08	363.36	347.57	339.45	335.14	332.81
34000	431.35	418.69	408.06	399.07	391.42	384.87	379.24	374.37	358.10	349.73	345.29	342.89
35000	444.04	431.01	420.06	410.81	402.93	396.19	390.39	385.39	368.63	360.02	355.45	352.98
36000	456.72	443.32	432.07	422.55	414.44	407.51	401.54	396.40	379.17	370.31	365.60	363.06
37000	469.41	455.63	444.07	434.28	425.95	418.83	412.70	407.41	389.70	380.59	375.76	373.15
38000	482.10	467.95	456.07	446.02	437.47	430.15	423.85	418.42	400.23	390.88	385.91	383.23
39000	494.78	480.26	468.07	457.76	448.98	441.47	435.01	429.43	410.76	401.16	396.07	393.32
40000	507.47	492.58	480.07	469.50	460.49	452.79	446.16	440.44	421.29	411.45	406.22	403.40
41000	520.16	504.89	492.07	481.23	472.00	464.10	457.31	451.45	431.83	421.74	416.38	413.49
42000	532.84	517.21	504.08	492.97	483.52	475.42	468.47	462.46	442.36	432.02	426.54	423.57
43000	545.53	529.52	516.08	504.71	495.03	486.74	479.62	473.47	452.89	442.31	436.69	433.66
44000	558.22	541.83	528.08	516.44	506.54	498.06	490.77	484.48	463.42	452.59	446.85	443.74
45000	570.90	554.15	540.08	528.18	518.05	509.38	501.93	495.49	473.96	462.88	457.00	453.83
46000	583.59	566.46	552.08	539.92	529.56	520.70	513.08	506.50	484.49	473.17	467.16	463.91
47000	596.28	578.78	564.08	551.66	541.08	532.02	524.24	517.52	495.02	483.45	477.31	474.00
48000	608.96	591.09	576.09	563.39	552.59	543.34	535.39	528.53	505.55	493.74	487.47	484.08
49000	621.65	603.41	588.09	575.13	564.10	554.66	546.54	539.54	516.08	504.03	497.62	494.17
50000	634.34	615.72	600.09	586.87	575.61	565.98	557.70	550.55	526.62	514.31	507.78	504.25
55000	697.77	677.29	660.10	645.55	633.17	622.58	613.47	605.60	579.28	565.74	558.56	554.68
60000	761.20	738.86	720.11	704.24	690.73	679.18	669.24	660.66	631.94	617.17	609.33	605.10
65000	824.64	800.43	780.11	762.93	748.30	735.77	725.01	715.71	684.60	668.60	660.11	655.53
70000	888.07	862.01	840.12	821.61	805.86	792.37	780.77	770.77	737.26	720.03	710.89	705.95
75000	951.50	923.58	900.13	880.30	863.42	848.97	836.54	825.82	789.92	771.46	761.67	756.38
80000	1014.94	985.15	960.14	938.99	920.98	905.57	892.31	880.87	842.58	822.90	812.44	806.80
85000	1078.37	1046.72	1020.15	997.67	978.54	962.16	948.08	935.93	895.25	874.33	863.22	857.23
90000	1141.80	1108.29	1080.16	1056.36	1036.10	1018.76	1003.85	990.98	947.91	925.76	914.00	907.65
95000	1205.24	1169.86	1140.16	1115.04	1093.66	1075.36	1059.62	1046.04	1000.57	977.19	964.78	958.08
100000	1268.67	1231.43	1200.17	1173.73	1151.22	1131.96	1115.39	1101.09	1053.23	1028.62	1015.55	1008.50

12.50% MONTHLY
PAYMENT REQUIRED TO AMORTIZE A LOAN

TERM AMOUNT	1 year	2 years	3 years	4 years	5 years	6 years	7 years	8 years	9 years	10 years	11 years	12 years
50	4.46	2.37	1.68	1.33	1.13	1.00	.90	.83	.78	.74	.70	.68
100	8.91	4.74	3.35	2.66	2.25	1.99	1.80	1.66	1.55	1.47	1.40	1.35
200	17.82	9.47	6.70	5.32	4.50	3.97	3.59	3.31	3.10	2.93	2.80	2.69
300	26.73	14.20	10.04	7.98	6.75	5.95	5.38	4.96	4.65	4.40	4.20	4.04
400	35.64	18.93	13.39	10.64	9.00	7.93	7.17	6.62	6.19	5.86	5.60	5.38
500	44.55	23.66	16.73	13.29	11.25	9.91	8.97	8.27	7.74	7.32	6.99	6.72
600	53.45	28.39	20.08	15.95	13.50	11.89	10.76	9.92	9.29	8.79	8.39	8.07
700	62.36	33.12	23.42	18.61	15.75	13.87	12.55	11.58	10.83	10.25	9.79	9.41
800	71.27	37.85	26.77	21.27	18.00	15.85	14.34	13.23	12.38	11.72	11.19	10.76
900	80.18	42.58	30.11	23.93	20.25	17.84	16.13	14.88	13.93	13.18	12.58	12.10
1000	89.09	47.31	33.46	26.58	22.50	19.82	17.93	16.53	15.47	14.64	13.98	13.44
2000	178.17	94.62	66.91	53.16	45.00	39.63	35.85	33.06	30.94	29.28	27.96	26.88
3000	267.25	141.93	100.37	79.74	67.50	59.44	53.77	49.59	46.41	43.92	41.93	40.32
4000	356.34	189.23	133.82	106.32	90.00	79.25	71.69	66.12	61.88	58.56	55.91	53.76
5000	445.42	236.54	167.27	132.90	112.49	99.06	89.61	82.65	77.34	73.19	69.88	67.20
6000	534.50	283.85	200.73	159.48	134.99	118.87	107.53	99.18	92.81	87.83	83.86	80.64
7000	623.59	331.16	234.18	186.06	157.49	138.68	125.45	115.71	108.28	102.47	97.83	94.08
8000	712.67	378.46	267.63	212.64	179.99	158.49	143.37	132.24	123.75	117.11	111.81	107.51
9000	801.75	425.77	301.09	239.22	202.49	178.31	161.30	148.76	139.21	131.74	125.78	120.95
10000	890.83	473.08	334.54	265.80	224.98	198.12	179.22	165.29	154.68	146.38	139.76	134.39
11000	979.92	520.39	367.99	292.38	247.48	217.93	197.14	181.82	170.15	161.02	153.73	147.83
12000	1069.00	567.69	401.45	318.96	269.98	237.74	215.06	198.35	185.62	175.66	167.71	161.27
13000	1158.08	615.00	434.90	345.54	292.48	257.55	232.98	214.88	201.08	190.29	181.69	174.71
14000	1247.17	662.31	468.36	372.12	314.98	277.36	250.90	231.41	216.55	204.93	195.66	188.15
15000	1336.25	709.61	501.81	398.70	337.47	297.17	268.82	247.94	232.02	219.57	209.64	201.58
16000	1425.33	756.92	535.26	425.28	359.97	316.98	286.74	264.47	247.49	234.21	223.61	215.02
17000	1514.41	804.23	568.72	451.86	382.47	336.80	304.67	280.99	262.95	248.84	237.59	228.46
18000	1603.50	851.54	602.17	478.44	404.97	356.61	322.59	297.52	278.42	263.48	251.56	241.90
19000	1692.58	898.84	635.62	505.02	427.47	376.42	340.51	314.05	293.89	278.12	265.54	255.34
20000	1781.66	946.15	669.08	531.60	449.96	396.23	358.43	330.58	309.36	292.76	279.51	268.78
21000	1870.75	993.46	702.53	558.18	472.46	416.04	376.35	347.11	324.82	307.39	293.49	282.22
22000	1959.83	1040.77	735.98	584.76	494.96	435.85	394.27	363.64	340.29	322.03	307.46	295.65
23000	2048.91	1088.07	769.44	611.34	517.46	455.66	412.19	380.17	355.76	336.67	321.44	309.09
24000	2137.99	1135.38	802.89	637.92	539.96	475.47	430.11	396.70	371.23	351.31	335.42	322.53
25000	2227.08	1182.69	836.35	664.50	562.45	495.28	448.04	413.23	386.69	365.95	349.39	335.97
26000	2316.16	1230.00	869.80	691.08	584.95	515.10	465.96	429.75	402.16	380.58	363.37	349.41
27000	2405.24	1277.30	903.25	717.66	607.45	534.91	483.88	446.28	417.63	395.22	377.34	362.85
28000	2494.33	1324.61	936.71	744.24	629.95	554.72	501.80	462.81	433.10	409.86	391.32	376.29
29000	2583.41	1371.92	970.16	770.82	652.45	574.53	519.72	479.34	448.56	424.50	405.29	389.72
30000	2672.49	1419.22	1003.61	797.40	674.94	594.34	537.64	495.87	464.03	439.13	419.27	403.16
31000	2761.57	1466.53	1037.07	823.98	697.44	614.15	555.56	512.40	479.50	453.77	433.24	416.60
32000	2850.66	1513.84	1070.52	850.56	719.94	633.96	573.48	528.93	494.97	468.41	447.22	430.04
33000	2939.74	1561.15	1103.97	877.14	742.44	653.77	591.41	545.46	510.43	483.05	461.19	443.48
34000	3028.82	1608.45	1137.43	903.72	764.93	673.59	609.33	561.98	525.90	497.68	475.17	456.92
35000	3117.91	1655.76	1170.88	930.30	787.43	693.40	627.25	578.51	541.37	512.32	489.15	470.36
36000	3206.99	1703.07	1204.34	956.88	809.93	713.21	645.17	595.04	556.84	526.96	503.12	483.79
37000	3296.07	1750.38	1237.79	983.46	832.43	733.02	663.09	611.57	572.30	541.60	517.10	497.23
38000	3385.15	1797.68	1271.24	1010.04	854.93	752.83	681.01	628.10	587.77	556.23	531.07	510.67
39000	3474.24	1844.99	1304.70	1036.63	877.42	772.64	698.93	644.63	603.24	570.87	545.05	524.11
40000	3563.32	1892.30	1338.15	1063.20	899.92	792.45	716.85	661.16	618.71	585.51	559.02	537.55
41000	3652.40	1939.60	1371.60	1089.78	922.42	812.26	734.78	677.69	634.17	600.15	573.00	550.99
42000	3741.49	1986.91	1405.06	1116.36	944.92	832.07	752.70	694.21	649.64	614.78	586.97	564.43
43000	3830.57	2034.22	1438.51	1142.94	967.42	851.89	770.62	710.74	665.11	629.42	600.95	577.86
44000	3919.65	2081.53	1471.96	1169.52	989.91	871.70	788.54	727.27	680.58	644.06	614.92	591.30
45000	4008.73	2128.83	1505.42	1196.10	1012.41	891.51	806.46	743.80	696.04	658.70	628.90	604.74
46000	4097.82	2176.14	1538.87	1222.68	1034.91	911.32	824.38	760.33	711.51	673.34	642.87	618.18
47000	4186.90	2223.45	1572.33	1249.26	1057.41	931.13	842.30	776.86	726.98	687.97	656.85	631.62
48000	4275.98	2270.76	1605.78	1275.84	1079.91	950.94	860.22	793.39	742.45	702.61	670.83	645.06
49000	4365.07	2318.06	1639.23	1302.42	1102.40	970.75	878.15	809.92	757.91	717.25	684.80	658.50
50000	4454.15	2365.37	1672.69	1329.00	1124.90	990.56	896.07	826.45	773.38	731.89	698.78	671.93
55000	4899.56	2601.91	1839.95	1461.90	1237.39	1089.62	985.67	909.09	850.72	805.07	768.65	739.13
60000	5344.98	2838.44	2007.22	1594.80	1349.88	1188.68	1075.28	991.73	928.06	878.26	838.53	806.32
65000	5790.39	3074.98	2174.49	1727.70	1462.37	1287.73	1164.89	1074.38	1005.40	951.45	908.41	873.51
70000	6235.81	3311.52	2341.76	1860.60	1574.86	1386.79	1254.49	1157.02	1082.73	1024.64	978.29	940.71
75000	6681.22	3548.05	2509.03	1993.50	1687.35	1485.84	1344.10	1239.67	1160.07	1097.83	1048.16	1007.90
80000	7126.63	3784.59	2676.30	2126.40	1799.84	1584.90	1433.70	1322.31	1237.41	1171.01	1118.04	1075.09
85000	7572.05	4021.13	2843.56	2259.30	1912.33	1683.96	1523.31	1404.95	1314.75	1244.20	1187.92	1142.28
90000	8017.46	4257.66	3010.83	2392.20	2024.82	1783.01	1612.92	1487.60	1392.08	1317.39	1257.79	1209.48
95000	8462.88	4494.20	3178.10	2525.10	2137.31	1882.07	1702.52	1570.24	1469.42	1390.58	1327.67	1276.67
100000	8908.29	4730.74	3345.37	2658.00	2249.80	1981.12	1792.13	1652.89	1546.76	1463.77	1397.55	1343.86

MONTHLY 12.50%

PAYMENT REQUIRED TO AMORTIZE A LOAN

TERM AMOUNT	13 year	14 years	15 years	16 years	17 years	18 years	19 years	20 years	25 years	30 years	35 years	40 years
50	.65	.64	.62	.61	.60	.59	.58	.57	.55	.54	.53	.53
100	1.30	1.27	1.24	1.21	1.19	1.17	1.15	1.14	1.10	1.07	1.06	1.05
200	2.60	2.53	2.47	2.42	2.37	2.34	2.30	2.28	2.19	2.14	2.12	2.10
300	3.90	3.79	3.70	3.63	3.56	3.50	3.45	3.41	3.28	3.21	3.17	3.15
400	5.20	5.06	4.94	4.83	4.74	4.67	4.60	4.55	4.37	4.27	4.23	4.20
500	6.50	6.32	6.17	6.04	5.93	5.84	5.75	5.69	5.46	5.34	5.28	5.25
600	7.80	7.58	7.40	7.25	7.11	7.00	6.90	6.82	6.55	6.41	6.34	6.30
700	9.10	8.85	8.63	8.45	8.30	8.17	8.05	7.96	7.64	7.48	7.39	7.35
800	10.40	10.11	9.87	9.66	9.48	9.33	9.20	9.09	8.73	8.54	8.45	8.40
900	11.70	11.37	11.10	10.87	10.67	10.50	10.35	10.23	9.82	9.61	9.50	9.45
1000	13.00	12.64	12.33	12.07	11.85	11.67	11.50	11.37	10.91	10.68	10.56	10.49
2000	26.00	25.27	24.66	24.14	23.70	23.33	23.00	22.73	21.81	21.35	21.11	20.98
3000	39.00	37.90	36.98	36.21	35.55	34.99	34.50	34.09	32.72	32.02	31.66	31.47
4000	52.00	50.53	49.31	48.27	47.39	46.65	46.00	45.45	43.62	42.70	42.22	41.96
5000	64.99	63.16	61.63	60.34	59.24	58.31	57.50	56.81	54.52	53.37	52.77	52.45
6000	77.99	75.80	73.96	72.41	71.09	69.97	69.00	68.17	65.43	64.04	63.32	62.94
7000	90.99	88.43	86.28	84.47	82.94	81.63	80.50	79.53	76.33	74.71	73.87	73.43
8000	103.99	101.06	98.61	96.54	94.78	93.29	92.00	90.90	87.23	85.39	84.43	83.92
9000	116.98	113.69	110.93	108.61	106.63	104.95	103.50	102.26	98.14	96.06	94.98	94.41
10000	129.98	126.32	123.26	120.67	118.48	116.61	115.00	113.62	109.04	106.73	105.53	104.90
11000	142.98	138.95	135.58	132.74	130.32	128.27	126.50	124.98	119.94	117.40	116.08	115.39
12000	155.98	151.59	147.91	144.81	142.17	139.93	138.00	136.34	130.85	128.08	126.64	125.88
13000	168.97	164.22	160.23	156.87	154.02	151.59	149.50	147.70	141.75	138.75	137.19	136.36
14000	181.97	176.85	172.56	168.94	165.87	163.25	161.00	159.06	152.65	149.42	147.74	146.85
15000	194.97	189.48	184.88	181.01	177.71	174.91	172.50	170.43	163.56	160.09	158.29	157.34
16000	207.97	202.11	197.21	193.07	189.56	186.57	184.00	181.79	174.46	170.77	168.85	167.83
17000	220.97	214.74	209.53	205.14	201.41	198.23	195.50	193.15	185.37	181.44	179.40	178.32
18000	233.96	227.38	221.86	217.21	213.26	209.89	207.00	204.51	196.27	192.11	189.95	188.81
19000	246.96	240.01	234.18	229.27	225.10	221.55	218.50	215.87	207.17	202.78	200.50	199.30
20000	259.96	252.64	246.51	241.34	236.95	233.21	230.00	227.23	218.08	213.46	211.06	209.79
21000	272.96	265.27	258.83	253.41	248.80	244.87	241.49	238.59	228.98	224.13	221.61	220.28
22000	285.95	277.90	271.16	265.47	260.64	256.53	252.99	249.96	239.88	234.80	232.16	230.77
23000	298.95	290.53	283.49	277.54	272.49	268.19	264.49	261.32	250.79	245.47	242.71	241.26
24000	311.95	303.17	295.81	289.61	284.34	279.85	275.99	272.68	261.69	256.15	253.27	251.75
25000	324.95	315.80	308.14	301.67	296.19	291.51	287.49	284.04	272.59	266.82	263.82	262.23
26000	337.94	328.43	320.46	313.74	308.03	303.17	298.99	295.40	283.50	277.49	274.37	272.72
27000	350.94	341.06	332.79	325.81	319.88	314.83	310.49	306.76	294.40	288.16	284.92	283.21
28000	363.94	353.69	345.11	337.87	331.73	326.49	321.99	318.12	305.30	298.84	295.48	293.70
29000	376.94	366.32	357.44	349.94	343.58	338.15	333.49	329.48	316.21	309.51	306.03	304.19
30000	389.93	378.96	369.76	362.01	355.42	349.81	344.99	340.85	327.11	320.18	316.58	314.68
31000	402.93	391.59	382.09	374.07	367.27	361.47	356.49	352.21	338.01	330.85	327.13	325.17
32000	415.93	404.22	394.41	386.14	379.12	373.13	367.99	363.57	348.92	341.53	337.69	335.66
33000	428.93	416.85	406.74	398.21	390.96	384.79	379.49	374.93	359.82	352.20	348.24	346.15
34000	441.93	429.48	419.06	410.27	402.81	396.45	390.99	386.29	370.73	362.87	358.79	356.64
35000	454.92	442.11	431.39	422.34	414.66	408.11	402.49	397.65	381.63	373.55	369.34	367.13
36000	467.92	454.75	443.71	434.41	426.51	419.77	413.99	409.02	392.53	384.22	379.90	377.62
37000	480.92	467.38	456.04	446.47	438.35	431.43	425.49	420.38	403.44	394.89	390.45	388.11
38000	493.92	480.01	468.36	458.54	450.20	443.09	436.99	431.74	414.34	405.56	401.00	398.59
39000	506.91	492.64	480.69	470.61	462.05	454.75	448.49	443.10	425.24	416.24	411.55	409.08
40000	519.91	505.27	493.01	482.67	473.90	466.41	459.99	454.46	436.15	426.91	422.11	419.57
41000	532.91	517.90	505.34	494.74	485.74	478.07	471.48	465.82	447.05	437.58	432.66	430.06
42000	545.91	530.54	517.66	506.81	497.59	489.73	482.98	477.18	457.95	448.25	443.21	440.55
43000	558.90	543.17	529.99	518.87	509.44	501.39	494.48	488.55	468.86	458.93	453.76	451.04
44000	571.90	555.80	542.31	530.94	521.28	513.05	505.98	499.91	479.76	469.60	464.32	461.53
45000	584.90	568.43	554.64	543.01	533.13	524.71	517.48	511.27	490.66	480.27	474.87	472.02
46000	597.90	581.06	566.97	555.07	544.98	536.37	528.98	522.63	501.57	490.94	485.42	482.51
47000	610.90	593.69	579.29	567.14	556.83	548.03	540.48	533.99	512.47	501.62	495.97	493.00
48000	623.89	606.33	591.62	579.21	568.67	559.69	551.98	545.35	523.37	512.29	506.53	503.49
49000	636.89	618.96	603.94	591.27	580.52	571.35	563.48	556.71	534.28	522.96	517.08	513.98
50000	649.89	631.59	616.27	603.34	592.37	583.01	574.98	568.08	545.18	533.63	527.63	524.46
55000	714.88	694.75	677.89	663.67	651.60	641.31	632.48	624.88	599.70	587.00	580.39	576.91
60000	779.86	757.91	739.52	724.01	710.84	699.61	689.98	681.69	654.22	640.36	633.16	629.36
65000	844.85	821.06	801.14	784.34	770.08	757.91	747.47	738.50	708.74	693.72	685.92	681.80
70000	909.84	884.22	862.77	844.67	829.31	816.21	804.97	795.30	763.25	747.09	738.68	734.25
75000	974.83	947.38	924.40	905.01	888.55	874.51	862.47	852.11	817.77	800.45	791.45	786.69
80000	1039.82	1010.54	986.02	965.34	947.79	932.81	919.97	908.92	872.29	853.81	844.21	839.14
85000	1104.81	1073.70	1047.65	1025.67	1007.02	991.11	977.46	965.72	926.81	907.17	896.97	891.59
90000	1169.79	1136.86	1109.27	1086.01	1066.26	1049.41	1034.96	1022.53	981.32	960.54	949.73	944.03
95000	1234.78	1200.01	1170.90	1146.34	1125.49	1107.71	1092.46	1079.34	1035.84	1013.90	1002.50	996.48
100000	1299.77	1263.17	1232.53	1206.67	1184.73	1166.01	1149.96	1136.15	1090.36	1067.26	1055.26	1048.92

13.00% MONTHLY
PAYMENT REQUIRED TO AMORTIZE A LOAN

TERM AMOUNT	1 year	2 years	3 years	4 years	5 years	6 years	7 years	8 years	9 years	10 years	11 years	12 years
50	4.47	2.38	1.69	1.35	1.14	1.01	.91	.85	.79	.75	.72	.69
100	8.94	4.76	3.37	2.69	2.28	2.01	1.82	1.69	1.58	1.50	1.43	1.38
200	17.87	9.51	6.74	5.37	4.56	4.02	3.64	3.37	3.16	2.99	2.86	2.75
300	26.80	14.27	10.11	8.05	6.83	6.03	5.46	5.05	4.73	4.48	4.29	4.13
400	35.73	19.02	13.48	10.74	9.11	8.03	7.28	6.73	6.31	5.98	5.72	5.50
500	44.66	23.78	16.85	13.42	11.38	10.04	9.10	8.41	7.88	7.47	7.14	6.88
600	53.60	28.53	20.22	16.10	13.66	12.05	10.92	10.09	9.46	8.96	8.57	8.25
700	62.53	33.28	23.59	18.78	15.93	14.06	12.74	11.77	11.03	10.46	10.00	9.63
800	71.46	38.04	26.96	21.47	18.21	16.06	14.56	13.45	12.61	11.95	11.43	11.00
900	80.39	42.79	30.33	24.15	20.48	18.07	16.38	15.13	14.18	13.44	12.85	12.38
1000	89.32	47.55	33.70	26.83	22.76	20.08	18.20	16.81	15.76	14.94	14.28	13.75
2000	178.64	95.09	67.39	53.66	45.51	40.15	36.39	33.62	31.51	29.87	28.56	27.50
3000	267.96	142.63	101.09	80.49	68.26	60.23	54.58	50.43	47.27	44.80	42.83	41.24
4000	357.27	190.17	134.78	107.31	91.02	80.30	72.77	67.23	63.02	59.73	57.11	54.99
5000	446.59	237.71	168.47	134.14	113.77	100.38	90.96	84.04	78.77	74.66	71.39	68.74
6000	535.91	285.26	202.17	160.97	136.52	120.45	109.16	100.85	94.53	89.59	85.66	82.48
7000	625.23	332.80	235.86	187.80	159.28	140.52	127.35	117.66	110.28	104.52	99.94	96.23
8000	714.54	380.34	269.56	214.62	182.03	160.60	145.54	134.46	126.03	119.45	114.21	109.98
9000	803.86	427.88	303.25	241.45	204.78	180.67	163.73	151.27	141.79	134.38	128.49	123.72
10000	893.18	475.42	336.94	268.28	227.54	200.75	181.92	168.08	157.54	149.32	142.77	137.47
11000	982.50	522.97	370.64	295.11	250.29	220.82	200.12	184.88	173.29	164.25	157.04	151.21
12000	1071.81	570.51	404.33	321.93	273.04	240.89	218.31	201.69	189.05	179.18	171.32	164.96
13000	1161.13	618.05	438.03	348.76	295.79	260.97	236.50	218.50	204.80	194.11	185.59	178.71
14000	1250.45	665.59	471.72	375.59	318.55	281.04	254.69	235.31	220.56	209.04	199.87	192.45
15000	1339.76	713.13	505.41	402.42	341.30	301.12	272.88	252.11	236.31	223.97	214.15	206.20
16000	1429.08	760.67	539.11	429.24	364.05	321.19	291.08	268.92	252.06	238.90	228.42	219.95
17000	1518.40	808.22	572.80	456.07	386.81	341.26	309.27	285.73	267.82	253.83	242.70	233.69
18000	1607.72	855.76	606.50	482.90	409.56	361.34	327.46	302.54	283.57	268.76	256.97	247.44
19000	1697.03	903.30	640.19	509.73	432.31	381.41	345.65	319.34	299.32	283.70	271.25	261.18
20000	1786.35	950.84	673.88	536.55	455.07	401.49	363.84	336.15	315.08	298.63	285.53	274.93
21000	1875.67	998.38	707.58	563.38	477.82	421.56	382.04	352.96	330.83	313.56	299.80	288.68
22000	1964.99	1045.93	741.27	590.21	500.57	441.64	400.23	369.76	346.58	328.49	314.08	302.42
23000	2054.30	1093.47	774.97	617.04	523.33	461.71	418.42	386.57	362.34	343.42	328.36	316.17
24000	2143.62	1141.01	808.66	643.86	546.08	481.78	436.61	403.38	378.09	358.35	342.63	329.92
25000	2232.94	1188.55	842.35	670.69	568.83	501.86	454.80	420.19	393.84	373.28	356.91	343.66
26000	2322.25	1236.09	876.05	697.52	591.58	521.93	473.00	436.99	409.60	388.21	371.18	357.41
27000	2411.57	1283.63	909.74	724.35	614.34	542.01	491.19	453.80	425.35	403.14	385.46	371.15
28000	2500.89	1331.18	943.44	751.17	637.09	562.08	509.38	470.61	441.11	418.08	399.74	384.90
29000	2590.21	1378.72	977.13	778.00	659.84	582.15	527.57	487.42	456.86	433.01	414.01	398.65
30000	2679.52	1426.26	1010.82	804.83	682.60	602.23	545.76	504.22	472.61	447.94	428.29	412.39
31000	2768.84	1473.80	1044.52	831.66	705.35	622.30	563.96	521.03	488.37	462.87	442.56	426.14
32000	2858.16	1521.34	1078.21	858.48	728.10	642.38	582.15	537.84	504.12	477.80	456.84	439.89
33000	2947.48	1568.89	1111.91	885.31	750.86	662.45	600.34	554.64	519.87	492.73	471.12	453.63
34000	3036.79	1616.43	1145.60	912.14	773.61	682.52	618.53	571.45	535.63	507.66	485.39	467.38
35000	3126.11	1663.97	1179.29	938.97	796.36	702.60	636.72	588.26	551.38	522.59	499.67	481.12
36000	3215.43	1711.51	1212.99	965.79	819.12	722.67	654.92	605.07	567.13	537.52	513.94	494.87
37000	3304.74	1759.05	1246.68	992.62	841.87	742.75	673.11	621.87	582.89	552.45	528.22	508.62
38000	3394.06	1806.59	1280.38	1019.45	864.62	762.82	691.30	638.68	598.64	567.39	542.50	522.36
39000	3483.38	1854.14	1314.07	1046.28	887.37	782.90	709.49	655.49	614.39	582.32	556.77	536.11
40000	3572.70	1901.68	1347.76	1073.10	910.13	802.97	727.68	672.30	630.15	597.25	571.05	549.86
41000	3662.01	1949.22	1381.46	1099.93	932.88	823.04	745.88	689.10	645.90	612.18	585.33	563.60
42000	3751.33	1996.76	1415.15	1126.76	955.63	843.12	764.07	705.91	661.66	627.11	599.60	577.35
43000	3840.65	2044.30	1448.84	1153.59	978.39	863.19	782.26	722.72	677.41	642.04	613.88	591.09
44000	3929.97	2091.85	1482.54	1180.41	1001.14	883.27	800.45	739.52	693.16	656.97	628.15	604.84
45000	4019.28	2139.39	1516.23	1207.24	1023.89	903.34	818.64	756.33	708.92	671.90	642.43	618.59
46000	4108.60	2186.93	1549.93	1234.07	1046.65	923.41	836.84	773.14	724.67	686.83	656.71	632.33
47000	4197.92	2234.47	1583.62	1260.90	1069.40	943.49	855.03	789.95	740.42	701.77	670.98	646.08
48000	4287.23	2282.01	1617.31	1287.72	1092.15	963.56	873.22	806.75	756.18	716.70	685.26	659.83
49000	4376.55	2329.55	1651.01	1314.55	1114.91	983.64	891.41	823.56	771.93	731.63	699.53	673.57
50000	4465.87	2377.10	1684.70	1341.38	1137.66	1003.71	909.60	840.37	787.68	746.56	713.81	687.32
55000	4912.46	2614.81	1853.17	1475.52	1251.42	1104.08	1000.56	924.40	866.45	821.21	785.19	756.05
60000	5359.04	2852.51	2021.64	1609.65	1365.19	1204.45	1091.52	1008.44	945.22	895.87	856.57	824.78
65000	5805.63	3090.22	2190.11	1743.79	1478.95	1304.82	1182.48	1092.48	1023.99	970.52	927.95	893.51
70000	6252.21	3327.93	2358.58	1877.93	1592.72	1405.19	1273.44	1176.51	1102.76	1045.18	999.33	962.24
75000	6698.80	3565.64	2527.05	2012.07	1706.49	1505.56	1364.40	1260.55	1181.52	1119.84	1070.71	1030.97
80000	7145.39	3803.35	2695.52	2146.20	1820.25	1605.93	1455.36	1344.59	1260.29	1194.49	1142.09	1099.71
85000	7591.97	4041.06	2863.99	2280.34	1934.02	1706.30	1546.32	1428.62	1339.06	1269.15	1213.47	1168.44
90000	8038.56	4278.77	3032.46	2414.48	2047.78	1806.67	1637.28	1512.66	1417.83	1343.80	1284.85	1237.17
95000	8485.15	4516.48	3200.93	2548.62	2161.55	1907.05	1728.24	1596.69	1496.60	1418.46	1356.24	1305.90
100000	8931.73	4754.19	3369.40	2682.75	2275.31	2007.42	1819.20	1680.73	1575.36	1493.11	1427.62	1374.63

MONTHLY

13.00%

PAYMENT REQUIRED TO AMORTIZE A LOAN

TERM AMOUNT	13 year	14 years	15 years	16 years	17 years	18 years	19 years	20 years	25 years	30 years	35 years	40 years
50	.67	.65	.64	.62	.61	.61	.60	.59	.57	.56	.55	.55
100	1.34	1.30	1.27	1.24	1.22	1.21	1.19	1.18	1.13	1.11	1.10	1.09
200	2.67	2.60	2.54	2.48	2.44	2.41	2.37	2.35	2.26	2.22	2.20	2.18
300	4.00	3.89	3.80	3.72	3.66	3.61	3.56	3.52	3.39	3.32	3.29	3.27
400	5.33	5.19	5.07	4.96	4.88	4.81	4.74	4.69	4.52	4.43	4.39	4.36
500	6.66	6.48	6.33	6.20	6.10	6.01	5.93	5.86	5.64	5.54	5.48	5.45
600	7.99	7.78	7.60	7.44	7.32	7.21	7.11	7.03	6.77	6.64	6.58	6.54
700	9.32	9.07	8.86	8.68	8.54	8.41	8.30	8.21	7.90	7.75	7.67	7.63
800	10.65	10.37	10.13	9.92	9.75	9.61	9.48	9.38	9.03	8.85	8.77	8.72
900	11.99	11.66	11.39	11.16	10.97	10.81	10.67	10.55	10.16	9.96	9.86	9.81
1000	13.32	12.96	12.66	12.40	12.19	12.01	11.85	11.72	11.28	11.07	10.96	10.90
2000	26.63	25.91	25.31	24.80	24.38	24.01	23.70	23.44	22.56	22.13	21.91	21.80
3000	39.94	38.86	37.96	37.20	36.56	36.02	35.55	35.15	33.84	33.19	32.86	32.69
4000	53.25	51.82	50.61	49.60	48.75	48.02	47.40	46.87	45.12	44.25	43.81	43.59
5000	66.57	64.77	63.27	62.00	60.94	60.03	59.25	58.58	56.40	55.31	54.76	54.48
6000	79.88	77.72	75.92	74.40	73.12	72.03	71.10	70.30	67.68	66.38	65.72	65.38
7000	93.19	90.67	88.57	86.80	85.31	84.04	82.95	82.02	78.95	77.44	76.67	76.27
8000	106.50	103.63	101.22	99.20	97.49	96.04	94.80	93.73	90.23	88.50	87.62	87.17
9000	119.81	116.58	113.88	111.60	109.68	108.04	106.65	105.45	101.51	99.56	98.57	98.06
10000	133.13	129.53	126.53	124.00	121.87	120.05	118.49	117.16	112.79	110.62	109.52	108.96
11000	146.44	142.48	139.18	136.40	134.05	132.05	130.34	128.88	124.07	121.69	120.48	119.85
12000	159.75	155.44	151.83	148.80	146.24	144.06	142.19	140.59	135.35	132.75	131.43	130.75
13000	173.06	168.39	164.49	161.20	158.42	156.06	154.04	152.31	146.62	143.81	142.38	141.64
14000	186.37	181.34	177.14	173.60	170.61	168.07	165.89	164.03	157.90	154.87	153.33	152.54
15000	199.69	194.29	189.79	186.00	182.80	180.07	177.74	175.74	169.18	165.93	164.28	163.43
16000	213.00	207.25	202.44	198.40	194.98	192.07	189.59	187.46	180.46	177.00	175.24	174.33
17000	226.31	220.20	215.10	210.80	207.17	204.08	201.44	199.17	191.74	188.06	186.19	185.22
18000	239.62	233.15	227.75	223.20	219.36	216.08	213.29	210.89	203.02	199.12	197.14	196.12
19000	252.93	246.11	240.40	235.60	231.54	228.09	225.14	222.60	214.29	210.18	208.09	207.01
20000	266.25	259.06	253.05	248.00	243.73	240.09	236.98	234.32	225.57	221.24	219.04	217.91
21000	279.56	272.01	265.71	260.40	255.91	252.10	248.83	246.04	236.85	232.31	230.00	228.80
22000	292.87	284.96	278.36	272.80	268.10	264.10	260.68	257.75	248.13	243.37	240.95	239.70
23000	306.18	297.92	291.01	285.20	280.29	276.10	272.53	269.47	259.41	254.43	251.90	250.59
24000	319.50	310.87	303.66	297.60	292.47	288.11	284.38	281.18	270.69	265.49	262.85	261.49
25000	332.81	323.82	316.32	310.00	304.66	300.11	296.23	292.90	281.96	276.55	273.80	272.38
26000	346.12	336.77	328.97	322.40	316.84	312.12	308.08	304.61	293.24	287.62	284.76	283.28
27000	359.43	349.73	341.62	334.80	329.03	324.12	319.93	316.33	304.52	298.68	295.71	294.17
28000	372.74	362.68	354.27	347.20	341.22	336.13	331.78	328.05	315.80	309.74	306.66	305.07
29000	386.06	375.63	366.93	359.60	353.40	348.13	343.63	339.76	327.08	320.80	317.61	315.96
30000	399.37	388.58	379.58	372.00	365.59	360.13	355.47	351.48	338.36	331.86	328.56	326.86
31000	412.68	401.54	392.23	384.40	377.78	372.14	367.32	363.19	349.63	342.93	339.51	337.75
32000	425.99	414.49	404.88	396.80	389.96	384.14	379.17	374.91	360.91	353.99	350.47	348.65
33000	439.30	427.44	417.53	409.20	402.15	396.15	391.02	386.62	372.19	365.05	361.42	359.54
34000	452.62	440.39	430.19	421.60	414.33	408.15	402.87	398.34	383.47	376.11	372.37	370.44
35000	465.93	453.35	442.84	434.00	426.52	420.16	414.72	410.06	394.75	387.17	383.32	381.33
36000	479.24	466.30	455.49	446.40	438.71	432.16	426.57	421.77	406.03	398.24	394.27	392.23
37000	492.55	479.25	468.14	458.80	450.89	444.17	438.42	433.49	417.30	409.30	405.23	403.13
38000	505.86	492.21	480.80	471.20	463.08	456.17	450.27	445.20	428.58	420.36	416.18	414.02
39000	519.18	505.16	493.45	483.60	475.26	468.17	462.12	456.92	439.86	431.42	427.13	424.92
40000	532.49	518.11	506.10	496.00	487.45	480.18	473.96	468.64	451.14	442.48	438.08	435.81
41000	545.80	531.06	518.75	508.40	499.64	492.18	485.81	480.35	462.42	453.55	449.03	446.71
42000	559.11	544.02	531.41	520.80	511.82	504.19	497.66	492.07	473.70	464.61	459.99	457.60
43000	572.43	556.97	544.06	533.20	524.01	516.19	509.51	503.78	484.97	475.67	470.94	468.50
44000	585.74	569.92	556.71	545.60	536.20	528.20	521.36	515.50	496.25	486.73	481.89	479.39
45000	599.05	582.87	569.36	558.00	548.38	540.20	533.21	527.21	507.53	497.79	492.84	490.29
46000	612.36	595.83	582.02	570.40	560.57	552.20	545.06	538.93	518.81	508.86	503.79	501.18
47000	625.67	608.78	594.67	582.80	572.75	564.21	556.91	550.65	530.09	519.92	514.75	512.08
48000	638.99	621.73	607.32	595.20	584.94	576.21	568.76	562.36	541.37	530.98	525.70	522.97
49000	652.30	634.68	619.97	607.60	597.13	588.22	580.61	574.08	552.64	542.04	536.65	533.87
50000	665.61	647.64	632.63	620.00	609.31	600.22	592.45	585.79	563.92	553.10	547.60	544.76
55000	732.17	712.40	695.89	682.00	670.24	660.24	651.70	644.37	620.31	608.41	602.36	599.24
60000	798.73	777.16	759.15	744.00	731.17	720.26	710.94	702.95	676.71	663.72	657.12	653.71
65000	865.29	841.93	822.41	806.00	792.10	780.29	770.19	761.53	733.10	719.03	711.88	708.19
70000	931.85	906.69	885.67	868.00	853.04	840.31	829.43	820.11	789.49	774.34	766.64	762.66
75000	998.41	971.45	948.94	930.00	913.97	900.33	888.68	878.69	845.88	829.65	821.40	817.14
80000	1064.97	1036.22	1012.20	992.00	974.90	960.35	947.92	937.27	902.27	884.96	876.16	871.62
85000	1131.53	1100.98	1075.46	1053.99	1035.83	1020.37	1007.17	995.84	958.67	940.27	930.92	926.09
90000	1198.09	1165.74	1138.72	1115.99	1096.76	1080.39	1066.41	1054.42	1015.06	995.58	985.68	980.57
95000	1264.65	1230.51	1201.99	1177.99	1157.69	1140.42	1125.66	1113.00	1071.45	1050.89	1040.44	1035.04
100000	1331.22	1295.27	1265.25	1239.99	1218.62	1200.44	1184.90	1171.58	1127.84	1106.20	1095.20	1089.52

REAL ESTATE GLOSSARY

□   □   □

A

ABSOLUTE TITLE—Exclusive claim, right, or interest to a property described in a title.

ABSTRACT—A short summary which contains the history of the ownership and title to a property, a listing of conveyances and legal proceedings, and a description of the land and conditions of ownership. Referred to sometimes as an *Abstract of Title* or an *Abstractor's Certificate.*

ABUT—To border, adjoin, or touch; adjacent to.

ACCEPT—To receive with approval, satisfaction, or the intention to keep.

ACCEPTANCE—Voluntarily agreeing to the price and terms of an offer and becoming bound to its terms. For example, a buyer offers to buy and a seller accepts the offer. See also CONTRACT.

Note: These definitions have been excerpted from *The Real Estate Greenbook* by Marc Stephen Garrison, copyright 1988, published by the National Committee for Real Estate Investment. Complete copies of the *Greenbook* are available by contacting M. S. Garrison and Company at (801) 225-8777, or by writing to P.O. Box 1096, Orem, Utah 84057. The price, including shipping, is $24.95.

ACCESS—The ability to approach a property. For example, most city lots have access to the street. Access also implies the right to approach. The public is also guaranteed the right of access to public records.

ACCESS RIGHTS—The right of an owner to passage over adjoining property in order to enter and leave his own property.

ACQUISITION—The process of obtaining property and becoming an owner.

ACQUISITION COST—The costs involved in acquiring a property other than the purchase price. Examples would be points, title insurance fees, closing costs, and recording fees.

ACT OF GOD—Damage caused entirely by acts of nature (floods, tornadoes, storms, etc.) rather than caused by man.

ACTUAL POSSESSION—Physically occupying or controlling a property. This is a legal term which compares with the saying "possession is nine tenths of the law." Actual possession is differentiated from constructive possession, which comes about from possession of a title.

ADDENDUM—Something added to a document, letter, contractual agreement, etc. *See also* AMENDMENT.

ADDITION—A part of a building added on after the original structure was built.

ADD-ON INTEREST—The interest that is added to the principal of a loan.

ADDRESS—Also known as street address. This refers to the common description of a property location for mailing purposes. It denotes the street name and number where the property lies, as well as the city, state, and postal zip code.

ADJUSTABLE MORTGAGE LOAN—Established in 1981 by the Federal Home Loan Bank Board to be used by savings and loans. It provides maximum flexibility in term selection. See also ADJUSTABLE RATE MORTGAGE.

ADJUSTABLE RATE MORTGAGE (ARM)—Mortgage wherein the interest rate fluctuates according to different factors. An example of a factor which some ARMs are tied to is the prime interest rate. Care should be taken before taking responsibility for an Adjustable Rate Mortgage to fully understand the factors which can increase your interest rate. You should also check the limits (if any) called for by the ARM on both the annual and loan duration interest rate increases. Many good ARMs limit the yearly increase to 1.5 percent or less and put a ceiling on interest that the loan can charge at 15 percent. See also the Latin expression CAVEAT EMPTOR.

ADJUSTED SALES PRICE—The sale price minus both the costs of "fixing up" and of selling a property.

ADMINISTRATOR'S DEED—The court document that specifies the conveyance of real property when a person dies intestate (without leaving a will).

ADULT—A person old enough to legally act without the consent of a parent or guardian. The legal age of adulthood varies between eighteen and twenty-one from state to state. An adult may enter into a binding contractual relationship, as opposed to a minor, whose contracts are voidable.

AD VALOREM—Taxes based "according to property value." See ASSESSED VALUATION.

ADVANCE FEE—A nonrefundable fee charged by a realtor to a seller to cover the broker's costs of marketing a property. The fee would be credited against commissions upon sale of the property.

ADVERSE TITLE—A property title which is claimed to differ or oppose another title or claim.

AESTHETIC VALUE—The added value placed on a property because of the beauty of the features or surroundings.

AGENCY—A legal relationship in which one person (the agent) acts on behalf of another (the principal) in business or legal affairs with third parties.

AGENT CLAUSE—A clause contained within or added to a listing agreement or a purchase agreement which outlines the terms and conditions of a realtor's listing. Examples of two agent clauses are:

"In addition to the purchase price, purchaser agrees to pay a commission to _____ in the sum of $_____ to be paid as follows _____ for services rendered with this transaction."

"Seller agrees to sell the property on the terms and conditions specified herein and further agrees to pay a commission of ____% of the sales price. Total commission not to exceed $_____."

AGREEMENT OF SALE CONTRACT—A contract whereby the purchaser agrees to buy and the seller agrees to sell under specific terms and conditions. Title remains with the seller until all conditions of the contract have been fulfilled. In some states this is synonymous with a purchase agreement. Also called *Conditional Sales Contract, Land Contract, or Sales Contract.*

ALIENATION—The process by which title is transferred from one owner to another.

ALL-INCLUSIVE TRUST DEED (AITD, WRAPAROUND MORTGAGE)—A junior mortgage with a face value of both the amount it secures and the balance due under the existing loans. The mortgagee himself—or through a trust company—collects payments on its face value, then pays the payments on the underlying existing loans. The difference between the amount he collects and the amount he pays out in loans serves as his income. It is most effective when the underlying loans have a lower interest rate than the rate which is charged on the "wrap." The use of an all-inclusive trust deed in creative real estate investing has been made popular by Wade B. Cook in his book *How to build a Real Estate Money Machine.*

AMERICAN INSTITUTE OF REAL ESTATE APPRAISERS (AIREA)—A part of the National Association of Realtors, which publishes reference materials on appraising properties and trains people in this field.

AMERICAN LAND TITLE INSURANCE (ALTA)—A group of title insurance companies which promotes and issues title insurance.

AMERICAN SOCIETY OF APPRAISERS—A professional society of real estate appraisers. Their address is Dulles International Airport, P.O. Box 17265, Washington, D.C., 20041.

AMERICAN SOCIETY OF REAL ESTATE COUNSELORS—An affiliate organization of the National Association of Realtors (NAR) whose members specialize in giving fee-based advice and counsel on real estate matters.

AMORTIZED LOAN—A loan in which the payments are to be made in certain, specified, usually equal payments.

ANNUAL PERCENTAGE RATE (APR)—The "true" percentage rate (stated as a yearly percentage) that a person pays a lender for the use of money. To comply with Federal Regulation Z of the truth-in-lending-law, the APR must be accurately stated.

APPOINTMENTS—Furnishings and features of a building (usually thought of as nonessential decorative features).

APPRAISAL—An estimate of quality, quantity, and value of an asset, as of a specific date, made by a qualified, unbiased, and disinterested person. See APPRAISAL METHODS.

APPRAISAL METHODS—The processes by which the market value of a specific piece of property is determined. There are three basic methods of appraisal:

- Replacement Cost (cost approach): The process of determining the cost for building and improving an identical structure at current market prices.

- Market Comparison: This is the most commonly used of the three methods. This approach involves an analysis of the recent sales prices of comparable properties in similar locations. Three or four comparable properties are usually used as a base for comparison. Adjustments should be made to the prices of these comparable properties to provide an accurate base.

- Capitalization of Income Approach: This method determines the market value of a property in terms of its ability to produce income. Income means net operating income (NOI). Capitalization means to relate future income to its present future net income, before depreciation.

APPRAISAL REPORT—A written report by an appraiser containing his determination of value and his method or reasoning in arriving at value.

APPRAISED VALUE—The appraiser's determination of value or price, given specific conditions of the property at the time of the appraisal.

APPRAISER—A person who, for a fee, estimates property values. Care should be taken to check the appraiser's qualifications, experience, and training.

APPRECIATION—Increase in value of a property, excluding increases due to improvements.

APPURTENANCE—Anything attached to or incident to the land and part of the property, such as an easement to some land or a garage to a house. It is part of the property and passes with it upon sale or transfer of title.

ARREARS—A loan, rental, or lease agreement for which payments have not been made according to the schedule called for in the legal contract.

AS-IS CONDITION—Property that is accepted by either the buyer or tenant to be conveyed or rented in the state existing at the time of the sale or lease. Selling "as is" is not binding in the case of an illegal or unenforceable contract.

ASKING PRICE—The price quoted by a seller as the amount for which he will part with a property. The asking price is usually considered the starting price for negotiations with a seller. Also called upset price.

ASSESSED VALUATION—Value placed upon a property for the purpose of determining property taxes by an assessor.

ASSESSMENT—This is the charge or tax levied against a property by a unit of government.

ASSESSMENT TAX DISTRICT—An area, such as a county or a city, which is used for tax assessment purposes.

ASSESSOR—The government official or appointee whose duty it is to appraise, value, or access property for taxation.

ASSIGNABILITY—Any property which may be transferred by assignment. Some contracts have a clause restricting assignability.

ASSIGNMENT—To transfer an interest in any property, real or personal, or of any estate or right therein.

ASSIGNMENT CLAUSE—A clause contained within or added to a purchase agreement which outlines how agreement may be assigned. Examples of two assignment clauses are:

> Seller reserves the right to transfer his interest herein described or assign his interest under this contract, but such assignment or transfer shall not affect any right or interest of purchase hereunder and shall be made subject to all the terms and provisions of this contract.

> Any attempted assignment or transfer by purchaser in violation of the foregoing provisions may at seller's option be deemed a default by purchaser under this contract, and seller may pursue such remedy as may be available to seller for material breach by purchaser.

ASSUMPTION—Purchase of property with the buyer taking over the existing mortgage and assuming liability for the payments. See ASSUMPTION OF MORTGAGE.

ASSUMPTION CLAUSE—A clause contained within or added to a purchase agreement which outlines the terms and rights of both the buyer and the seller concerning an assumption of the existing loan or loans. Examples of two assumption clauses are:

> If there is a conflict in assuming the existing loans, purchasers agree to secure financing to pay the above amount.

> Purchaser agrees to assume and pay said mortgage according to its own terms and conditions.

ASSUMPTION FEE—The loan institution's charge for the assumption report and paperwork involved in processing the assumption of a mortgage.

ASSUMPTION OF MORTGAGE—Taking over the payments and terms of a mortgage. Two common ways of assuming a mortgage are:

> Simple Assumption: Common in many FHA and VA loans. The loan is taken over without qualification or formal application and approval. The original holder of the note still retains some liability for the loan.

> Formal assumption: Taking over a loan through application, credit check, and approval by the lender who holds the note. The original holder of the note is released from all liability of the note.

ATTRACTIVE NUISANCE—Anything on a property which may attract small children and be a hazard to them. Examples of attractive nuisances would be swimming pools, old refrigerators, broken glass. These items should be fenced off, locked up, and, if necessary, cleaned up to prevent injury to children.

AUTOMATIC RENEWAL CLAUSE—A clause contained within a contract that specifies an automatic renewal or rollover unless specific action is taken to stop it.

B

BACKFILL—Soil and other nondecomposing material used to fill in around a foundation or low area.

BACKUP OFFER—An offer that would be considered second to another offer.

BALLOON PAYMENT—A payment larger than the usual payment which is due at the end of a note's payment schedule.

BALLOON PAYMENT MORTGAGE—A mortgage in which payments are structured in such a way as to require a large lump sum payment at the end of its payment schedule.

BANKRUPTCY—A legal motion on behalf of a person or company unable to pay debts. The person filing bankruptcy is asking the court for protection from creditors. There are several forms of bankruptcy, called "chapters." The subject is much too complex to be treated in a few sentences. For more information on your own state's laws, seek competent local legal advice.

BARTER—To trade or exchange goods for services for something else of equal value. (An example would be negotiating a trade of something other than cash for a down payment on a house.)

BASE AND MERIDIAN LINES—Survey lines used to describe the location of a property.

BASEBOARD—A strip of wood or some other material installed on the wall where it meets the floor.

BASIS—Basis is a way of measuring your investment in property for tax purposes. You must know the basis of your property to calculate depreciation, amortization, depletion, casualty losses, or whether you have a gain or loss on its sale or exchange. The basis of a property is usually its cost. The cost is the amount of cash you pay for it, the fair market value of other property or services you provide in the transaction, and all settlement fees or closing costs. Some special points concerning the determination of basis are:

- Unstated Interest: If you buy property on any time-payment plan that charges little or no interest, the basis of your property is your purchase price, less the amount considered to be interest.

- Real Estate Taxes: If you buy real property and agree to pay taxes that were owed by the seller, the taxes you pay are treated as part of the cost of the property.

- Fair Market Value: There are times when you cannot use cost as a basis. In these cases fair market value may be important. Several examples of these cases are: partial and nontaxable exchanges, property trades, discounted property purchases from employers, or if you receive property for services rendered.

BASIS POINT—One point + 1/100 of 1% (.01).

BEAM/BEAMS—The main horizontal supports of a building.

BEARING WALL—A main supporting wall that helps carry the weight of the structure.

BETTERMENT—A city or state improvement that adds to the value of real estate, such as sidewalks, street lights, sewers, and streets.

BID—The amount offered by the buyer.

BINDER—An agreement to cover part or all of the down payment for buying real estate. See also EARNEST MONEY.

BLENDED RATE—An interest rate applied to a refinanced loan that is higher than the old loan but lower than the existing loan.

BOOK VALUE—The value of a property that is shown in the financial records of an individual or a corporation. This is usually purchase price plus any improvement minus any accrued depreciation.

BOUNDARY—A natural or artificial separation which marks the property line between two adjacent properties.

BREACH OF CONTRACT—Failure to perform a contract without proper legal excuse.

BREACH OF WARRANTY—In real estate, this means the failure to pass clear title as implied in the purchase offer and closing documents.

BROKER—A state-licensed person, who for compensation or expectation of compensation acts as an agent in buying, selling, leasing, renting, and exchanging properties.

BUDGET MORTGAGE—A mortgage that includes monthly payments for taxes, insurance, principal, and interest.

BUFFER ZONE—An area of transition between areas of different land usage. (Home versus freeway, for example.)

BUILDING CODE—The federal, state, and local rules regulating the construction of a building. These codes are adopted and enforced by the local city or county.

BUNDLE OF RIGHTS—The rights that a person has to enjoy, use, and dispose of his real or personal property.

BUY-BACK AGREEMENT—A clause in which the seller agrees to repurchase the property on the occurrence of an event specified. (A time limit or price or both may be specified.)

BUYER—A purchaser; an agent responsible for purchasing something for another party.

BUYER'S MARKET—A housing market in which there is an oversupply of houses for sale. This oversupply drives down the prices of the properties for sale.

C

CAE (CERTIFIED ASSESSMENT EVALUATOR)—A title earned by examination, experience, and course study given to property assessors by the International Association of Assessing Officers.

CALLED MORTGAGE—A loan that is due and payable at the demand of the lender as a result of an acceleration or due-on-sale clause that has been acted upon.

CANCELLATION CLAUSE—A clause canceling the contract when a specified event(s) or condition(s) is not met.

CAP—A term referring to either the maximum interest rate allowed to be charged on an adjustable rate mortgage or the largest maximum increase in charged interest.

CARPORT—A roof supported by pillars used to shelter cars. Typically there are no supporting or enclosing walls.

CARRYING CHARGES—Costs that are incidental to ownership, such as insurance, taxes, maintenance.

CASH FLOW—A person's spendable income from an investment after operating expenses and loan payments are made.

CASHING OUT—Sale of a property in which the buyer pays the seller for his total equity. An example would be when a person bought a home for $60,000 and assumed the existing loan for $52,000. If the buyer were to cash out the seller, he would pay the entire $8,000 equity in cash at closing.

CAVEAT EMPTOR—A Latin term meaning "Let the buyer beware!" The buyer takes the risk when purchasing a property or an item without the protection of title insurance or warranties.

CELLAR—A room or group of rooms beneath a home under ground level; sometimes called a basement.

CEMENT BLOCK—A hollow block made of cement used in building homes and buildings.

CERTIFICATE OF OCCUPANCY—A certificate issued by the local city or county building inspection department stating that a building is approved for occupancy. Many home insurance policies are null and void in the event of a fire if the certificate of occupancy has never been issued for the insured structure.

CHAIN OF TITLE—A documented history of encumbrances and conveyances affecting the title of a property as far back as records are available.

CHATTEL—Personal property. Any item of property other than real estate.

CHATTEL MORTGAGE—A mortgage on personal property.

CHECKLIST—A list of important things to consider and check when buying and/or closing a home or property.

CIRCUIT BREAKER—An electrical device which limits the flow of electricity on a conductor under abnormal conditions. Circuit breakers are usually found in the outside electrical disconnect and the electrical distribution panel.

CLAUSES—A particular part of a legal document, such as a purchase agreement, clarifying, describing, and outlining a specific plan of action. Clauses in real estate transactions cover such areas as agents, assignment, assumption, closing, closing costs, collateral, deposits, down payments, earnest money, escrow agents, financing, owner financing, personal property, possession, price, subject to, subordination, and title. *For examples of these clauses refer to the specific titles, such as FINANCING CLAUSE.*

CLAIM—A right or title to a property.

CLEAR TITLE—A title not clouded with encumbrances, liens, or other defects.

CLOSED MORTGAGE—A mortgage containing the provision that it cannot be paid off until it matures.

CLOSING—A term used to refer to the final signing of papers to purchase a home or property. A closing usually takes place at a title office, lending institution, or attorney's office.

CLOSING CHECKLIST—A checklist used by a purchaser or closing officer to make sure that everything has been done to insure the proper sale or transfer of a property.

CLOSING COST CLAUSE—A clause contained within or added to a purchase agreement which refers to the payment or terms of a property's closing. Two examples of closing cost clauses are:

> Buyer and seller to split equally the costs for title insurance, closing fee, and all recording fees.

> Seller shall pay the following costs and expenses of the transaction on close of escrow:_____
> _____
> (Specify charges, such as title insurance, assumption fees, closing fees, transfer tax, legal fees, etc.)

CLOSING COSTS—The fees required to finalize the purchase of a home or property. These fees usually include remainder of down payment, property insurance, property taxes, title insurance, points, assumption fee, mortgage insurance premium, and filing and recording fees.

CLOSING STATEMENT—A final itemized statement of all disbursements. There is a closing statement for the buyer and another for the seller, listing the final financial settlement between them.

CLOUD ON TITLE—A lien, encumbrance, or legal action against the title of a property that comes up during a sale that the purchaser or seller was previously unaware of. The cloud on title usually comes through a recording mistake or invalid claim.

CODE OF ETHICS—The set of standards to which every broker and agent must adhere.

COLLATERAL—Personal property that a person pledges as security for an obligation. In real estate the collateral for a mortgage is usually the mortgaged property.

COLOR OF TITLE—This term is used to refer to a defect in a property's title that is not obvious. See CLOUDED TITLE.

COMMITMENT—A written promise or oral affirmation to act according to an agreed-upon commitment. This commitment is most common with government FHA loans. After applying for a loan and being approved by the FHA, you would then receive a firm commitment for the loan. This firm commitment would require that you close by a certain date, etc.

COMPOUND INTEREST—Paying interest on both the principal and the accumulated interest on a note. An example would be a bank deposit of $100 which earned 10-percent annual interest. After one year the note with interest would be worth $110. The next year that $110 would earn $11 interest, the extra $1 being the interest paid on interest —the compound interest.

CONDITIONAL COMMITMENT—A loan commitment given on the condition of the mortgagee meeting certain conditions set by the lender.

CONSIDERATION—Something of value given to bind a promise. All contracts, to be legal, must include consideration. In real estate transactions earnest money is given to bind the purchase offer.

CONTINGENCY—An act which is dependent on the prior completion of another act. An example would be a purchase offer which is contingent on the purchaser being able to sell his own home within a certain amount of time (subject-to clause).

CONTRACT—1. An agreement between two parties, oral or written, usually based on one person (the offeree) accepting the offer of another person (the offeror). 2. In real estate, the idea of "selling on contract" or "taking a contract" means that the seller is willing to take monthly payments from the buyer, rather than a lump-sum payment for his equity. See ALL-INCLUSIVE TRUST DEED.

CONTRACT ACCEPTANCE CLAUSE—A clause contained within or added to a purchase agreement which describes terms relating to the acceptance of the contract. Examples of two contract acceptance clauses are:

> Said counter offer expires on _____ date, at __ _____am/pm.

> Seller reserves the right to accept offers from other buyers. All offers must be accepted junior to this offer. If the following conditions are not met _____
> _____

then this offer will be considered null and void and the offer junior to this one will be considered valid. Time is of the essence.

CONVENTIONAL LOAN—A loan that is insured by real estate and not guaranteed by an agency of the government, such as the Veterans Administration or the Federal Housing Authority.

CO-OWNERSHIP—The ownership of a property by two or more people.

CORRECTION DEED (DEED OF CONFIRMATION OR REFORMATION DEED)—A correction of an error in a deed which is both written and recorded.

COUNTEROFFER—An offer given by the seller in response to a purchase offer by a prospective buyer. An example would be a seller who received a purchase offer on his home for $59,000 with $5,000 down. He might agree with the down payment but feel that the sales price was too low. He might then counter back with a sales price of $62,000 with the same down payment. A counteroffer is *always* a rejection of the original offer, combined with a new offer.

COVENANT—An agreement between two or more people who are legally bound to either perform or not perform a certain act, or that a given state of things does or does not exist.

COVENANTS—In all contracts there are five basic covenants that give full "warranty" to the property. These five basic covenants are:

- The owner has a right to convey the property.

- The owner will "forever" warrant the title.

- The owner will obtain title insurance.

- The property is encumbered only by the liens listed in the purchase offer.

- The owner has the right of quiet enjoyment.

CREATIVE FINANCING—Financing a property using methods other than traditional bank financing. Creative financing usually refers to owner financing. Wade B. Cook, Dr. Albert Lowry, Mark O. Haroldsen and myself are just four of the authors who have written books which have helped change the direction of real estate investing, away from reliance on the high interest rates associated in the eighties with traditional financing.

CREDIT REPORT—A report on the credit history of an individual. Increasingly today, many sellers are finding it necessary to check the credit record of the people interested in their properties.

CURING THE TITLE—Clearing up or rectifying a defect in a property's title.

D

DEBT SERVICE—The amount of money required to make the payments on a loan according to the payment schedule.

DEBTOR—A person who owes a debt.

DEED—A written document, properly made out, executed, and under proper seal. Types of commonly used deeds are the administrator's, condominium, corporation, county, executor's, foreclosure, gift, grant, guardian's, mineral, quick claim, reconveyance, referee's, sheriff's, trust, and warranty.

DEED, BARGAIN AND SALE—A simple deed conveying property ownership but not guaranteeing the title, right, or interest. See also QUITCLAIM DEED.

DEED, QUITCLAIM—A simple deed which conveys all claims that a person possesses in a property to another. See also DEED, BARGAIN AND SALE.

DEED IN LIEU OF FORECLOSURE—A property owner in a distressed situation may find it advantageous to deed his property back to the creditor rather than have the creditor complete the foreclosure process at auction. Using a deed like this may save the property owner's credit rating. Seek competent local legal advice for more information on this process.

DEED OF TRUST (TRUST DEED, TRUST DEED MORTGAGE, OR TRUST INDENTURE)—This is a form of deed on a mortgaged property in which a third party (trustee) holds the deed. Upon payment of the note in full, the trustee delivers the deed to the property owner. The use of trust deeds in the United States is fast becoming the rule because of the ease of foreclosure in default situations and the advantages of having a third party holding the deed.

DEFAULT—Failure to perform according to the terms of a note or an obligation.

DEFECTS IN TITLE—Flaws or problems in a property's title. See also CLOUD ON TITLE.

DEFEASANCE—An instrument or clause which defeats or alters a deed, or a mortgage.

DEFERRED INTEREST MORTGAGE—A mortgage where the loan payment is initially lower to begin with than a normal amortization schedule would require. The deficit, or deferred interest, is added on to the principal of the loan. This negative amortization is most commonly seen in the Federal Housing Administration's 245 loan. Benefits include being able to qualify for a higher loan on a home than you would normally. Problems include having your loan actually increase in value every month for the first several years.

DEFERRED PAYMENTS—Payments to be made at a future date.

DEPARTMENT OF REAL ESTATE—Each state and district has a government body that administers and regulates local state real estate laws.

DEPOSIT—Money placed in trust to show good faith; also known as earnest money.

DESCRIPTION—A legal method of giving dimensions to the property. See DEED.

DIRECT REDUCTION MORTGAGE—A loan in which level payments include a set amount to be attributed to principal and interest at an amount which will reduce the loan balance to zero by the end of its payment schedule.

DISCOUNT—To sell a note or home for less than its face or market value.

DISCOUNT POINTS—The percentage of a loan's value that upon closing must be given to the lender to secure the loan. In essence, discount points represent what you have to pay to get a loan at a certain interest rate.

DISCRIMINATION IN REAL ESTATE (CIVIL RIGHTS ACTS OF 1866 AND 1968)—These laws forbid any racial discrimination in the sale, lease, or rental of property. The 1968 civil rights act extended this to include race, color, religion, sex, or national origin.

DISTRESSED PROPERTY—In real estate terms a distressed property refers to a property which is in danger of being foreclosed on by a lender because of nonpayment of a loan.

DOCUMENT—A written instrument. In order for a document to be legally binding it must be properly prepared, witnessed, and recorded. For more information, seek competent local legal counsel.

DOMICILE—A legal term signifying a place which an individual calls his legal residence; a home.

DOWN PAYMENT—The amount of payment (either cash or services) required to secure the purchase of a property.

DOWN PAYMENT CLAUSE—A clause contained within or added to a purchase agreement which refers to the form and amount of a purchaser's down payment. Examples of two down payment clauses would be:

Said down payment of $_____ will be paid in full in the form of personal property described as follows:_____.

_____

The down payment of $_____ will be paid in the following manner. $_____ including earnest money, will be paid on closing. The balance of $_____ to be paid _____ from closing date. Above total down payment of $_____ to be considered a payment of interest in advance toward said property.

DRAINAGE—The flowing of water off a property.

DRY MORTGAGE—A mortgage which places no personal liability on the mortgagor, looking only to the property as collateral for the loan.

DUE-ON-SALE (CLAUSE)—A clause calling for a debt under a deed of trust or a mortgage to be due upon sale or transfer of title of the secured property. Also called an Acceleration or Alienation Clause.

DUTY TO RECONVEY—The responsibility of a party to return property and/or fill out the necessary papers when a note is paid in full.

E

EARNEST MONEY—A payment made as evidence of a purchaser's good faith to go through with the purchase of real estate. It is given along with an earnest money, or binder, agreement, outlining the terms and conditions of the sale and payment for the property.

EARNEST MONEY CLAUSE—A clause contained within or added to a purchase agreement which refers to the form and terms of a buyer's earnest money. Two examples of earnest money clauses are:

> Earnest money and this agreement shall be held by broker or _____ for the benefit of the parties hereto.

> The parties agree to refund earnest money in full in the event financing contemplated by the purchaser is not obtainable.

EASEMENT—The right of a person to use someone else's land for a particular purpose, such as access to property. The right of easement is inherent with ownership of certain properties.

EASEMENT APPURTENANT—An easement for the benefit of another property. An example would be an easement which allowed the right to cross a property to get to another property.

EASEMENT BY NECESSITY—The right to cross a property of another person because of a necessity which is apparent.

EASEMENT IN GROSS—An easement granted to a utility company which is not specifically attached to any parcel of land.

EFFECTIVE AGE—The age of property based upon wear and tear. Example: A house is fifteen years old but current remodeling gives an effective age of two years.

EGRESS—The right to exit from your own property by crossing another property.

ELECTRICAL PROBLEMS—Most electrical repairs and problems require a competent state licensed electrician to repair them. If in any doubt at all about how to fix an electrical problem, call in a licensed professional.

ELIGIBLE—Properly qualified; worthy to apply.

ENCROACHMENT—Anything, such as a building overhang, that extends over the property line into another person's property. Encroachment can also refer to building a structure partly or wholly on another's property.

ENCUMBRANCE—Any claim against or attached to a property, such as a judgment, mortgage, lien, or easement.

EQUITABLE TITLE—The interest or share of ownership that a party holds in a property. This equity increase can be attributed to mortgage reduction through amortization of a loan; property improvements; outside factors, such as city street lighting, a new school, paved streets, a general rise in property values, locational value; and goodwill.

ESCALATOR CLAUSE—A clause contained in most adjustable rate mortgages which allows for certain changes in the mortgage in conjunction with specified eventualities, i.e., inflation rate, T Bill rates, etc.

ESCROW—A deed, bond, or something of value held by a third party for delivery to the grantee upon the completion of a prescribed event. A common example of an escrow would be the tax and insurance funds that a mortgage company holds for property owners. Each month a portion of most first mortgage payments includes one twelfth of the yearly anticipated tax assessments and insurance costs. These amounts are held in escrow by the mortgage company and paid yearly.

ESCROW ACCOUNT—Same as a trust account, in which a broker, by law, deposits all monies collected for a client.

ESCROW AGENT—The party or concern who holds the items of value in escrow and administers the escrow transactions.

ESCROW CLAUSE—A clause contained within or added to a purchase agreement which refers to the use of an escrow agent or trustee. Two examples of escrow clauses are:

> Seller agrees to deliver to an escrow agent at closing a warranty deed
> to be released to buyer, his assigns or heirs upon final payment of all
> obligations at the time and manner described.

> All costs and fees of the escrow agent shall be split equally between
> the buyer and the seller.

ESCROW CLOSING—A closing in which an item may be missing. The closing will take place, but the satisfactory items are held in escrow pending receipt of the missing items.

ESTATE—The extent of legal interest a party has in real property.

EXCEPTION TO TITLE—The situation in which a title is found to be clouded or with a defect.

EXCLUSIVE AGENT—A real estate broker who is under written contract with the seller to be the only broker with the right to sell a certain property within a certain time in exchange for an agreed-upon percentage of the sale price.

EXCLUSIVE LISTING—In most listing contracts the broker is granted the "exclusive right to sell the property." This right to sell means that if the seller makes the sale himself, he must pay the broker the regular commission.

EXCULPATORY CLAUSE—A clause contained within a note or mortgage meaning to release the holder from any personal liability in the event of default. An example of an exculpatory clause would be, "The property mentioned herein shall be the sole collateral for this note or mortgage."

EXISTING LIEN—A lien that has not yet been satisfied.

EXISTING MORTGAGE—A mortgage that has not yet been satisfied.

F

FAILURE OF CONSIDERATION—Giving a bad check as earnest money or not putting any money with it. This would render the earnest money or contract invalid.

FAILURE TO PERFORM—The failure of one of the parties in a contract to perform according to agreement.

FAIR CREDIT REPORTING ACT—A federal law intended to protect the public from having inaccurate information reported by credit agencies concerning their credit ratings. Under this law, an individual has the right to inspect information in his or her files at their local credit bureau and request to amend any incorrect information. This act also requires a lender who refuses credit to an individual to disclose to the individual the credit bureau they based their decision on.

FANNIE MAE—A nickname for the Federal National Mortgage Association. See FEDERAL NATIONAL MORTGAGE ASSOCIATION.

FEDERAL HOME LOAN MORTGAGE CORPORATION—A federally sponsored agency which buys and sells government-backed and conventional mortgages. A common name for this agency is "Freddie Mac."

FEDERAL HOUSING ADMINISTRATION (FHA)—A federal agency that insures private banks, mortgage companies, and savings and loans against loss on real estate loans under the Federal Housing Administration loan programs. In the past this FHA insurance on a loan was paid for by the property buyer in the form of one-half percentage point extra interest charged on the loan. Beginning in 1984, buyers who get new FHA loans are charged one-half point interest in advance, rather than a higher rate over the course of the loan.

FEDERAL NATIONAL MORTGAGE ASSOCIATION (FNMA, FANNIE MAE)—The purpose of the federally sponsored agency which buys mortgages from institutions, such as banks, savings and loans, and insurance companies in order to provide a degree of liquidity in the mortgage market by establishing a secondary market.

FEDERAL SAVINGS AND LOAN ASSOCIATION—A privately or publicly owned savings and loan which is federally chartered.

FEDERAL SAVINGS AND LOAN INSURANCE CORPORATION (FSLIC)—A private corporation which provides insurance (up to $100,000) on accounts deposited in a savings and loan association.

FEE (ABSOLUTE, CONDITIONAL, DETERMINABLE, SIMPLE)—Ownership of real estate free and clear from all mortgages, liens, conditions, or limitations.

FIDUCIARY—A relationship of trust; for example, a real estate broker who has the duty to represent and act in the best interests of the seller.

FILE—To place an original document on public record.

FINANCE CHARGE—The sum of all costs charged directly or indirectly by the creditor and payable either directly or indirectly by the customer as defined by the federal truth-in-lending laws.

FINANCING CLAUSE—A clause contained within or added to a purchase agreement which refers to the terms and conditions of the financing involved in the transaction. Examples of two financing clauses are:

> Buyer to obtain and qualify for a new _____ year _____ loan in the amount of $_____. Sellers costs in obtaining the loan are not to exceed _____.

> Seller is to obtain a new loan against the property for the maximum amount allowable. Buyer is to assume this loan and pay the seller the balance of the purchase price according to the following terms:
>
> _____
> _____
> _____

FINANCING STATEMENT—A brief statement in the public record for recording and establishing a creditor's interest or lien on a personal property.

FIRM COMMITMENT—A definite commitment by a lender to loan a set amount of money at a set interest rate for a set period of time. Time should be taken to verify that the interest rate has been locked in with the lender.

FIRST MORTGAGE—The senior mortgage attached to a property. It is essentially the lien which has been recorded first against the property, and is not necessarily the largest or longest to amortize.

FIXTURE—Personal property, such as an air conditioner or stove, which has become real estate either because it is attached to the property or because of custom in that area.

FLAT FEE BROKER—A broker who lists and sells a home for a set fee rather than a percentage of sale price.

FORBEARANCE—Not taking legal action in the situation where a mortgage or deed of trust is in arrears. Forbearance is usually only granted in a case where a borrower makes a satisfactory arrangement in which he will make up the late payments by an agreed upon future date.

FORCE MAJEURE—An unavoidable delay in performing a contract obligation in the specified time.

FORECLOSURE—A legal procedure initiated by a lender because of nonpayment of a debt to take property from the present person, who has it mortgaged. The procedure of foreclosure varies from state to state. For more information on your own area, seek competent legal advice from an attorney.

FOUNDATION WALL—The basic supporting structure of a home or building. In most modern homes this wall is made of concrete or cinderblock. In many older homes it is made out of wood. Care should be taken to inspect the condition of the foundation on older homes to see that, if it is made out of wood, it is free from any dry rot or termite damage.

FREE AND CLEAR TITLE—A title to a real property which is free from any liens, mortgages, defects, clouds, or other encumbrances.

FURTHER ASSURANCE—A warranty that is expressly stated in a deed. This warranty states that the grantor will be liable for, and will cure, any defect that is discovered in a title after the property is sold.

G

GENERAL LIEN—A lien directed by a court against the entire estate of a debtor.

GIFT LETTER—Most lending institutions require that the borrower show proof of sufficient deposits to cover the proposed down payment on closing. These funds must usually be free and clear and, in the case of FHA loans, not borrowed from another source. In the case of many young home purchasers, their parents lend them the money for the down payment. In this instance, the bank usually requires a letter from the donee (parent) stating that the money given is specifically a gift and not a loan.

GOOD FAITH MONEY—A deposit, such as earnest money, used to bind a contract.

GOOD RECORD TITLE—A title that has been researched and found to have no encumbrances that would adversely affect a sale or transfer.

GOVERNMENT NATIONAL MORTGAGE ASSOCIATION (GNMA, GINNIE MAE)—A federally chartered agency organized in 1968 as a result of a reorganization of the Federal National Mortgage Association, FNMA. GINNIE MAE is a corporation without capital stock which serves to stabilize mortgage lending and residential construction by buying, selling, and servicing residential construction.

GRACE PERIOD—The time period between the due date and the date when a mortgage payment is assessed late charges. An example would be mortgages which are due by the first of each month and which are assessed late charges if the payment is received after the fifteenth of each month.

GRANT DEED—A type of deed which warrants the property being conveyed by the grantor to be free from any defects in title or encumbrances other than those addressed for in the sales contract. The grant deed also conveys all rights to the property that may come to the grantor at any time in the future.

GRANTOR—The seller in a deed or a party conveying property.

GRANTOR'S LIEN—A lien which goes into effect whenever all of the selling price of a property is not paid upon closing or transfer of title. The balance of the seller's equity automatically becomes a grantor's deed.

GROWING EQUITY MORTGAGE (GEM)—A loan in which the payment increases by a predetermined amount yearly. This makes the payoff time shorter.

GUARANTEED MORTGAGE—A mortgage that is guaranteed against default. Examples of guaranteed mortgages are government-insured FHA and VA loans. This guarantee is paid for by the mortgagee in the form of a mortgage insurance premium. Also known as an insured mortgage.

H

HAND MONEY—A term meaning earnest money. See EARNEST MONEY.

HAZARD INSURANCE—Insurance to cover catastrophic events or acts of God such as tornadoes, floods, earthquakes, fires, wind, or workman injury.

HOMEOWNER POLICY—Property insurance protecting a homeowner against all expected perils such as fire, theft, personal liability, and wind.

HOME WARRANTY INSURANCE—Private insurance that insures a buyer of either a new or used home against defects such as plumbing, heating, and electrical problems in the home purchased.

HOUSING AND URBAN DEVELOPMENT—A branch of the federal government responsible for most major housing programs in the United States.

I

IMPOUND ACCOUNT—A trust account established to hold funds which may be required at a future time. An example would be the impound accounts set up for FHA loans in which a tax reserve of six months and an insurance reserve of one full year are held by the lender.

IMPROVEMENTS—Additions to a property or building which are more than basic repairs. Examples of improvements would be a new fireplace, a new fence, adding on a garage, etc.

INDENTURE DEED—A deed between a grantor and a grantee guaranteeing that both parties will work together according to agreement.

INDEXED LOAN—A long term loan in which the terms may be adjusted periodically per a specified index as stated in the mortgage contract.

INSPECTION—A visit to a property or building to check and review it. Examples of inspections would be an inspection by the city building inspector to check for safety- or building-code violations. Another type is the inspection of a property by a partner which a purchase agreement was contingent upon.

INSTITUTIONAL LENDERS—A bank, savings and loan, mortgage company, or insurance company which loans money and is regulated by law.

INSTRUMENT—A legal document, such as a deed, lease agreement, contract of sale, or will.

INSURANCE—Protection against loss from a specific hazard or peril. Examples of real estate insurance would be a title insurance policy, liability insurance against theft and vandalism, and hazard insurance protecting against flood, fire, or other hazard.

INTEREST RATE—The annualized percentage rate that is charged for the use of a sum of money, as in a mortgage loan.

INVOLUNTARY LIEN—A lien put against a person's property by a creditor. An example of an involuntary lien would be a mechanic's or tax lien put against a property because of nonpayment.

IRONCLAD AGREEMENT—A contract that cannot be broken by the parties involved.

J

JOINT NOTE—A note signed by two or more people who are both equally liable for repayment.

JOINT TENANTS (TENANCY)—Property held by two or more parties with each having the legal right to assume full title upon the death of the other. Under joint tenancy probate is avoided. See TENANTS IN COMMON for another form of property ownership by two or more parties.

JUDGMENT LIEN—A court-appointed lien against a property. The property cannot be sold without resolving this judgment.

JUNIOR LIEN—A lien subordinate (junior) to another lien against a property.

JUNIOR MORTGAGE—A mortgage which falls in title claim behind another mortgage. Also known as a secondary mortgage. An example would be a second mortgage whose mortgage rights fall in line after the first mortgagee's rights.

K

KEY LOT—A lot which has a premium price because of its location.

L

LAND CERTIFICATE—A document held by a landowner, giving the legal description of the property and the name and address of the current owner.

LAND CONTRACT—An installment contract for the sale of a property in which the seller retains legal title until paid in full. The buyer holds only equitable title on the property during the payment period.

LAND DESCRIPTION—A description of a particular piece of real property; should be a complete legal description.

LAND TRUST—The title held by a trustee. Under this arrangement, the actual land-owner is not recorded on public records. Only the name of the trustee (third party) is known.

LATENT DEFECT—1. Titles which appear originally to be sound but are found later to contain a fault. 2. Hidden structural defects resulting from faulty construction materials or inferior craftsmanship.

LEGAL DESCRIPTION—A land description measured in metes (measurements) and bounds (boundaries) recognized by law.

LEGAL RATE OF INTEREST—The maximum rate of interest permitted by law in each local state. Charging of interest above the legal rate is illegal and in violation of state usury laws.

LEGAL TITLE—Any title that would be or has been recognized as valid by a court of law.

LETTER OF INTENT—The expressed desire to enter into a contract without actually doing so.

LEVEL PAYMENT—A payment which is made in equal installments during the full payment period of a loan.

LIABILITY INSURANCE—Insurance to protect a property owner from claims due to injury on the property.

LIEN—The claim one party has on the property of another as the result of a legal judgment, or as security for a debt. Examples of types of liens would be tax liens, mortgage liens, judgment liens, and other specified liens.

LIEN WAIVER—A legal document releasing a lien.

LIQUIDATED DAMAGES—A clause contained within a contract specifying payment in the eventuality of default on a contract. An example of liquidated damages would be where a seller would retain a buyer's earnest money in the event of default.

LOAN APPLICATION—Documents required before a loan commitment is issued. It is an in-depth information sheet.

LOAN BROKERAGE FEE—A charge or premium given to an individual or company for arranging for a loan.

LOAN-TO-VALUE RATIO—The ratio of a property's appraised value to the amount of proposed financing.

LOAN VALUE—1. The current amount needed to pay a loan in full. 2. The current maximum of money that could be borrowed against a property.

M

MAINTENANCE—Necessary repairs that are made to a property to preserve the property at its present condition.

MARKETABLE TITLE—A title free from any unusual or unreasonable attachment which a court would require a buyer to assume. Also known as merchantable title.

MARKET VALUE (fair market value)—The price at which a property can realistically be sold. The highest price a buyer will pay and the lowest price a seller will take for a property when both are acting free from any compulsion and collusion.

MATURITY—The time at which a loan or note becomes due.

MECHANIC'S LIEN—A lien placed by a contractor against a property as the result of nonpayment for services or materials supplied by the contractor or mechanic to the property owner.

MORTGAGE—A conditional contract in which real estate is given as security for repayment of a loan. In some states the mortgagee holds a lien only, not a legal title.

MORTGAGE BANKER—A private company that finds borrowers for money obtained from the secondary mortgage market or private investors.

MORTGAGE COMMITMENT—A firm commitment by a lending institution stating that it will lend money against a property according to certain conditions.

MORTGAGE GUARANTY INSURANCE CORPORATION (MGIC)—A private organization which serves as a secondary market for conventional mortgages.

MORTGAGE LIEN—The lien which is recorded against a property when a mortgage is owed against it.

N

NATIONAL ASSOCIATION OF REALTORS—The largest and most prestigious real estate association in the United States. Its membership includes real estate professionals in all fifty states. It serves as an association which promotes modern techniques and education as well as professional standards within its membership. For more information, write the National Association of Realtors, 430 North Michigan, Chicago, Illinois 60611.

NEGATIVE AMORTIZATION—Increase in the outstanding balance of the loan resulting from the failure of periodic debt service. Negative Amortization will occur if the indexed interest rate increases.

NEGOTIATION—When people meet for the purpose of resolving differences so that agreement can be achieved.

NONASSUMPTION CLAUSE—A clause in a mortgage or loan stating that it is due on sale.

NO-RECOURSE CLAUSE—A clause in a purchase offer or a loan stating that the mortgaged property is sole collateral for the loan.

NOTE—A legal instrument which acknowledges a debt and guarantees payment.

O

OCCUPANCY CODE—A local law enforced by police power designed to establish socially acceptable minimum standards for safety and health in both newly constructed buildings and existing structures.

OFFER—A written document signed by a buyer offering to purchase a specific property at a specific price under a specific set of terms. When a seller signs and accepts the terms of the offer, the written document becomes a contract. See also CONTRACT.

OPEN END MORTGAGE—In an open end mortgage the borrower has the right to pay off the loan at any time without penalty and also to refinance it and receive additional funds prior to its maturity date.

OPINION OF TITLE—The legal opinion which is rendered by a title company or attorney about the condition of a property's title. This opinion is rendered by studying an abstract of title and done to determine whether the title is invalid and defective or good and marketable.

OPTION—An option is the right to purchase a property at a certain price, during a certain period of time, under some set of specified terms. To conform with legal requirements, an option must:

1. Involve some consideration to bind the agreement.

2. Contain a legal description of the property involved.

3. Specify conditions and terms.

4. Specify time period for exercising the option.

5. Be in writing and in many cases witnessed.

ORAL CONTRACT—An agreement that is verbal, not written. These are unenforceable as far as property is concerned.

ORIGINAL COST—The total amount of money, consideration, and sweat equity extended out to purchase a property.

ORIGINATION FEE—A fee charged by a mortgage company for processing the paperwork on a loan. This origination fee is above and beyond the "points" which may be charged.

OVERALL CAP RATE—This term means both the maximum interest rate increase that an adjustable rate mortgage may rise during the life of the loan and also the capitalization formula which is found by dividing net operating income by the market price of a property.

OWNER-FINANCING CLAUSES—A clause contained within or added to a purchase agreement which refers to the form and terms of the owner financing involved in the sale. Two examples of owner financing clauses are:

> Seller to carry back a second trust deed in the approximate amount of $_____ bearing _____% interest per annum on the remaining equity in the property. Payments to be made as follows:
>
> _____.
>
> Purchasers agree to pay a $_____ late charge if payment is not received within 10 days of due date.

P

PACKAGE MORTGAGE—A mortgage which covers both real and personal property.

PASSING TITLE—The act of transferring the title of a property to another. A title may be passed by will, gift, or sale.

PERMANENT MORTGAGE—A long-term (more than ten years) mortgage.

PERSONAL PROPERTY—Property which is not designated as real property. Examples of personal property in a home are a stereo, clothing, and lawn equipment. Examples of real property in a home would be a dishwasher, a garbage disposal, or a heater.

PITI—A term meaning Principal, Interest, Taxes, and Insurance. See BUDGET MORTGAGE.

POINT—One percentage point. The typical use of points is in reference to discount points that a lender charges a buyer for the "right to borrow money."

PREPAYMENT CLAUSE/PENALTY—A penalty which a lender may assess a party for paying off a loan before the due date.

PRICE—The amount of money or consideration paid in exchange for a property.

PRICE CLAUSE—A clause contained within or added to a purchase agreement which sets up conditions to the agreement concerning the property's price. Examples of two price clauses are:

> Purchase price for the property is _____ dollars ($_____), which shall be paid on delivery of warranty deed and satisfactory evidence of good and marketable title conveyed thereby to the purchaser.

> Price to be established by the average of three independent appraisals.

PRIME RATE—The rate charged by lending institutions on short-term loans to their best customers.

PROPERTY CLAUSE—A clause contained within or added to a purchase agreement which refers to the disposition of personal property located on the ground and in the structure being purchased. Examples of two property clauses are:

> Buyer accepts the property in its present condition subject only to
> _____.

> Purchaser agrees to pay for remaining oil in fuel tank provided that, prior to closing, seller obtains a written statement as to the quantity and price thereof from his regular supplier.

PROPERTY LINES—The boundary of a property.

PROPERTY TAX—A tax which is assessed against both real and personal properties by the local governments.

PRORATE—To separate something, such as property taxes or insurance, into the actual amounts that a seller is responsible for at the closing.

PUNCH LIST—A list of items that must be corrected prior to the sale.

PURCHASE MONEY MORTGAGE—A mortgage made by the buyer to make a down payment on a specific property or as part of the purchase price.

Q

QUALIFYING—The process of determining whether a buyer is financially able to assume the responsibility of ownership of a property and paying the required debt service. This process may include checking credit history, employment, past landlords, and other sources of financial history which may help determine the capability of the buyer.

R

RATE—The annual percentage rate of a loan. An example would be a thirty-year FHA loan with an annual percentage rate of 12.5% interest.

REAL ESTATE—The land and everything built on it, attached to it with the intention of its becoming a permanent part of the property and passing with it upon sale, or growing on it.

REAL ESTATE BOARD—A local organization whose membership consists primarily of real estate brokers and salesmen.

REAL ESTATE COMMISSION (STATE)—A state agency which regulates and licenses real estate brokers and salespeople. Many state agencies are also responsible for making the local state's real estate rules and regulations.

REAL ESTATE LIEN NOTE—The document which attests to an existing mortgage or lien.

REAL PROPERTY LAWS—The local and federal laws which regulate the real estate market.

RECONVEYANCE—The process of transferring the title of a property back to the original owner.

RECOURSE—The ability for a lender to reclaim money from a borrower who is in default and the property used as collateral as well.

REFINANCING—To obtain a new loan and pay off the existing financing. People usually refinance to get the equity out of their homes.

REGULATION Z—A federal truth-in-lending law which requires that consumers be made aware of the costs of financing.

RELEASE OF LIEN—The removal of a lien, judgment, mortgage, or claim from a certain property.

RESCIND—The right to withdraw from an offer/contract. Regulation Z gives the consumer/buyer three days to change his/her mind.

RESIDENTIAL—Property or land which is zoned to be used for single-family homes or other living quarters.

RIDER—An attached amendment to a contract.

RIGHT-OF-WAY—The easement that a person may have to cross another's property in order to gain access to his own property.

ROOT OF TITLE—The record of initial ownership in a property.

S

SETTLEMENT AGENT—The party which administers the actual signing of the sales documents of a property transaction.

SIMPLE INTEREST—Interest which is computed on the principal of a loan only. Another type of interest is compound interest, in which interest is charged not only on the remaining principal but also on the accumulated interest.

SPECIAL ASSESSMENT—A special charge placed against property owners to pay for public improvements or repairs.

SREA—Senior Real Estate Appraiser. The highest award given in this field.

STANDBY FEE—The fee required by a lender to provide a commitment. It is nonrefundable if the loan is not closed within a specified period of time.

STANDBY LOAN—A lender's commitment to loan a sum of money for a fixed period of time and a fixed interest. A fee is charged for this, and the borrower retains the option of closing or lapsing the loan commitment.

STATUTE OF FRAUDS—A doctrine of contract law which requires certain contracts, including all real estate contracts, to be in writing to be enforceable.

STATUTORY QUITCLAIM DEED—A quitclaim deed form designated and approved by local state statute.

SUBORDINATE—Making a senior lien junior to another lien. An example would be if you held a first mortgage against a lot, and the owner needed to get a construction loan for it. You would most likely be asked to "subordinate" or move your first position mortgage into second position behind the construction loan. This changing of positions in the line of title is called subordination.

SUBORDINATION CLAUSE—A clause contained within or added to a purchase agreement which refers to the subordination of existing financing. Two examples of subordination clauses are:

> Seller agrees to subordinate seller's equity to buyer's new mortgage.

> Seller hereby agrees to subordinate said note and trust deed to buyer's new loan; both parties agree that the loan amount of the new deed of trust or mortgage will not be greater than the increase of the value of the property as a result of, but not exclusively from, the new improvements made by buyer from the proceeds of buyer's new loan.

T

TAX LIEN—A lien placed against a property because of nonpayment of taxes.

TENANCY BY THE ENTIRETY—A type of ownership for married partners wherein they own property as a sole owner if married at the time of receiving the deed.

TENANTS IN COMMON—Two or more parties who own equal shares of a property. If one partner dies, his share goes to his estate. For another form of joint property ownership, see JOINT TENANCY.

TENDER—An offer made in the form of money.

TENURE—The right or act of owning or occupying real estate.

TERM AMORTIZATION—A type of debt service where the entire debt is paid in one final payment at maturity. See also BALLOON PAYMENT.

TERMITE BOND—An insurance policy issued against future termite damage to a property after a satisfactory inspection and treatment by a licensed pest control company.

TERMITE INSPECTION—An inspection of a property by a licensed pest control company in which a written statement is issued stating whether the property is free from termite damage or not.

TIME-IS-OF-THE-ESSENCE CLAUSE—The phrase, when put into a contract, gives specific legally binding commitments and cannot be subordinated by the recalcitrant party. Failure to insert this phrase can cause serious delays.

TITLE—The formal document which establishes legal right to ownership or a lien against a property.

TITLE CLAUSE—A clause contained within or added to a purchase agreement which refers to a property's title. Examples of two title clauses are:

> Purchaser and seller agree that if the title to the above property be defective, ninety (90) days from the date hereof, it shall be given to the seller, or his agent, to perfect same. If said title cannot be perfected within said time limit, the earnest money receipted for herein shall, upon the demand of purchaser, be returned to purchaser in full and the contract cancelled.

> The land contract shall be completed and executed by the parties at the close of escrow. Title to property shall be reserved to seller, his heirs, personal representatives, and assigns, until full payment of the balance is made, as provided in the land contract.

TITLE COMPANY—A private company that prepares real estate title abstracts, helps in property closings, and provides title insurance.

TITLE INSURANCE—Insurance protection sold to the purchaser of a property by an insurance company to cover any loss from undiscovered defects in title.

TITLE REPORT—A record stating the current condition of the title. (For example: easements, liens, defects of title, covenants, etc.)

TITLE SEARCH—An examination of public records showing encumbrances on the real property.

TRUTH-IN-LENDING LAWS—See REGULATION Z.

U

UNENCUMBERED—Property that is "free and clear." An unencumbered property is said to have no mortgages, liens, claims, or other attachments or limitations of rights placed against it.

UNRECORDED DEED—An instrument that transfers title but is not publicly recorded. This can be *very* dangerous; recording a title protects your interest.

USEFUL LIFE—The time period over which real property may be termed "of use." Useful life for a home is eighteen years under federal depreciation laws. (This is subject to change.)

UTILITY EASEMENT—The use of property, by utility companies, to lay service lines. The easement gives them access to work on these services.

V

VALID—A document or instrument which has been prepared according to law and is legally binding.

VA LOAN—A loan, of low interest, backed by the government that is given to qualified veterans.

VALUABLE CONSIDERATION—A note that stipulates a promised payment on which the bearer can enforce a claim against the party signing the note. This can be a promise of money, chattel, time, or other consideration for the grantor of the note.

VALUATION—The estimated worth of a property. It should be noted that estimations or valuations are subjective and subject to error.

VARIABLE RATE MORTGAGE (VRM)—A mortgage in which the borrower allows the lender to alter the interest rate and monthly payments under prespecified criteria. Most variable rate mortgages contain "caps" which limit both the annual interest rate increase and the total interest rate increase which a loan may jump over its lifetime.

VARIANCE—An exception to a zoning ordinance.

VENDEE—The buyer of real estate under a purchase agreement. Often referred to as the purchaser or the party of the first part.

VENDEE's LIEN—A lien brought against property by a contract of sale, to secure the deposit paid by the purchaser. This keeps the seller from selling to someone else.

VETERANS ADMINISTRATION—A government agency that administers benefits to qualified veterans.

VOID—A contract that is not legally enforceable.

VOLUNTARY LIEN—A debt against the property that the owner agrees to have recorded.

W

WAIVER—The voluntary surrender or abandonment of a right, claim, or privilege.

WARRANT—To promise; to certify.

WARRANTY DEED—A legal document which contains guarantees that the grantor is the legal owner and has the right to sell a property.

WARRANTY OF HABITABILITY—A deed which warrants that a property is habitable.

WEASEL CLAUSE—A clause contained within or added to a purchase agreement which makes the offer subject to the performance of an act or some other event. Subject-to clauses are also know as weasel clauses. Examples of two subject-to clauses are:

> Offer subject to partners approval.

> Subject to buyer's approval of appraisal.

WITHOUT RECOURSE—Usually written in endorsing a note/contract denoting that the holder cannot go to the debtor personally if payment of note/contract is not fulfilled. The creditor has recourse only to the property.

WRAPAROUND MORTGAGE—See ALL-INCLUSIVE TRUST DEED.

Z

ZONING (BOARD/COMMISSION/ORDINANCES)—Rules pertaining to the usage of real estate imposed by the local city or county government. See VARIANCE.

ZONING MAP—A map showing where the zones lie within an area. It will show C (commercial), R (residential), and I (industrial) areas within a city.

INDEX

□ □ □

ABOUT THE AUTHOR

Marc Stephen Garrison lectures nationwide at real estate seminars, publishes a newsletter called *The Real Estate Advisor,* and is the author of *Financially Free.* He lives with his wife, DeAnn, and their children, Ryan, Kelly, and Hunter, in Orem, Utah.

GETTING STARTED MAKING MONEY IN REAL ESTATE INVESTMENT

Ninety-seven percent of all American millionaires made their money in real estate investment. If you'd like to learn the techniques and strategies that will get you started making money in real estate, the most lucrative investment that exists today, simply complete and mail this coupon (or a copy of it) to the address below. For faster service just call our office and request this free special report, Getting Started Making Money in Real Estate Investment.

Name _____

Address _____

City, State _____

Zip Code _____ Phone _____

Return To:

M. S. Garrison & Company
P.O. Box 1096
Orem, Utah 84057

or call 801-225-8777